AMERICA'S
SOARING BOOK

AMERICA'S SOARING BOOK

BY THE EDITORS
OF FLYING MAGAZINE

Charles Scribner's Sons / New York

Copyright © 1974, 1975 Ziff-Davis Publishing Co.

Library of Congress Cataloging in Publication Data

Main entry under title:

America's soaring book.

    Continues America's flying book.
    Bibliography: p. 264
    Includes index.
    1. Gliding and soaring. I. Flying.
TL760.A64   629.132'523   74–32016
ISBN 0–684–14208–2

1 3 5 7 9 11 13 15 17 19 C/MD 20 18 16 14 12 10 8 6 4 2

Printed in the United States of America

CONTENTS

LIST OF ILLUSTRATIONS

Grateful acknowledgment is made for pictures used from the following sources:

ACKNOWLEDGMENTS

We at *Flying Magazine* feel particularly fortunate that among our editors and contributors there is a wealth of knowledge of and experience in soaring that has enabled us to create this sequel to *America*'s *Flying Book*, which was also published by Charles Scribner's Sons. Among the writers and editors whose expertise is found in these pages are Peter Garrison, John W. Olcott, Peter Lert, and Ann Welch. Anna Babij, Jennifer Richardson, and Jerry Sablo helped greatly in the preparation of the manuscript. Managing Editor of the project was Norbert Slepyan.

The Soaring Society of America was helpful in providing some of the photographs and directory materials. We are particularly grateful to Douglas Lamont and Lloyd Licher, of the SSA, for their cooperation. The Schweizer Aircraft Corporation also provided valuable assistance.

To Laurie Graham and Dorothy Coover at Scribners go our thanks for their guidance and help in seeing *America's Soaring Book* through to publication.

And a word of gratitude is also due the soaring community—the pilots, students, base operators, and crew members—who, through their participation in the sport, provided the inspiration for our endeavors.

ROBERT B. PARKE
Editor and Publisher,
Flying Magazine

PREFACE

Somehow, you've become interested in gliders. Perhaps you've seen a newspaper or magazine article or a film about them. Maybe a friend has extolled the joys of motorless flight to you. If you're a power pilot, you may have landed at some small rural strip and seen a row of sailplanes tied down like sleeping birds. Perhaps you've glanced upward and suddenly seen one drifting gracefully along the hills or circling among the clouds.

Whatever the reason, you've started to wonder what it must be like to be alone in the air, dependent on no source of power other than the movement of the medium through which you pass. Isn't it dangerous? How does one stay up, anyway? Can anyone learn how, or does it require superhuman skill? These are some of the questions we intend to answer in this book, which is not so much a how-to manual as it is a source of consolidated information that you can use as a springboard toward your own development and accomplishment as a soaring pilot.

Soaring certainly is not everyone's cup of tea. Those attracted to it, whether as pilots or as interested observers, are usually individualists, and there are so many facets to soaring that it can be a different experience for each enthusiast. Some are so enamored of the simple sensation of flight, of freedom from the shackles of gravity, that an hour aloft within a mile or so of the home airfield may suffice; others test themselves against nature and each other in cross-country flights of hundreds of miles or in sailplane competition. For some, the beauty of soaring is the main lure—some sailplanes must surely rank among man's loveliest and most graceful works. For others, the quiet and solitude of soaring flight offer opportunities for introspection and meditation—the sailplane, like the bow of the Zen archer, becomes a vehicle that carries the pilot closer and closer to nature and deeper and deeper within himself, as well as from place to place in the real world.

Many powered-airplane pilots find learning to soar a most revealing experience. Sequestered in a plush cabin, impelled through the air by powerful engines, guided and counseled by needles flicking over dials, it's easy to lose touch with the atmosphere in which we fly, as well as with the quintessential feeling of flight itself. A sailplane, with its quiet progress and its immediate response to the slightest stirring of the air, reminds its pilot constantly that the atmosphere is a live, breathing thing. Its equally immediate response to both proper and improper use of its controls puts the pilot on a one-to-one basis with his craft and its reactions.

For some, soaring is a means to find freedom. Learning to fly a sailplane and taking the first solo flight add a new dimension (in the most literal sense) to life and provide an invaluable base of experience and understanding to those who may go on to other forms of flight. Those who have learned from scratch range from barely teen-age children, who can legally solo a glider at fourteen (two years before many can drive a car) to octogenarians. It needn't cost much, either; soaring clubs and school groups can bring the expense within anyone's range.

There's a special camaraderie among soaring pilots, too. The shared experience of silent flight—an experience often very difficult to put into words—creates a special bond among those whose common interests and goals have already brought them together. This camaraderie often extends beyond flight; pilots gather to help one another on cross-country flights, to work on privately or mutually owned sailplanes, to organize soaring meets and gatherings, or just to talk about past, present, and future soaring experiences.

Learning to fly; the people in and around soaring; cross-country flight; competition; weather; places to fly; practical aspects and organizations . . . the list of topics goes on and on. In this book, the editors of *Flying Magazine* can touch on many of them, can give pilot and nonpilot alike the information they need to begin soaring and to continue to grow and develop in the sport; but the central experience cannot be completely described in words. We can only hope that the look at motorless flight that we offer here may move you to sample its many facets and delights.

AMERICA'S
SOARING BOOK

1 PURE FLIGHT

The fantasy of flying like birds has always possessed men, and even though human flight is now commonplace, fliers continue to envy the immediacy and individuality of the flight of birds. Various kinds of recreational flying—parachute jumping, gyrocoptering, and others—claim to offer a closer approximation to bird flight, but it is probably the soaring pilot who makes the least fanciful claim to fraternity with the birds. Not that the sailplane permits direct contact between the body and the wind, or that it maneuvers especially handily, or that it muscles itself aloft—on the contrary, many sailplanes are cocoonlike, cumbersome to maneuver, and all sailplanes require assistance to get them aloft—but there comes a moment when the pilot, pulling the cable-release handle, suddenly severs his ties with the earth and makes a more precious, *personal* connection with the sky.

It is that intimate connection between a man and the enveloping air that makes soaring like the flight of birds. To power pilots, the only part of the atmosphere that matters is the visible cloudbank or thunderhead; he ignores the rest. The parachutist rests on an air cushion smaller than a mattress and deals only with it. The soaring pilot, however, spins a web in the air about him, feeling for vibrations of lift and shunning the caverns of sink. The relevant air extends for miles, sometimes as far as he can see; nothing is insignificant. Each cloud has something to tell him, and the shape of the landscape below hints at invisible air structures through which he must make his way. Nor is it enough for him to know the rules of the road by rote, or to analyze conditions by cold logic; to succeed, he must have a feel for the air, and he must sublimate his knowledge into the stuff of which intuition, hunches, and luck are made.

Primitive men must have had such a sense of the earth; modern urbanites perhaps have a similar prescience about conditions on freeways.

2

Nevertheless, we are generally estranged from the natural world. Soaring requires that we become intimate with it again.

It is often said that the atmosphere is a sea of air in which we are bottom dwellers, and through the middle depths of which our fliers swim. Like the ocean, this sea of air has its currents, and because of the lightness—the "airiness"—of it, the atmosphere stirs more nervously and more constantly than does the ocean. In the course of an average day, a cycle of heating, rising, condensing, cooling, stagnating, sinking, cooling, and settling is repeated again and again. If air of different temperatures were color coded, we might see the Great Plains on a midsummer day picketed by armies of pink columns thousands of feet high leaning with the wind in a matrix of blue-green. The pink is warm air, which produces thermal lift, the basic staple of soaring; the blue-green is cool air, which produces sink, the nemesis of soaring.

It is not only the heating of the ground and ground-level air by the sun, however, that produces lift; winds rising over hills, ridges, or entire mountain ranges produce lift ranging in magnitude from a hint to giant waves that can carry a sailplane upward with eerie smoothness into the stratosphere, until cold and lack of oxygen drive the pilot back toward the earth.

The air is invisible, but the puffy clouds that mark the tops of rising columns of warm air, the smoothly curved and shelved lenticulars that loom over mountain ridges and, at intervals, downwind of them, the smokestacks and flags that signal the direction of the wind, the birds circling and rising over a field, the hills and cliffs themselves—these producers and by-products of lift are visible, and it is around them that the soaring pilot constructs his imaginary model of the air. Sometimes clues are abundant; sometimes they are lacking, and he must feel his way through the air, hoping to catch the shudder and bump of an upcurrent and then to turn into it and remain circling within it, all by instinct, feel, or luck. On some days he will find himself towed to release altitude only to glide back to the field; on others he will feel nibbles throughout the tow, and on release will quickly hook a big thermal and be up and away. There is not always lift to be found, only certain combinations of weather and terrain allow it, and when it is not plentiful, skill is required to discover and exploit it.

Aloft in sunlight, the soaring pilot can see for miles, tracing sources of lift in the farmland patchwork below and in puffs of clouds.

Accompanying the pilot's art is that of the designer. The paramount considerations in sailplane design are rate of sink and glide ratio or glide angle—the latter being a measure of aerodynamic efficiency, the proportion of a sailplane's lift to its drag. For sailplanes, the basic configuration inevitably means a fuselage of the smallest possible cross section, and therefore a reclining or even supine pilot position; extremely long, slender wings; and surfaces of extreme smoothness. Only considerations of cost, intended market, and serviceability may limit the degree of fanaticism with which designers may pursue their ends; the most exotic sailplanes today may have all-plastic structures, wings more than 100 feet from tip to tip that can change their shape and size in flight, and even small jet engines for launching without a tow plane.

As the equipment grows in sophistication, the goals that sailplane pilots set for themselves become more demanding. The current record for altitude stands at almost nine miles; for straight-line distance, nearly one thousand miles. One current design project involves a pressurized sailplane, the cockpit of which is sealed and maintained under pressure from an oxygen bottle capable of operating at phenomenal altitudes of twelve miles or more. It might catch a ride on a Rocky Mountain wave and be shot before a spring tailwind six hundred, eight hundred, perhaps one thousand miles out over the Great Plains. One barely says so aloud, but the crowning ambition of the most Faustian soaring pilots is to fly a sailplane nonstop from coast to coast.

Though soaring is a competitive sport, it is also thermal-hopping on a Sunday afternoon; a teen-age girl who has neither the money nor the need for powered aircraft getting her pilot's license for the sheer thrill of it; a retired man who likes to relax around the airport swapping stories and going up once or twice a day when the lift is good and the traffic is light; or a young mathematician stepping off a mountaintop into empty air hanging beneath a sailwing of his own design. Various gliderports cater to different tastes and have different ambiences. Some, because of their geographical locations, support principally local soaring—fliers riding from thermal to thermal, never far from the airport. Others serve mainly as bases for cross-country flights, with the airplanes leaving in droves in the midmorning, not to be seen again until late afternoon. Mountain waves, which are to be found in some measure anywhere that a strong wind and a large mountain meet but most powerfully and reliably at a few well-known locations, bring together seasonal camps of serious pilots with their down underwear, oxygen systems, and transponders, ready to climb into the rarefied and icy regions of the stratosphere. When the wave or the thermal is not cooperative, folding chairs come out of the campers and the confraternity of sailplane pilots and their families and crews settles down to some serious jawing. It turns out that once you have been up there and wrestled personally with the refractory air, you have a surprisingly strong bond with others who have done so.

People usually get started in soaring through a friend. Rides in sailplanes are appealingly cheap, and to a newcomer, they lack the sense of peril that automatically arises in the power pilot when he is confronted with the problem of landing at a specified point without the aid of an engine. Often you stay up as long as you like, seemingly without effort, and then you come down easily, landing precisely where you ought to and rolling with an automobilist's precision to a place in the tow queue behind another sailplane.

Once caught by the thing, you go back again and again, and even if you at first thought of nothing other than going up for a few rides with an experienced pilot now and then, you eventually find yourself so tantalizingly close to soloing that you cannot turn away. When you have soloed, turning away is all the harder. You might go on to power flying, or just keep renting sailplanes, until one day you notice that you have spent as much on rentals as you would have on your own sailplane, so you might eventually buy your own ship and trailer or go into partnership with some of your soaring friends. The more serious you become, the more likely you are to get into competitive flying.

Soaring contests take place on every level, from the casually local to the uptightly national and international. Since you do not need a particular kind of physique to compete, anyone, of any sex or age, could theoretically become a champion. There are intangibles involved, of course, including what Joseph Conrad dubbed "ability in the abstract" and a powerful competitive spirit. As in all sports, a touch of the egomaniac is helpful as one sets out to butcher the competition. A passion for winning, a terror

Above: On the ground, a sailplane looks like an unlikely candidate for graceful flight. Its strange appearance may belie its charm, or it may be part of it. Below: From the cockpit, the ground seems to slide by as the strangely silent towplane bobs and weaves, gently tugging the sailplane to altitude.

of losing, like the imminence of the gallows, concentrates a person wonderfully. In fact, the ingenuity of contestants in international competition has been a constant challenge to judges. Enthusiastic entrants have not been above resorting to dishonest means to appear to have made better times and distances than they in fact made. The present safeguards against excessive zeal are quite complicated and apparently airtight; it is only a matter of time, though, until some aerial Houdini will contrive to defeat them.

At less Olympian levels, however, the competition proceeds at a congenial simmer. Many of the activities of soaring pilots center around the performance of "tasks," which are broken down into silver, gold, and diamond grades according to their degree of difficulty, and for the completion of which badges of the appropriate metal or surrogate gemstone are issued. These include distances in a straight line and around a triangular course, altitude gains, and a flat requirement for any badge of the "big sit," an endurance flight of five hours. Naturally, there is some unfairness in the uniform application of these requirements to different regions, since what may be quite difficult to achieve in weak northeastern conditions may be easy fare for any beginner in the mountainous terrain and powerful lift of southern California. It is accordingly considered unsporting to make the 3,000-meter altitude gain required for the Gold and Diamond badges in wave, since to do so requires practically no ability at all. It is *de rigueur* to make the 3,000 meters in thermals—though it is still easier to do so in the Southwest than in the Northeast.

In addition to the winning of badges, constant assaults, frequently successful, are made upon state, national, and international records. There are two principal tools for the verification of flight claims. One is the turnpoint camera, with which the pilot photographs a landmark to prove that he has been to it. The other is the sealed barograph, which is a combination altimeter and clockwork drive that records a plot of altitude against time for the entire flight, revealing how high the pilot went if he is seeking an altitude mark, or whether he stopped for a tow along the way if he was trying for distance.

Local and regional contests are open to all comers and involve tasks of moderate difficulty. Generally, superior equipment confers upon its

When the lift fails and an off-airport landing is necessary, the pilot seeks out a carpet of cushioning grass on which to put his plane.

owner a better chance of success, though some tasks are designed to tax the judgment and weather sense of the pilot more than the quality of his ship. When the competing ships in a contest are well matched, the sport becomes what it is meant to be: a challenge to the pilot's knowledge and instinct and to his ability to make the right decisions at the right time. So piloting technique is inferior in importance both to the quality of the airplane and to the pilot's decision-making ability. One well-known championship pilot is said to be unusually clumsy at the controls of his aircraft but remarkably cunning in his decision making. Contest soaring is for the quick thinker who can do his mental calculations, plan his strategies, and season them with a good hunch or two, while at the same time making the best of the present situation.

Cross-country soaring is mainly a matter of proceeding from one thermal to another, of speeding through intervening areas of sink in order to minimize the time spent in them, and of slowing and circling within the thermals one finds. Thermals in a given air mass are likely to be similar in size, strength, and spacing, with these features varying in a predictable way throughout the day. Since the sailplane has predetermined physical properties that cause its rate of sink to vary in a fixed relation to its forward speed, there is a calculus that combines all of this information—the knowns and the estimates—and determines the manner in which the task should be flown. The pilot can choose the altitudes at which he enters and leaves thermals and the speeds at which to fly between them. When thermals are frequent, strong, and easily found, it is not necessary to stay with each of them very long in order to maintain height, and the pilot can fly from one to the next at an unusually high speed. When thermals are weak and far apart, it is necessary to stay with them up to a higher altitude and to fly between them at more conservative speeds, in order to minimize the risk of having to land en route. Various sorts of calculators are available to solve height band and interthermal speed problems for the less-than-omniscient pilot. These range from specialized circular slide rules, carried in the pocket, to elaborate, semiautomatic panel-mounted devices costing hundreds of dollars.

When all the intuitions and gadgets go awry, the sailplane pilot is faced with an eventuality for which his training has prepared him, but the mere

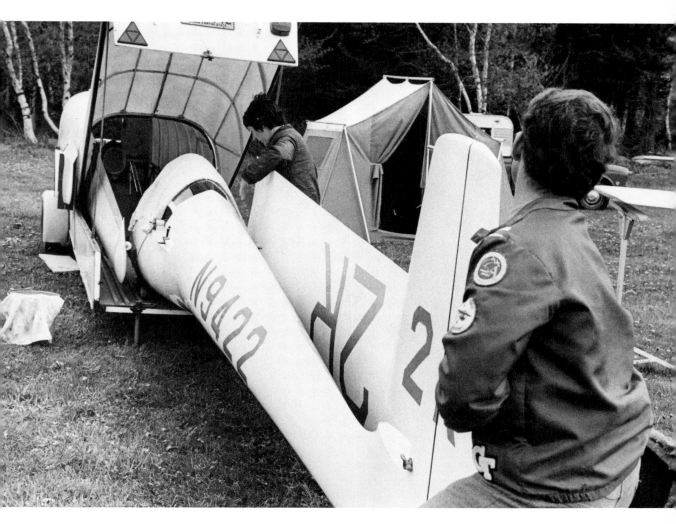

Into the mouth of its trailer go the dismantled fuselage and wings of a Libelle.

Hugging a slope for lift, a sailplane tries for a few more passes in the waning day before gliding home.

thought of which makes a power pilot blanch—an off-airport landing. Ideally, he may land in a field large and firm enough for a tow plane to land and pull him out. More typically, it will be a farmer's field, complete with a perhaps intrigued or perhaps enraged farmer leading a horde of curious bystanders trampling the sprouts on their way to the plane. When peace is restored, the crew is notified of the pilot's position and arrives with the trailer. The sailplane is dismantled and loaded aboard, sometimes after being carried piecemeal out of the field to the nearest road. Because wing panels may weigh a couple of hundred pounds each, crewing can be quite a chore, especially since the time not spent sweating and grunting out an actual retrieve is generally spent doing nothing at all.

Either the pilot must share crewing duties with partners in a ship or with fellow club members, or he must enlist a team of relatives, spouses, interested observers, or teen-age beginners to do his donkey work for him. In either case, several people get stuck with an unromantic, boring, and strenuous job so that another person may commune with the clouds. The determination to pursue that communion must be great, and the conviction of its importance must imbue the crew to prevent disgruntlement. Normally it does, and they accept without complaint their role as supporters of a single individual whose one-seat airplane offers no room for hope that he will ever take anyone up for a ride. It is taken for granted among soaring pilots, because they have been there, that the journey alone through the unseen streets of the sky is worth any inconvenience. The nature of the journey is such that it almost must be made alone. The pilot must be able to forget himself, shed his social position and roles, in order to melt into the act of flying. His attention and awareness must be complete. There is lift somewhere, silent and invisible; he must find and exploit it. To be able to use the air freely, and not to be defeated by its caprice and elusiveness, is soaring's great personal challenge. It is what draws pilots to powerless flight and holds them; for if the powered airplane represents the conquest by man of the problem of flight, the sailplane represents the extension of that conquest into nature, usurping the techniques and devices of birds to capitalize, like a sailboat, on divinely provided energy. Soaring flight is as exotic and yet as pure a liaison with the sky as men will ever find.

2 THE FIRST GOLDEN AGE

It was inevitable that man, captivated by the seeming effortlessness of soaring flight, would try to imitate the birds. He quickly built into his mythologies images of manlike deities who could move through the skies at will. Phoebus Apollo used the sun as a airborne chariot; angels, ranging from tiny cherubim to adult-sized heavenly hosts, were part of the Judeo-Christian tradition, flying by the strength of their wings alone, as do the birds. However, they were supernatural. Man's supposed bondage to the earth was all too apparent in ancient times, as the myth of Daedalus and Icarus indicates. According to the Greek tale, they sought to imitate the birds by fashioning wings of feathers bonded by wax. Apparently the design was successful, because they did fly. Unfortunately, Icarus tried to stretch the performance of his invention too far. As he flew too close to the sun, the wax bonding of his wings melted, and he became the first recorded case of fatal pilot error. He was the first but certainly not the last pilot to come to grief by failing to respect the limitations of flight.

The notebooks of Leonardo da Vinci reveal that he spent considerable time observing the techniques of soaring birds and of examining the construction and form of their wings. Apparently, none of his designs reached the construction stage, which was a pity, for one or two of them might have flown fairly well.

While heavier-than-air flight remained an ambition of man, it was subsequently neglected until the mid-nineteenth century, overshadowed by the spectacular emergence of manned hot-air balloon flight in the 1780s. By the mid-1850s, however, research into glider designs was again underway, most notably by Sir George Cayley, who was the first man to describe the principles of heavier-than-air flight and to design workable airplanes. He apparently wasn't keen on flying them, however, for when,

16

THE FIRST GOLDEN AGE / 17

in 1852, his invention was ready for its first test flight, he volunteered the services of a ten-year-old boy, the son of one of his servants, for the mission. The young prodigy actually survived this combination of firsts —first flight by the boy, first heavier-than-air flight by anyone, first flight of that particular design and machine. According to tradition, the first adult to fly was John Appleby, Cayley's coachman at Brompton Hall, Yorkshire, also in 1852. The account that has come down to us has him landing successfully but then giving notice with the complaint, "Sir George, I was hired to drive, not to fly." He thus became the first pilot dropout.

In America, John Montgomery claimed to have made 600-foot flights in his tandem-winged biplanes as early as 1884, while engineer Octave Chanute developed the biplane design later adapted by the Wright brothers. In Germany, the indefatigable Otto Lilienthal built an artificial hill from which to launch his birdlike folding monoplanes and made thousands of flights before his death from injuries received in a crash. All of these early devices were devoid of controls as we know them, but were steered—if the pilot was lucky—by frantic shifts of body weight. The first major innovation came from the Wright brothers, who decided that weight-shifting was a decidedly inefficient method of control, as was the practice of taking off and landing on one's own feet. Their early gliders, developed in the late 1800s and early 1900s, featured wooden skids for takeoffs and landings and an elaborate system of levers and wires that could actually warp the wing curvature for positive control. The pilot lay prone on the wing. These gliders looked very similar to the later powered Wright Flyer and were flown both as captive kites and as manned ships gliding free from the sandhills of Kitty Hawk.

After their historic first powered flight, made in the Flyer on December 17, 1903, the Wrights temporarily abandoned gliders. In 1911, they returned to the dunes and made the first real soaring flight; its duration of nine minutes and forty-five seconds was to be the world record until after World War I.

In 1911, 1912, and 1913, hang-gliders appeared in Germany, all flown by university students from Darmstadt. The students had discovered an ideal gliding site in a mountainous area of southern Germany called the

Virtually tossed into the air and struggling to stay airborne, the Wright gliders made possible enormous advances in the knowledge of aerodynamics.

Rhön. There, on a hill called the Wasserkuppe, they started the practice of summer-soaring encampments.

With the cessation of hostilities, flying activity commenced again in the Rhön. Model builders and future glider pilots began wondering whether it would be possible to use the wind for power to remain aloft; in the summer of 1920, the first Rhön competition included more than twenty-five aircraft, some of them very strange devices. Some of these designs were based loosely on those of powered aircraft; others resembled Chanute's hang-glider. The most successful design was the Schwarzer Teufel (Black Devil), a thoroughly modern-looking cantilever monoplane with faired fuselage and streamlined landing skids, which turned in a flight of two minutes, twenty-two seconds. An improved version built in 1921, the Blaue Maus, flew for thirteen minutes, breaking the Wrights' 1911 record; a few days later, a Harth-Messerschmitt glider flew over twenty-two minutes and landed at its takeoff point. Ninteen-twenty-two marked the beginning of what we now consider to be true soaring. Sailplanes were designed for minimum drag and sink speed, and one new design, the Vampyr, became the first powerless aircraft to break the one-hour barrier. Recognition of the possibilities of soaring began to spread throughout the world.

The period from the end of World War I to the beginning of World War II may well come to be regarded as soaring's first golden age. During this twenty-year period, soaring evolved from a crude means of slightly retarding one's headlong plummet from the rim of a hill to a highly refined and technologically advanced science. The aircraft themselves changed relatively early during the period from crude and stubby contraptions into the slender, long-winged creations we are familiar with today. Although refinement continues constantly, a definitive form of aircraft was created in those exciting years, and not many external differences are visible when some of today's best sailplanes are compared with their ancestors of three or four decades ago. By the mid-1930s, almost all the flying techniques and devices in common use today had been well researched and established. Not until the mid- to late-1960s would development even approach the pitch of the years between the world wars, and only now does it appear that we may again be on the verge of major breakthroughs into new fields of soaring capability.

This burst of development early in the century becomes all the more impressive when we consider that the overwhelmingly major portion was the work of a relatively small group of people. The soaring nations of the world between the wars can be divided into two basic classes: Class One —Germany; and Class Two—everyone else. This came about for political reasons. With the signing of the Treaty of Versailles at the end of World War I, Germany found itself forbidden to have an air force or to engage in aerial commerce; German powered aircraft were legislated almost out of existence, at least temporarily. However, the treaty made no mention of gliders, which still existed only in primitive forms. Having once enjoyed freedom of the air, Germans, especially those of the younger generation, were reluctant to relinquish it. During the first few years after the war, the fledgling soarers had to go it pretty much alone, impelled only by their enthusiasm and camaraderie. It was not too long, however, before the German government stepped in to offer considerable support in both research and sport soaring. Scouting programs and, a bit later, the Hitler *jugend* made it possible for any youngster seriously interested in flying to pursue this interest at almost no cost to himself. Such support now exists, incidentally, in almost every major soaring nation except the United States.

A second major factor in Germany's importance—and another that continues into the present—was the formation of aeronautics departments and associated sport and research soaring operations at a number of German universities. These *Akafliegs* (short for *Akademische Fliegergruppen*) offered talented individuals a chance to realize their ideas and designs at state cost; even today, most of the current crop of German superships come from the *Akafliegs* and earn their designers not only modest fame and fortune but academic degrees as well.

Of course, the Germans didn't have a total monopoly on talent, and valuable contributions came from other countries, notably England and the United States. Many of these contributions were in the development of flying techniques rather than in construction concepts. German sailplanes were always the cream of the crop, and many of them were exported.

At this time, soaring became a distinct area of aviation, as opposed to powered flight.

Of course, a great deal of what went on in the mid-1920s was still quite primitive. The average sailplane was very lightly built and was launched by a team of men on the ground: a length of rubber shock cord was hooked to the nose; the takeoff team ran as hard as it could down the hill and—just as they were about to be snatched backward off their feet—the glider would be released to leap into the air. Such launches had to be carried out at the top of a hill or ridge, for the only known source of lift then was wind-deflected upward by sloping land. No real cross-country flights were made. The pilots always stayed close to the hill and its known lift. After landing at the bottom of the hill, the glider would be carried back to the top by muscle power.

By 1925, the picture had changed a good deal. It had been discovered that, for a given wing area, a long, slender wing had much less drag than a short, broad version. Unfortunately, because a slender wing also has to be thinner from top to bottom, there is less room for structural members inside. To make matters worse, the extra length requires far greater strength. Nonetheless, by 1928, wingspans had increased to almost 60 feet and aspect ratios (a mathematical convention expressing the relation of a wing's length to its width) had reached to over 21, compared to the humble Blaue Maus with a 28-foot span and an aspect ratio of 5.6. The direct result of these higher aspect ratios—meaning longer, thinner wings—was dramatically improved performance.

An important change in pilot technique came about in 1928. Early flying had been entirely by the "seat-of-the-pants" method; now, instruments started to appear. The most important of these was the variometer, an ultrasensitive rate-of-climb indicator, which lets the pilot know his exact vertical speed at all times. Still the most important soaring instrument, it allowed pilots to discover that hills weren't the only source of rising air. One lucky pilot had discovered earlier that air rises before an advancing squall line, but unless a line happened to come through the area while a glider was aloft on the slope lift, it was of no use. Now pilots discovered the existence of thermals under cumulus clouds. However, it would be two years before Wolf Hirth, flying during a goodwill visit at Elmira, New York, would discover the technique of circling within a thermal updraft to remain within it as it drifted downwind. By now, considerable interest in gliding was manifested in the United States—the

A German Rhönsperber (foreground) at Harris Hill, near Elmira, New York, in the 1930s.

first German pilots and aircraft had visited America in 1928—and numerous Americans were planning their own designs.

Flight training was also much more rugged in those halcyon days. Dual instruction, in which the instructor flies with the student, was unheard of; in fact, there were no two-place ships. Students got their start in so-called primaries, which were little more than a wing and a set of tail surfaces linked by a sticklike truss fuselage; the pilot sat completely exposed just ahead of the wing. The shock-cord launch and landing were carried out on a sturdy barrel-stave-like skid which formed the bottom fuselage member. After a few dry runs on the ground to learn the controls and their functions, the new student was catapulted into the air by his eager comrades on the shock cord and wobbled along, regaled by his safely earthbound instructor with lusty shouts of encouragement or criticism. Remarkably few novices were killed or injured by this practice, largely because the ground crews didn't pull the shock cord very tight for one's first flights. In a good upslope wind these ungainly contraptions could actually stay aloft for hours at a time. Unfortunately, the early gliders had a very bad safety record in the United States, where publication of their

In early open-cockpit trainers such as this Franklin, students quickly became intimate with the sharp sensations of flight.

plans in such magazines as *Popular Mechanics* made it possible for every farm boy to lash one up out of whatever materials came to hand and, without benefit of the German training program, go out and break it and/or his neck.

Those students who survived their apprenticeship in the primaries moved on to secondaries, which were gliders with longer, slimmer wings, enclosed fuselages, and much better performance. Modest cross-country flights, a few miles along a ridge, for instance, could be carried out in these machines, which had glide ratios (distance traveled forward for each foot of altitude lost) of up to 15 to 1. This meant that for every foot of altitude the glider would descend, it would progress fifteen feet farther along its course.

In the more advanced areas of motorless flight, major milestones were being passed. New launching methods were developed: automobile tow, in which the glider is pulled aloft at the end of a cable by a car, and airplane tow, which was first demonstrated in early 1910 but left fallow until 1930, when American Frank Hawks had a Waco biplane tow him in

The handiwork of the great designer, W. Hawley Bowlus: the Baby Albatross (above) and the first high-performance American sailplane, the Senior Albatross (following page).

his Franklin Eaglet across the entire United States. At the same time, Wolf Hirth's discovery of the circling technique that allowed the variometer-equipped pilot to utilize thermals joined with the above factors to free the sailplane from the hills and allow ever-longer cross-country flights. The 100-kilometer barrier soon fell, and by the 1932 Rhön competition, flights as long as 160 kilometers (100 statute miles) were made, using thermals only.

Equipment kept pace with techniques. Glide ratios exceeded the magic 20 and continued to climb; the *Akafliegs* spent more and more time and effort on their brainchildren, creating such products as the graceful gull-winged Fafnir (one of the first long-span, cantilever aircraft) and the incredible Austria. The latter sailplane—called *das Elefant* by its weary ground crew—spanned over one hundred feet and boasted such technical refinements as full-span trailing-edge flaperons that not only controlled roll but reduced the strong wing camber for high-speed flight, a practice that was to reappear in the mid-1960s.

By now, sailplanes carried blind-flying gear. The flights they made in cumulus clouds and in thunderstorms contributed not only to knowledge of soaring technique but also provided invaluable meteorological data. At the time, very little was known about the violent processes that roil in a thundercloud; although only a few fatalities were recorded, a number of sailplanes, including the proud Austria, suffered what the German pilots understatedly called *demontierung*—inflight disassembly—leaving their pilots to try out their newfangled parachutes.

In the United States, new directions independent of German progress were being taken. Airplane and automobile tow were very common; although dual instruction was still rare, the Americans eschewed separate primary and secondary trainers and instead combined the functions in the utility glider, whose steel-tube fuselage and convertible nose—it could be either open, as in the primary, or closed, as in the secondary—fitted it to either role. It was also much more rugged than the German design; its descendants, the Schweizer 2–22 and 2–33 series, are still in service.

Training in the utilities was much safer than the "kick-them-out-of-the-nest" technique of Europe. Equipped with a wheel rather than a skid, the utility ship could be towed along behind a car or truck at a speed high enough for control effectiveness but insufficient for actual flight; the instructor, riding in the car, could watch and correct the student. Later, flights of gradually increasing altitude could be made behind the car before the student graduated to high launches or airplane tows.

While many of the advanced pilots in America owned German sailplanes, some Americans had their own designs. Probably the most important of these designers was W. Hawley Bowlus, factory manager of Ryan Aircraft and builder of the *Spirit of St. Louis;* his early sailplanes were successfully soared off Pt. Loma near San Diego, California. His Senior Albatross was the best American ship of its day, while the smaller Baby Albatross combined wings from the German Grunau Baby transition trainer with Bowlus's own streamlined pod-and-boom fuselage to provide what was then considered excellent performance for a small sailplane. The Senior now hangs in the Smithsonian Institution; a number of Babies are still flying.

Development continued in Germany in competition classes and in a series of moderate-performance sailplanes built for club use. By now, a number of manufacturers had joined the *Akafliegs;* several, such as Alexander Schleicher and Egon Scheibe, remain active today. Flights of more than 300 kilometers (180 miles) in length were made, while further experience in thunderstorm and mountain-wave flying pushed achieved altitudes toward 10,000 feet. Distance flights had been carried out by whole swarms of sailplanes flying together. Pilots had started flying cross-country to specific goals rather than drifting downwind and hoping for the best. In America, Elmira, New York, had become "Wasserkuppe West" and had hosted the U.S. National Soaring Championships since 1931.

A few technical innovations deserve special mention. In the quest for less and less drag, the Germans had always done without a landing wheel, preferring a faired skid for landing and a droppable dolly for takeoff; in the mid-1930s, a few retractable landing-gear installations started to appear. More important was the development of the dive brake and spoiler combination with which almost all modern sailplanes are equipped; this combination of devices not only allows landings in extremely small fields by reducing the tendency for the clean, long-winged sailplane to "float" near the ground, it also allows the pilot to hold the speed to safe limits

A British design of the 1930s, the Slingsby Kirby Kite.

Top: Another British 1930s design, the Kirby Gull 1. This Gull, NX 41829, was homebuilt from the manufacturer's plans in 1938 and is still flying. Bottom: A Corcoran Cinema I on takeoff, one of the American prewar ships later modified for use as military trainers.

should he become disoriented and lose control of the sailplane in clouds or during aerobatics. (While one doesn't normally imagine a sailplane looping and rolling without power, many are capable of such maneuvers.)

By 1936, competition soaring had become a popular European sport. Weeks-long contests occurred at several sites, often involving round-robin flights that took the pilots over hundreds of kilometers in a few days. Goal flights and goal-and-return flights added to the challenge. Soaring was demonstrated at the 1936 Olympics in Berlin and was accepted for the 1940 Olympics, which were not held. Mass cross-country flights became a regular feature, including some from the Rhön to Berlin.

The last few years before World War II brought soaring to a point which it would not surpass until well after the conflict was over. In America, Harland Ross's Zanonia became the first sailplane to exceed a glide ratio of 30. In Germany, research and competition designs started to go their separate ways. As an example of the former, the *Akaflieg* Darmstadt's D–30 Cirrus was the first attempt at metal construction. With its extremely thin wings (its aspect ratio was over 30 and was unmatched

At the 1936 Olympic Games, held in Berlin, soaring was recognized as a sport worthy of competition in the next Olympics. The combination of the Olympic symbol and the swastika was ironic, for the 1940 Games were canceled by the onset of World War II.

The gull-wing Minimoa, designed by the great Wolf Hirth, was introduced in 1936. It set an American altitude record of 19,434 feet.

until 1970) and its pod-and-boom fuselage, its appearance was as striking as its performance. Spoilers and a full-span flap system simplified landing, while the dihedral could be changed *in flight* from ten degrees to a three-degree droop for research purposes. With its many features and nearly 70-foot span, the D–30 represented a major change from Darmstadt's earlier Windspiel light-air sailplane, which had a span of just over 35 feet and an empty weight of about 125 pounds. Meanwhile, the German Soaring Research Institute had developed the Reiher competition sailplane, perhaps the prettiest sailplane ever built until the advent of fiberglass gliders in the 1960s. Although only three were built, they remained unbeatable until the war. While the Reihers were all destroyed during or after the war, a contemporary design—the eerie 85-foot Horten IV flying wing—reached over 25,000 feet in a thunderstorm and was later brought to the United States for postwar research at the University of Mississippi. It even competed in a United States National Championship meet.

World War II was destined to have a particularly devastating effect on soaring development. Many fine pilots on both sides were drafted into

Above: One of the American products of the first golden age of soaring, the Schweizer 1-19. What was to become the Schweizer company's domination of American sailplane design was already developing. Below: The Laister-Kauffmann CG–10A Trojan was one of the last of the giant World War II glider designs.

military troopglider projects and lost their lives either in development or in glider operations such as in Belgium and Crete (German) or Burma and the Normandy Invasion (Allied).

A few small trainers for troopglider pilots were derived more or less directly from the existing sport sailplane technology and could be soared; however, the actual combat craft were much more like aerial semitrailers than sailplanes. They were designed for short-landing and high-load-carrying capabilities above all else and were of immense size compared to sport ships. The smallest, the German DFS–320 and the British Hotspur, carried eight combat-equipped troops, while the largest in common use, the British Hamilcar, was especially designed to transport the Tetrarch tank. Sailplanes were usually towed aloft by light two-seat sportplanes, but the Halifax bomber or C–47 transport (the military version of the DC–3 airliner) were the Allied planes most frequently used for towing troop gliders. One experimental German design, the Messerschmitt Gigant, was so huge that two medium bombers were bolted to a special mating section (with its own engine) to produce a bastard, five-engined towplane. Even this unlikely craft had to strain to haul the monster aloft, and engine fires were frequent. Ultimately, the Gigant was fitted with six engines of its own, as well as gun turrets here and there, to become the forerunner of the current jumbo transports.

The largest U.S. design to be used in combat was the Waco CG–4A, designed by Jack Laister, who is still a major force in American sport sailplane design. Thousands of these were built, many by nonaircraft firms chosen for their expertise in woodworking. ("What did you fly in the war, Daddy?"—"A Steinway, son.")

The effects were felt long after the war, particularly in the United States; while flying was restricted for several years in Germany, the glut of surplus troopglider trainers available for ridiculously low prices in the United States stifled development of new types until the mid-1950s. Such historic projects as the Sierra Wave Project were carried out almost entirely with these war-weary retreads.

Nonetheless, the stage had been set for the advent of sailplanes like the RJ–5 and the Sisu and for the exploration of the soaring sites of the southwestern United States. All the prior developments had prepared the way for the opening of soaring's second great era.

3 THE GREAT LIFT

World War II marked the end of the first golden age of soaring. While the war effectively halted the direct development of sailplanes and soaring until the end of hostilities, it also provided an immense impetus to aeronautical development in general. Many subsequent advances in design and technique have been direct or indirect spinoffs from wartime research and development programs.

Not that *all* powerless flight activity came to a halt, of course. The troopglider programs of several countries were direct outgrowths of the soaring movement, and while little was achieved in the way of epochal developments, a whole new generation of glider pilots got their start as military fliers. The Germans continued glider research, developing a number of rather exotic designs as test beds for experimental powered aircraft. Several German jet prototypes were derived from a series of tailless "flying wing" gliders developed by the Horten brothers; one of these gliders, the Horten IV, was brought to the United States at the end of the war. It placed among the top ten ships in a national soaring contest as late at 1954. The Americans also contemplated a flying-wing design as a towed fuel tank for powered aircraft, but the aircraft proved to have bad spin characteristics and the program was shelved.

On a more conventional level, both the troopglider programs and general aircraft development during the war led to major advances in aerodynamic knowledge, materials and construction techniques. Moreover, with the end of the war, large amounts of surplus aircraft materials became available at very low cost, fostering a spate of amateur designing and construction.

In a sense, though, the troopglider program and the subsequent availability of surplus trainers at ridiculously low costs served, at least for a time, to stifle development in the United States. The emotional climate

Above: The Horten glider was part of a surge of interest in the flying-wing designs at the end of World War II. Below: The Laister-Kauffmann company not only produced the CG-10 mammoth, but also made much lighter ships, such as this LK–10A, which was extremely popular in the early postwar years.

surrounding the sport in America before the war had been somewhat less intense than in Europe; while German groups were often out to build extremely advanced sailplanes and capture records for the fatherland, many American clubs and individuals were in soaring largely for the fun and camaraderie. Why should one, after the war, have labored for months or even years designing and constructing a fragile and temperamental new sailplane when he could pick up a brand-new TG–3 or LK–10A trainer in its original crate for a couple hundred dollars? While not exactly sylphlike, either of these stalwarts performed better than all but the best of prewar American sailplanes. Moreover, they were easy to fly and, if dinged, were easily repaired. In fact, some of these Army Air Force retreads are still doing yeoman service in soaring clubs and schools thirty years after the end of the war.

Gradually, though, pilots became dissatisfied with the surplus ships. Moreover, the supply started to give out. New designs began to appear and have continued to emerge at an accelerating pace that shows no sign of slowing down.

The first major effort was the modification of some of the surplus ships. The rugged Schweizer TG–3 was usually left more or less alone, apart from minor modifications, and used for training and utility soaring. The smaller and lighter LK–10A, however, came in for more than its share. One of the earliest modifications was the "bunny nose," in which the rather graceless front canopy was cleaned up and stretched. Soon tail surfaces were modified, fuselages were cut down and fitted with either single or tandem bubble canopies. Many homebuilders chose to retain only the original LK wings, building their own fuselages. This gave rise to such interesting hybrids as the LM–1—a single-place, monocoque fuselage with faired-in cockpit and hydraulically actuated dual-wheel retractable landing gear—or the "surplus special" Falcon—LK wings mated to a fuselage composed of a fighter drop-tank, an F–84 canopy, and the tail of a Cessna 140.

By now, though, many American pilots and designers were ready to embrace techniques of design and construction developed during the war, rather than continuing in earlier directions. This thinking gave rise to a number of exciting designs. While various projects were underway all

Above: Richard Johnson, eight times U.S. national champion. Below: In 1962 Richard Schreder introduced the HP-11, one of several important designs he has produced.

over the country, one of the most important centers of this new direction was the aeronautics department of the University of Mississippi, under the direction of Dr. August Raspet. Here, for the first time, newly developed advanced techniques of calculation and measurement could be applied to the special low-speed domain of powerless flight, and by the early 1950s, several important milestones had been passed. Among these was the magic 40-to-1 glide ratio, first reached with the RJ–5 sailplane, a joint project of Harland Ross and Richard Johnson, who has since won the U.S. National Soaring Championship no less than eight times in the RJ–5 and other sailplanes. The RJ–5 was one of the first sailplanes to use an advanced airfoil derived from calculation rather than trial and error. Basically a high aspect-ratio sailplane of fairly conventional design and composite construction (wood wings, metal monocoque fuselage), the RJ–5 was remarkable not only for its performance but for the thoroughness with which its builders documented the steps taken to achieve that performance. Pilots had always polished their wings to improve performance, but the extensive flight tests of the RJ–5 actually showed, in hard numbers, how important smoothness—spanwise as well as chordwise—and accuracy of contour are, particularly for the "laminar-flow" airfoils coming into general use at the time. By the same token, various modifications of fuselage shape were tried and their effects on drag and performance were carefully measured and recorded. While the RJ–5 has been surpassed by now, the documentation of its development and refinement remains a model for current practice.

The peculiarities of American soaring conditions gave rise to certain specialties of design. The promise of strong thermals in the western United States led to a series of new sailplanes that were much heavier in relation to their wing area than any sailplane had ever been before. These "lead sleds" sacrificed a certain amount of climb performance to improve penetration between thermals and achieved cross-country speeds that were phenomenal compared to even the best of earlier sailplanes. Richard Schreder, of Bryan, Ohio, embarked on a series of "HP" designs that still have a new addition every year or so. Some of them have been among the world's best sailplanes. The HP designs set several speed records and pioneered the use of flaps, which not only changed wing camber for better soaring performance but could also be deflected ninety degrees for very slow, steep landing approaches. Harland Ross came up with the R–6, a "convertible" that could be used as a single- or two-place sailplane (the rear cockpit, behind the wing spar, could be faired over when not required), while Richard Johnson, not to be outdone, constructed the wooden two-place "Adastra." In California, Irving Prue was exploring the strange realm of the V-tail, initially with a few very small sailplanes of tiny wing area and high wing loading despite their modest weight— the Prue 160, in fact, was named after its own empty weight—and later with competition designs like the Prue Standard and Super Standard. In Texas, Leonard Niemi was beginning work on the Sisu, one of the most graceful sailplanes of all time and the aircraft destined to be the first to break the 1,000-kilometer distance barrier. In fact, for several years to come, the progress of American sailplane design would be marked by a steady succession of speed record increases. Altitude achievements would keep pace, culminating with Paul Bikle's 1961 flight to 46,267 feet above sea level in a Schweizer 1–23.

Almost all of these ships, of course, were one-of-a-kind undertakings. Only the Sisu was ever reproduced, and even then, only ten were built. Development had not passed the field of consumer sailplanes, however. Even before the war, the Schweizer brothers, of Elmira, New York, had been the only major American sailplane manufacturer. With the end of hostilities they turned from mass-production of TG–3 trainers to their first love, sport soaring.

One of their first postwar designs, the all-metal 1–21, was a milestone in several different respects. It was the first time a competition sailplane had been built entirely from metal, and, though it was completed only six weeks before a National Soaring Championship meet, it won the contest quite handily. It also represented some major rethinking in the Schweizer Company's design philosophy. The Schweizers recognized that its high cost made the 1–21 available to only a few pilots, and they did not put it into production, choosing instead to produce a range of sailplanes that would broaden the base of soaring in the United States by providing clubs and schools with rugged, low-cost equipment of moderate performance.

The 1–21 was followed by designs that were essentially modernized

No American sailplane has been as successful in competition as the Sisu-1A, which was designed and built by Leonard Niemi. The prototype was introduced in 1958, and the ship has been modified often since.

versions of the prewar "utility" sailplanes, using more modern techniques. The most successful of these designs was the 2–22, the trainer in which a major proportion of the current generation of pilots first encountered the delights and terrors of the air. The 2–22 combines a rugged steel-tube fuselage with a simple constant-chord wing of fabric-covered aluminum. While its performance is, to say the least, modest, its low speed, tight turning radius, and docile performance make it a surprisingly good climber. While the sink rate of the 2–22 in a steep turn is rocklike, the tiny area traversed lets her remain in the very core of a thermal, while high-speed superships of a later era circle round the fringes in weaker lift. Of course, as soon as the 2–22 leaves the thermal and attempts what one may laughingly (or cryingly) call a cruise, a landing is soon in order unless another thermal is near.

The 2–22 was followed by the 1–23. This descendant of the 1–21 was a rugged and graceful all-metal, single-place aircraft and was, at the time of its appearance, the best production sailplane in the country. Various models remained in production until the early 1960s. An improved version, the 1–24, was designed, but only one was built. The next design, the

2–25, was another "one-off." Probably the highest-performing two-place in the world when it appeared, it would have been too expensive for production. It acquitted itself well in international competition, performed excellent service in high-altitude meteorological research, and is now owned and flown by the U.S. Air Force Academy.

Schweizer's next design represents a major factor in American soaring. The 1–26 was developed as an inexpensive single-place fun ship, using some features of an earlier single-place, one-off design, the 1–21. Small, nimble, and responsive, the 1–26 found an immediate popularity that has persisted through many refinements of the model. By now, almost seven hundred 1–26s are active, and they represent an important direction in competition: Regardless of the model, the performance of all 1–26s is essentially identical, providing an opportunity for uniquely fair soaring competition. The annual 1–26 championships often offer tighter and more exciting flying than open-class national or world contests as pilots strive to wring the maximum speed or distance from the 1–26's moderate (23:1) performance. It's an ideal ship for a young pilot or couple; a used 1–26 can be had from $3,000 up, and its light weight and small size make assembly a snap for a pilot and one helper.

While all of this development was going on in America, the Europeans were far from idle. During the first few years after the war, the problems of survival were pressing enough so that few people could spare much thought or effort for soaring, but by the early 1950s, the movement experienced an inevitable renaissance.

As might be expected, Germany was in the forefront of this development. Many designers and builders from the prewar days reappeared, and the *Akafliegs* were revived at the various universities. The FAI once again took an interest in soaring, and the first postwar World Championship took place at Samedan, Switzerland, in 1948.

One of the most important designs in the history of soaring appeared in Germany at this time, the Ka. 6, designed by Rudolf Kaiser and built by the firm of Alexander Schleicher. The FAI had designated new standards for a special competition class, the standard class. The Ka. 6 was one of the best new designs and was awarded a prize by the FAI. All plywood, the original Ka. 6 went into production as the Ka. 6B, followed soon by the Ka. 6BR (with its landing skid replaced by a wheel) and an improved version, the Ka. 6CR. A new airfoil, a lowered fuselage and an all-flying tail marked the Ka. 6E, one of the finest of the wooden standards and an excellent performer, not only in the moderate conditions of Europe but also in the powerful thermals of the western United States, where it made several 500-mile flights.

Germany did not hold a monopoly on soaring, of course. In England, the venerable firm of Slingsby continued the line of development based on the prewar Kirby Gull and Kite through various models of the Skylark. In France, such advanced designs as the Breguet 901 contained new improvements like flaps and retractable landing gear. Poland became a major power in the soaring world, producing such prize-winning designs as the lovely Foka (Seal) standard and the flap-equipped Zefir open-class wooden sailplanes. Standard-class designs were encouraged by the FAI, and countries such as Holland and Finland entered fine sailplanes like the Sagitta and Vasama, respectively.

For a time, with the development of the wooden standards, soaring seemed to have reached a sort of plateau of development. The pause was only transitory, though; both in the United States and in Europe, relatively young designers were preparing the next major step.

The standard ships were pretty well frozen by the rules of the class: wingspan was set at 15 meters (49.2 feet); retractable landing gear was not permitted, nor were flaps. The effect of these rules was to concentrate development, at least for a time, in the open ("anything goes") class of all-out competition, record, and research machines.

Flaps were one improvement. While a powered aircraft uses flaps to increase lift and drag for landing, the purpose of flaps in a sailplane is to modify the airfoil to accommodate the speed range and flight regime. Thus, flaps might be set below the wing for increased climb, but above the wing for less drag at high speeds. Advanced airfoils were designed for use with flaps, especially by Richard Eppler and F. X. Wortman of Germany. In America, the Sisu—first sailplane to fly over one thousand kilometers—had Fowler flaps that not only changed the curve of "camber" of the wing, but its area (and hence the wing loading) as well.

Reduction of drag was also improved. The frontal area of the fuselage

Two excellent standard-class ships from Poland are the SZD–24C Foka (above) and the SZD–30 Pirat (right). The Foka's introduction in 1960 did much to upgrade standard-class competition technologically and financially.

was reduced by placing the pilot in a semisupine or reclining position, rather than sitting upright; cockpit canopies were faired smoothly into the shape of the nose rather than protruding. Wheels and even towrope hooks were made retractable to reduce every possible vestige of drag, while great attention was paid to the most favorable arrangement of the wing-fuselage junction. Sailplanes started to look more and more streamlined and graceful, like idealized sketches instead of actual aircraft.

In the early 1960s, the *Akafliegs* of Germany made a major breakthrough: fiberglass construction. Until then, true high performance in a sailplane could be obtained only at the expense of months or years of painstaking construction to achieve the necessary accuracy of contour and smoothness of surface. With the advent of fiberglass, all of this changed. The structural qualities of the material allowed sailplanes to be made of only a few major parts, rather than hundreds; and the painstaking smoothing and finishing work was expended, not on a single sailplane, but on the master mold from which any number of aircraft could be made. Moreover, the advent of fiberglass coincided with a number of important devel-

One of the best of the fiberglass sailplanes, the Libelle.

The Bölkow Phoebus (shown here) was a descendant of the Phönix, which pioneered fiberglass-balsa sandwich construction.

opments in flaps and airfoils, so that even the first generation of fiberglass sailplanes represented a major improvement over any existing production sailplane of the time.

One of the first and finest of the new generation, and still one of the world's best sailplanes, was the Libelle (Dragonfly), designed by Wolfgang Hütter and later manufactured by the Glasflügel (literally, "glass wing") company. No larger than a standard, the dainty Libelle had retractable landing gear and camber-changing flaps and could actually fly rings around almost any wooden standard of contemporary vintage. Another *Akaflieg* product, the Phönix, went into production as the Phoebus, initially as a standard, later as a 17-meter retractable-gear open-class ship. In Switzerland, students at the Federal Technical University designed a reclining-pilot fiberglass fuselage that was originally outfitted with Ka. 6 wings. This proved so successful that it went into production with Libelle wings as the Diamant. Within a year or so, the manufacturers added their own wings, available in 16½ - or 18-meter sizes.

Meanwhile, in the United States, competition machines had become the domain of homebuilders and those who could afford one of the German or Swiss "flexible flyers." Schweizer, still the only real manufacturer, directed the thrust of its development toward a wider range of pilots. Several research machines were designed and a few constructed, including the 1–29, Schweizer's first foray into the world of laminar-flow airfoils, and the 1–30, a powered 1–26 designed as a towplane. Their next production design was the 2–32, a beautiful all-metal two-place with an outstandingly comfortable cockpit and performance to match the best of the wooden standards, even surpassing them in terms of speed. The 2–32 remained the world's best production two-place until quite recently, and still holds many multiplace records.

The club fliers and students didn't go unnoticed. Aware that the venerable 2–22 deserved honorable retirement, Schweizer developed the 2–33, a sailplane of similar construction, greater comfort, and performance similar to that of the 1–26. This was followed a couple of years later by the 1–34, an all-metal standard with performance similar to that of the Ka. 6 but of greater ruggedness suitable for club and school use.

An important impetus in American soaring during this period came

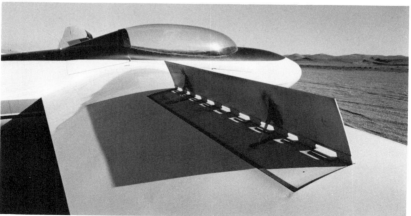

While European ships were reflecting striking new design concepts, the Schweizer 2–32 was establishing itself as America's outstanding high-performance multi-seat ship, setting many records after its introduction in the mid-1960s. Among its advanced design features were spoilers.

The Schweizer 2-33 was the product of a determined effort to bring more people into soaring. A much better performer than previous trainers, the ship became the basic training ship in the United States.

from the kit builders. The 1–26 was available in kit form, and a number were constructed as group projects by Air Explorer posts and the like. High-performance designs were available as well; in California, Gus Briegleb, one of the grand old men of American soaring, was producing kits for the wooden BG–12, an excellent standard, and Jack Laister—designer of the LK–10A wartime trainer as well as the CG–4 troopglider—was putting out the LP–49, a standard of composite construction (metal wings and tail, fiberglass shell). For those in search of all-out performance, Richard Schreder's fine HP–11 design was followed by the HP–14, an open-class machine with camber-changing flaps and retractable gear. Many of these kits were purchased by two or three pilots in partnership, who shared the construction work as well as the expense.

By the mid-1960s, another development step had been reached. Competition sailplanes began carrying water ballast—sometimes several hundred pounds of it—to improve high-speed performance while still allowing the pilot the option of taking off without ballast on weaker days or of lightening the ship en route if necessary. Instrumentation had kept pace with airframe development, and many ships now sported electronic rate-

Gus Briegleb flying one of his BG-12s over California.

A Schempp-Hirth Cirrus, with its drag parachute out to slow it for a landing.

of-climb indicators far more sensitive, faster to respond and more versatile than the heretofore ubiquitous variometer. There were even attempts at developing some sort of thermal sniffer that could sense lift at a distance, but so far, these attempts have remained as inconclusive as they are unsporting.

FAI rules changes have allowed standard-class sailplanes to partake of many of the refinements, such as retractable gear, flaps, and ballast, formerly the exclusive province of the open-class sailplanes. In fact, any of the current generation of glass standards, such as the standard-Libelle, the AS–W15, the Standard Cirrus, or the LS–1 will perform as well as—and cost more than—the first generation open-class fiberglass sailplanes. The original Libelles, Phoebi, and Diamants have themselves been superseded by second-generation open-class ships such as the Cirrus, the Kestrel, the AS–W12, and a subclass of very large and expensive superships such as the Glasflügel 604 (basically a 22-meter Kestrel), the Nimbus, or the BS–1B. The supremacy of the 2–32 has ended with the introduction of such sailplanes as the Italian Caproni, with a 67-foot wingspan and claimed performance of 43:1. For those who shun towplanes, a version of the Caproni is available outfitted with a 220-pound thrust turbojet.

Recent developments in the United States indicate that America may once again become a power in international design competition. Two firms are manufacturing high-performance standards, including Jack Laister's all-metal Nugget, and Schweizer's new 1–35, the firm's first truly competitive sailplane since the 1–21.

Another trend that's becoming increasingly important is the growth of the motorsailer idea; this is particularly attractive to the pilot who lives far from a sailplane base or towplane. Powered sailplanes that are currently available range from machines that are basically airplanes of rather modest power-off gliding—not soaring—performance to all-out machines, like the Caproni, which are among the world's best sailplanes but which can still launch themselves.

Electronics is playing an increasing role in the cockpit, particularly in competition. Integrated circuitry makes possible tiny onboard computers which tell the pilot how fast to cruise, when and how high to climb, and when to begin the final glide toward home base. Admittedly, these devices

Schweizer's 1-34, introduced in 1969, featured dive brakes beneath the wings and spoilers above them.

The new, all-metal 1-35 represents Schweizer's major effort to end standard-class dominance by European fiberglass ships in this country.

The Nelson Hummingbird is one of the early birds of the growing power-glider movement.

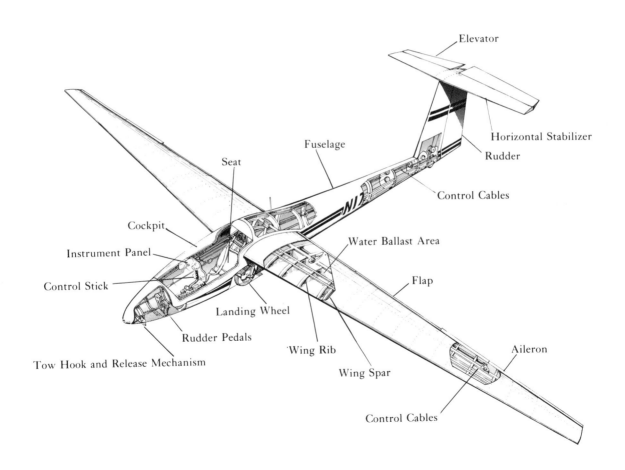

ANATOMY OF A MODERN SAILPLANE (Schweizer 1-35)

are no better than the quality of information fed into them, and so far they don't seem to affect contest scores very much, but they're bound to improve. Besides, they're impressive to watch and/or listen to as they flash lights, move dials, and whirp, click, buzz, and bleep to indicate various conditions or malfunctions.

It's not easy to say where the future will lead soaring. If it's anything like the past, it will lead us in several directions at once.

One direction will be past the present superships to what we could call "superduperships." Several such projects are already underway; for example, a German sailplane (the SB–10), which uses composite materials such as boron fibers to provide adequate stiffness for its 35-meter (115-foot) wingspan, or the home-built "Alcor," a Seattle-based 20-meter sailplane with pressurized, heated cabin for high-altitude exploration.

Another direction is exactly 180 degrees away: the trend toward simpler, less expensive sailplanes—a new standard class. This might be called the sport class, and it's anticipated that sailplanes within it might be restricted to a 13-meter wingspan. In the United States there is a low-performance approximation of such a class, the 1–26.

A further step along these lines might be that of self-launched, or foot-launched sailplanes, a development that looks more and more attractive in this age of pollution and fuel crises. The hang-glider movement is growing rapidly; in the few short years of hang-gliding's resurgence we've already seen amazing increases in sophistication and performance. Future breakthroughs in aerodynamics and materials may yet produce true sailplanes light enough to be carried to a hilltop and foot-launched, yet of sufficient performance for hours-long flights covering many cross-country miles.

In any case, the history of soaring and sailplane development since World War II has been one of steadily accelerating progress. By now the curve of advancement is rising exponentially, and it seems safe to say that the next ten years will be the most exciting the sport, art, and science of soaring have ever had.

4 A SPORT OF
GENEROSITY

Soaring can be a sport full of paradoxes and contrasts. One of the most obvious of these is that soaring is a sport at once solitary and gregarious. Many pilots are drawn to silent flight as much by the opportunities it offers for solitude, introspection, and even splendid isolation as by any other attraction. Yet soaring pilots tend to share a camaraderie that is lacking in many other sports.

There are many reasons for this social behavior. Soaring may always remain a sport of the fortunate few rather than a mass activity, as skiing and boating have become. This means that usually the sailplane pilots in a given area all know each other personally. Then there's the special passion that soaring seems to awaken in those who are serious about it. Such intense pleasure is much more easily shared with one who also has experienced it. The main reason, which constantly serves to reinforce the camaraderie of glider pilots, is their mutual interdependence. With the exception of hang-glider pilots, no one can soar without the aid of others, and most soaring pilots alternate between the roles of helper and helped.

Climbing effortlessly in a thermal or cruising silently cross-country, the sailplane is the epitome of freedom. From the instant its wheel touches the ground until the moment when the towline is dropped for the next flight, though, this lone eagle is metamorphosed into an ungainly, helpless creature. It is only through the aid of people that this change can be reversed.

There are two distinct levels of aid needed by any soaring pilot. Simply getting a sailplane aloft for a local flight can be a fairly major production. When a pilot sets out on a cross-country flight, his need for assistance makes an almost quantum jump. Should he be flying in competition, the demands placed on his helpers increase even more.

In many cases, soaring clubs help apportion the work evenly. In Europe such clubs are the rule rather than the exception, and it seems to go

60

without saying that every pilot will also spend a given number of hours in the workshop, at the field among the operations crew, or at any of a number of other tasks. In the United States, where individual ownership of sailplanes is rather more prevalent and clubs rarer, some of these functions are occasionally taken over by the commercial operators of gliderports. While this is anything but a thankless way of earning a living, it's certainly not an easy one.

For a typical day's soaring at an American gliderport, the pilot rises early and notes that the day looks good for soaring. His first step probably will be to call the weather bureau, or possibly phone his gliderport, to get a better idea of the conditions. Getting a promising report, he drives to the gliderport, which may be located in the country as much as eighty miles from his metropolitan home.

While glider operations are frequently carried out at general-aviation airports, many of the better gliderports are more or less entirely dedicated to soaring. Their construction and maintenance are carried out entirely by the commercial operators who run them. The local pilots are thus the fields' only source of income. Such fields typically offer such services as hangar space and/or tie-down facilities for protecting sailplanes, for sailplane rental, and for pilot instruction and sailplane launching by aero tow or winch. Some of the larger operators offer such added fillips as restaurants, some of which are excellent, others of which can be terrible, bunkhouses or motels, hot showers, swimming pools, camping facilities, and sailplane construction and repair shops. Sites located near wave-soaring areas usually provide oxygen and rental of special gear such as warm clothing, bail-out bottles, high-altitude barographs, and so forth. All of these services are surprisingly low in cost to the individual pilot as long as enough local pilots use the field and its services.

Arriving at his field, the pilot goes to the office/line shack. If he were a student pilot, he'd rent a sailplane owned and maintained by the field, signing out with the person who keeps track of flight times and tow rates. Usually, he owns a sailplane in partnership with two or three other local pilots, none of whom is at the field this day.

Some sailplanes are tied down outdoors at the field, but most owners of high-performance craft want more protection. This pilot's craft is kept

Above: From the beginning of the development of sophisticated ships, such as this Baby Albatross, the ritual of assembly and disassembly has been part and parcel of soaring. Below: Simple tools, concentration, and patience are usually what are needed to put together even a high-performance sailplane such as this Schweizer 1-34.

in its enclosed trailer at the airfield so that all three partners can have easy access to it. All three share in the maintenance and upkeep and occasionally meet at the field for nonflying workdays when the "things-to-do" list gets large enough. Last year, they kept their bird in the hangar, but have since decided on trailer storage instead: while it was nice to have the ship constantly assembled, it always seemed to be at the back of the hangar when needed. This meant dismantling a complex interlocking puzzle of nine other sailplanes—four with wingspans larger than the hangar door —and moving them all outside before they could get their own sailplane out.

As he heads for his trailer, he notices the pilot two trailers down the row starting to unlock the doors of his trailer, so he goes over to help the man rig his sailplane. It's a recent fiberglass ship with a sophisticated trailer, so the two of them have the wings on in less than ten minutes. Our pilot's glider is an older design, and his trailer doesn't have the automatic wing dollies and fuselage supports of the latest models, so he and the man he helped round up two more pilots, for the initial stages of assembling his glider require four people. One holds the fuselage upright while the other three carry the left wing over from the trailer; two hold the 160-pound root and one supports the tip. Once the wing is mounted to the fuselage, the fuselage man lets go, leaving the man at the left wingtip to hold the wing level and the fuselage erect. The fuselage man can now aid the other two in bringing the right wing out of the trailer and mounting it. The final step involves a man at each tip while our pilot inserts the main locking pins in the spar carry-through. Since these are ground to very close tolerances, there's a good deal of "Forward on the right tip . . . more . . . more . . . too much . . . okay, raise the left tip a little . . . now wiggle both of them . . ." until the pins are properly seated and safetied.

With the wings secured, the pilot can continue on his own. One wingtip is placed on the ground and weighted with a parachute as security against wind gusts; the horizontal tail is installed and the controls are connected —a job seldom left to anyone other than the pilot. The canopy is polished. The pilot may well help to assemble one or two other sailplanes, since this is a day for local flying and he's in no particular hurry to be aloft.

When it's finally time to fly, the pilot again will depend on the help of several people to prepare for takeoff. Since a sailplane cannot taxi, it will have to be walked or towed to the takeoff area. Even if it's pulled with a car, someone will have to walk holding up one wingtip, since there's only a single wheel in the center of the fuselage. Today both aero and winch tow are being used at different areas on the field.

At each takeoff area, the sailplanes are marshaled by a line chief, aided by one or two henchmen or APEs (this is not a derogatory term but stands for Aircraft Placement Engineers). Line crews are often high school students who work at the field and get paid in flying time and instruction; often, they stay on later as tow pilots or glider instructors. One by one, the sailplanes move up the line and are towed aloft by the towplane; after each tow, the towplane pilot makes a low pass over the takeoff line to drop the towrope before landing. As the sailplane pilot's turn approaches, an APE helps him move his sailplane into position and helps him in fastening his parachute and safety harness in the cramped cockpit while another gets a towrope from the rope-drop area and attaches it to the towhook under the sailplane's nose. The release mechanism of the plane is checked while the towplane is waved into position by the line chief; the towrope is connected to the towplane and the sailplane canopy is closed. At a signal from the pilot, an APE grasps a wingtip of the sailplane and holds it level; seeing this, the tow pilot taxis slowly forward until the rope is taut. The sailplane's rudder is moved back and forth vigorously to give the signal to launch. As the sailplane begins to roll, the APE at the wingtip runs alongside, supporting it until the speed is sufficient for aileron control to become effective.

With any luck, the tow pilot will also be glider-rated and know where to expect lift in the local area; he'll try to put the sailplane in a good area at the desired release altitude. At two thousand feet, the sailplane pilot feels a good thermal and releases; he's finally on his own, after being aided by as many as ten people. Of course, it's quite possible that he may fail to strike good lift and be on the ground again in half an hour for another try, helped uncomplainingly by the same crew.

Had he elected to use winch launch, the takeoff line would have been quite similar, again with a line chief and helpers. The tow pilot would have been supplanted by a winch operator, and there would be one addi-

Unlike powered planes, which can taxi, sailplanes have to be pushed or pulled into place, with the inevitable linemen keeping them upright.

It is always an exciting moment for a student when the towrope is attached to the trainer. The student sits up front, the instructor behind him.

tional helper, the driver of the retrieve car, which speeds down the runway after each winch launch to bring the end of the 3,000-foot steel winch wire back for the next launch. With continual trips down a straight, wide runway, many of these retrieve drivers develop speed-shifting skills that would be the envy of seasoned champion drag racers.

When the sailplane lands after a few hours of local soaring, the process is more or less reversed. Willing hands walk the glider back to the trailer and help in the disassembly process; the pilot, in turn, helps others. Finally, all repair to a nearby restaurant to rehash the day's flying.

A commercial operator charges for hangarage or trailer storage, sailplane rental, instruction and towing; the cost of the line crew is absorbed in tow charges. All of these operations can also be carried out by club members, who are not paid in money but in low rental and tow fees using club-owned equipment. Many clubs operate their own airports on a noncommercial, expenses-shared basis. For those with the time and inclination, there's no cheaper or pleasanter way to fly than with such a club.

So far, we've dealt only with the forces necessary to get a pilot into the

A crew member removes the tail dolly from a Cirrus.

air. When we start to think about cross-country and competition soaring, a new figure is introduced: the loyal crewman.

As soon as a pilot flies away from his home field, he's exposed to the possibility of landing out, either at some other airport or in a randomly chosen field of some sort. Many cross-country flights are planned as out-and-return or triangle-course ventures, but the possibility of off-field landing is still there, and if a pilot is trying for maximum distance, he's bound to land away. All of this means that he cannot merely venture forth alone, but must be followed by someone who'll help get him home. This is the responsibility of the crew.

A crew can be composed of as few as one person or as many as are required to handle disassembly of a sailplane in the field. Two may well be the ideal number: two crewmen help each other, share the tasks, and take turns driving the crew car; three people, including the pilot, are sufficient to disassemble and trailer-load almost any sailplane.

A crew often includes the pilot's spouse or close friend. Crewing can be an excellent testing ground for those considering marriage, since a rough stint at crewing can either cement a good relationship or dissolve a shaky one. Very often, pilots will crew for one another on an exchange basis. For a pilot, crewing can be lots of fun, and crewing for a more experienced pilot is one of the best ways to learn cross-country technique at minimal risk and expense.

The crew has two basic responsibilities: helping the pilot prepare for his flight, and getting him home after he lands. In return, a pilot pays all of his crew's expenses while they labor on his behalf.

Let us say that our pilot's two partners are going to crew for him on an attempt at the 500-kilometer (about 312 miles) flight required for the Distance Diamond award, one of several such awards for which he can try. A partnership is one of the best ways of ensuring crew availability; he and his two partners crew for one another on a regularly rotating basis. Today, the weather forecast looks excellent, so by ten o'clock in the morning they've assembled the sailplane and prepared it for a long flight. All the joints and gaps have been taped over to reduce drag; the wings have been washed and polished; the oxygen bottle has been filled; the battery has been charged overnight. Some extra equipment is loaded into

A typical sailplane rig: a trailer to house the ship, a crew car, and a friend to serve as crew. At soaring meets, competitors sometimes set up housekeeping at the field.

the sailplane's tiny baggage area: a compact survival kit, a set of tie-down stakes and ropes, and a thermos of ice water with a plastic tube leading to the cockpit. The elasticized pockets along both sides of the cockpit are loaded with maps of the planned route, the plastic glide-angle calculator, spare pencils, a Chap Stick and other necessities and conveniences. There is usually something to nibble on—perhaps some nonmelting hard candy or an apple or two, even a sandwich for the luxury-loving pilot, and, for long flights, some sort of relief tube or plastic bottle. Finally, the all-important barograph, a recording device that plots altitudes flown during the flight, is wound, started and carefully hung in its shockproof mount. Its trace must be submitted for the flight to be valid.

A good crew will attend to all these details, encouraging the pilot to relax somewhere. After all, he'll be in the cockpit as long as eight or nine hours, and every bit of rest he can get now will be a help late in the day.

After an hour or so, conditions begin to look promising. The sailplane is moved to the takeoff line and the crews help the pilot get set in the cockpit. Comfort is more a necessity than a luxury for a long flight, so the crew makes sure that all the parachute straps are smooth and unkinked, that everything the pilot will want is in easy reach, and that the all-important barograph is turned on and recording properly. The line boy arrives with the towrope and the flight begins.

As soon as the crew is certain that the sailplane will not land within a few minutes, they hook the trailer to the car and check to see that all is secure for the road. Modern pilots have a great aid to crewing in the form of a radio; the crew car has a transistorized transceiver that will operate on 123.3 mHz, the approved glider frequency. The car is fitted out to aid crewing, too: it has a compass, an altimeter, an extra-large radiator, and jerrycans of fuel and water. The crew members have added a well-filled picnic chest and soft-drink cooler and have an aero chart marked with the intended flight course. Every ten miles, the course is marked with a letter on both the crew's map and the pilot's; this simplifies position reporting for both. "I'm in fair lift three miles past Point J; proceed to Point L and wait there," the pilot may report.

With the glider aloft and the crew ready to roll, a waiting period may ensue. The pilot may not want to leave at once, but may stay above the field, preferring to watch conditions for a while or see how other sail-planes are doing. The crew might park the car-trailer rig in the shade and head for the airfield lunchroom, since they have a transistor aircraft-band radio to monitor when they're away from the car. On the other hand, the pilot may send the crew out ahead of him if he anticipates conditions strong enough to make his average speed higher than the crew's.

When the crew finally gets the signal to roll, they check out at the gliderport office; this sets into operation a communication system, which may be required later. Ideally, the crew will move along the highways closest to the course line, holding or proceeding according to the desires of the pilot. A good crew will do a great deal on its own initiative rather than bother the pilot, who may be pretty busy on his own. An unwritten rule is that a really good crew monitors the radio constantly but never initiates a call to the pilot unless they haven't heard from him after an hour or more.

On the road, the members take turns as driver and "navigator"; the latter handles all map reading, radio monitoring, bottle opening, and sandwich passing chores, since the driver often has his hands full with the 35-foot trailer in traffic. Both attempt to keep the sailplane in sight, but this is usually impossible if conditions are strong. They can discuss condi-tions and make educated guesses on the glider's position if they lose visual contact with it.

Sooner or later, particularly in mountainous areas, radio contact is likely to be lost as well. Now the contingency communications plan is put into effect: every half-hour, the crew finds a telephone and places a person-to-person call to the pilot at the home gliderport. As long as the glider's still airborne, the field will refuse the call. When the pilot finally lands, he'll get to a phone and call the field; within half an hour, the crew will call again and be advised of his position.

Of course, the crew members never turn their radio off; contact might be reestablished directly, or another pilot might relay a message. In fact, a number of airline pilots are soaring enthusiasts and habitually tune a radio to the glider frequency when flying over known soaring areas. Not a few crews are stunned when a powerful voice announces, "Three Bravo Ground, this is United 450 at forty thousand feet. I have a message from your pilot."

Meanwhile, the pilot has been doing his best to make miles. There was a bad scare about an hour ago when he was down to eight hundred feet above a small and apparently roadless meadow in the mountains; visions of a two-day hike to civilization loomed large. It wouldn't be the first time that an entire glider club had to turn out to carry wings and fuselage for miles to the nearest trailerable road. This time, though, the traditional last-minute bubble of lift has made a "save" possible, and now the pilot is running under a cloud street in good lift, making good about seventy miles per hour groundspeed. The cloudstreet eliminates the need for circling and he even has time for a sandwich and an apple before running to the end of the clouds.

Back on the road, the loyal crew forges on. Radio contact has been lost, but the conditions look good, so it's unlikely that the ship is down. There is another fruitless phone call to the field. The crew decides to refuel the car and press on about twenty miles to a point where the highway crests a high mountain pass. From this position, their radio range will be greatly increased and there'll be a good chance of contacting the glider now, hopefully, far ahead of them.

Every pilot who flies out of gliding distance to his home airport expects that he may have to put down in a farmer's field, a meadow, or some other less comfortable landing spot. It's a matter of landing, waiting for the crew, and dismantling the sailplane.

In weaker conditions, it could have been easier for the crew to remain more or less beneath their pilot; this can be an important landing aid. It can contribute greatly to the pilot's peace of mind to be able to ask the crew to scout a likely-looking landing field (that's why crew cars have altimeters), determine the ground wind speed and direction, or, in extremis, use the car and detached trailer to block off a few hundred feet of highway for landing.

By the time the crew reaches the top of the pass, the day's thermal activity is dying. The pilot is still short of five hundred kilometers, but he's planned for this: He's been staying higher and higher as the afternoon has waned. As he tops the last gentle thermal, he has sufficient altitude for a final straight glide of over thirty miles. Moreover, he's contacted the crew and told them to press on to an area near his assumed landing spot.

About forty-five minutes later, he jubilantly crosses the five hundred-kilometer point as marked on his chart; he's still two thousand feet above the ground. He's passed over some hills that have cut him off from the crew's radio once again, so he chooses a recently cut hayfield near a lighted farmhouse and lands. After securing the sailplane with his tie-down kit, he walks to the farmhouse, knocks on the door, and asks the astonished farmer and his wife to sign his landing card; this, with the barograph record, will substantiate his flight. Then he telephones the gliderport so that they'll be able to give his crew the exact coordinates from the aero chart of his landing point.

Within another half-hour, the crew arrive and congratulate him on his flight. They leave him to rest while they load the sailplane onto the trailer; after all, he's been in the cockpit almost seven hours. After thanking the farmer and his wife for an excellent country dinner, they drive away to start the six-hour drive home.

Today has been a day when everything went well. Every pilot and crew can regale you with tales of disaster: landing atop inaccessible peaks, a sobbing crewman pouring the last cold can of beer into a boiling radiator, pilots without radio changing their minds in flight and heading off on a new course ninety degrees different from what they had been flying. The list is endless. Perhaps the saddest tale is one of the novice crewman who radioed his terrifyingly low pilot that there was a smooth, green field just

For the dedicated, soaring is often very much a family affair.

past a row of trees, only to find too late that the green was algae growing atop a sewage-settling pond.

Also, today's flight was fairly easygoing. In competition, demands on crews become more severe. The crew must be ready to roll instantly when the pilot sets out on course and stay right under him for the first fifty miles or so, because if he goes down early enough in the day he'll want to try for a "relight"—a frantic return to the field and a reassembly of the sailplane for another try. Radio communication becomes difficult when there are up to eighty pilots and crews on the same channel, and pilot tempers fray during long competitions. A good crew is worth his or her weight in plutonium in a competition; the crew must combine total skill and dedication with Job-like patience and an immunity to imprecations delivered by an overwrought pilot. It has been said of one top-ranked pilot, "The longest list in soaring is those who've crewed once for him; the shortest, those who've crewed twice." The above notwithstanding, crewing is as rewarding in its own way as actual cross-country soaring; you won't be a real dyed-in-the-wool soaring buff until you've sampled the delights and despairs of both.

5 PRACTICAL MATTERS

Getting started in soaring is remarkably easy for the complete novice and even easier for those who already hold ratings for powered aircraft. If you're not familiar with a gliderport in your area, write to the Soaring Society of America at Box 66071, Los Angeles, California 90066. They'll send you a list of the clubs, schools, and commercial operators in your area. If you don't already hold a pilot's license, don't worry about a physical exam; none is required. Instead, at some point before you solo, you'll have to write in your logbook, "I certify that I have no known physical defect which would make me unable to pilot a glider," and sign your name.

Costs can vary, but most commercial operators charge between $12 and $15 per hour for rental of a two-place trainer. The services of the flight instructor, who is certified by the Federal Aviation Administration, will be another $6 to $8 per hour. A major factor in your training costs will be towing. For an airplane tow to two thousand feet—which is typical for a training flight—expect to pay $5 to $7. Assuming two tows per hour of dual instruction logged, your first ten hours at a commercial operation could cost between $330 and $440. Sometime during this period—probably after eight hours or so—you're likely to have soloed.

If you can spend more time participating on the ground than aloft and would like to spend less money, you may prefer to join a soaring club. You might pay $100 to join, and unless the club has a towplane, you'd be paying the same amount for tows as would a nonmember, so your first ten hours could cost between $200 and $240, even if the sailplane and instructor were free (with the exception of monthly dues). This is often the case; if not, charges are usually much smaller than at commercial operations: typically $5 per hour for the sailplane and similar or smaller amounts for the instructor. All this is not as expensive as it seems, though. Remember that the club initiation fee is usually refundable when a member resigns, so that costs for the first ten hours can actually be as low as $100. Some operations have their own towplanes, which can reduce the costs even further.

Before he or she allows you to solo, your instructor will make sure that you can handle the sailplane safely in all conditions, both on and off tow; that you can keep closely in position behind the towplane; that you can recognize and avoid dangerous flight conditions; and that you have the necessary skill, experience, and judgment to land safely at the training site.

It's an adage in aviation that you really start to learn after you solo. It's quite possible that you'll be allowed to attempt short cross-country flights of a few miles before you try for your private license.

There are, of course, regulations regarding your education as a glider pilot; they appear in Part 61 of the Federal Aviation Regulations. To solo, you must be at least fourteen years old, have certified that you have no physical defects, possess a current Student Pilot Certificate (obtainable from the FAA without examination for $2), and have the certificate and your logbook endorsed by your instructor for solo flight.

As a student pilot you cannot carry passengers, even though you'll probably still be flying the two-place sailplane you learned to fly in. By the time you've gained more experience, you should be ready for your private license. The FAA has various requirements for knowledge and experience, and you'll have to pass a flight test administered by an FAA inspector or designated pilot examiner.

One of the things you'll have to do is take a written test at the nearest FAA General Aviation District Office. There are only fifty multiple-choice questions, and you have three hours to answer them, so you can take your time. The questions will cover regulations, aeronautical knowledge, safe operating procedures, and weather and cross-country flight planning. The passing grade is 70. Incidentally, you needn't wait until you're ready for the flight test; the written test can be taken at any time. You'll get the results within a few weeks; if you don't pass the first time, you can try again in thirty days.

You'll have to have passed the written and be recommended by your

Many a casual first demonstration ride has led to the making of a new pilot, as the panorama and peacefulness of soaring flight seduce him or her.

instructor before you can face the FAA examiner. You'll also have to have logged at least seventy solo flights, including twenty during which you make a 360-degree turn, or seven hours of solo time, including thirty-five flights if launched by ground tow (winch or auto) or twenty if launched by airplane tow. During the flight test, you won't be expected to show superhuman skills, but to be in complete control of the glider at all times while executing normal maneuvers and recovering from potentially dangerous situations. You'll also have to land with the nose of the glider coming to a stop short of, but within two hundred feet of, a designated point or line on the runway. Even if you are already a power pilot, you'll have to take this flight test, but for you there's no written examination, and the experience requirement is only ten solo flights in which 360-degree turns were made.

Even if you don't plan on using them, obtaining commercial and/or instructor ratings can be a rewarding experience. Clubs encourage their members to go on to the advanced ratings, since most training is done by club members with instructor ratings rather than by paid outside instructors. Instructing is a whole world in itself; frequently the instructor can find himself learning as much as the student he's teaching, and soloing a student for the first time is often just as satisfying to the instructor as it is to his protégé. Moreover, should you someday have your own ship, your insurance rates will be lower if you have an advanced rating.

As in the case of the private license, the commercial license requires a written test. This one goes into much more detail on the subjects that appear on the private exam. The experience requirement is for twenty-five flying hours, of which at least twenty must be in gliders; one hundred flights as pilot in command, with at least twenty-five including a 360-degree turn; or, in the case of a commercial pilot making the conversion, twenty flights as pilot in command with the usual 360-degree turns.

The major difference is the flight test. Where the private applicant has to demonstrate his ability for only one sort of launch—usually airplane tow—the commercial applicant must demonstrate skill in both airplane tow and ground launches, unless he can be content with a license endorsed for only one or the other. The other required maneuvers are more or less similar to those required for the private license, but precision, rather than just competence, is the watchword; for example, the accuracy landing area in this test is 100 feet rather than 200.

The minimum age for the commercial or flight instructor rating is eighteen; that for the private, seventeen.

The flight-instructor rating is rather different from the others. While great emphasis has always been placed on precision flying as a requisite to being an instructor, today's instructor is expected to be just as well versed in the methods and psychology of the instruction process itself. The flight-experience requirements are the same as for the commercial license, since you must have one in order to become an instructor, but the main thrust of both the written examination and the flight test is toward effective instruction. It's not enough to be able to do the maneuvers; you must be able to explain them clearly. Unlike the other ratings, which do not expire (although a biennial proficiency review is required), the instructor rating expires after twenty-four months. It can be renewed, however, through retesting, by attending an FAA-sponsored Flight Instruction Clinic, or by showing sufficient logged instructional activity during the prior twenty-four months.

What about the soaring clubs themselves? To many pilots, soaring offers the epitome of solitude—while in flight. Nonetheless, soaring pilots tend to band together, and the sport is still one in which a great many of its adherents know each other personally. The bond of a shared experience as powerful and special as soaring is strong. Once a group begins to form, however casually, organization is frequently not long in coming.

Soaring clubs and groups don't form just for social reasons, though. Practical considerations are often paramount in the purposes of these groups, which range from informal flying partnerships of two or three pilots through local and regional clubs up to the 12,000-member Soaring Society of America, which, through the National Aeronautic Association, provides the American soaring movement liaison with the Fédération Aéronautique Internationale, the worldwide governing body for all sport aviation.

At the simplest level, informal partnerships are often formed for no higher purpose than to allow two or more pilots to fly together or share beer and hangar talk at the end of the day. Many two- or three-pilot groups

Above: Soaring is not only the experience of being aloft. Its pleasures also exist in solving mechanical problems with the help of one's friends. Right: People who soar are often quiet preservers of intense individuality.

are formed—usually informally, although sometimes with written agreements—to allow members to pool their resources and obtain a sailplane that none could afford to own individually. This is an ideal way to obtain a sailplane, since it's unusual that one person employed at a steady job finds enough flying time to justify sole ownership of an expensive sailplane.

A step beyond the partnership is the local soaring club. These clubs span a wide range of size and complexity, ranging from larger versions of partnerships to formal legal entities that own many sailplanes, often a few towplanes and sometimes a club soaring site of their own. More often, large clubs will own or lease hangars and other facilities on an existing gliderport or airport.

A few clubs represent outgrowths of partnerships and own high-performance sailplanes only. Such clubs often require considerable experience and proficiency as entrance requirements and also fairly sizable entrance fees and monthly dues payments. For example, a club consisting of twenty-five members owning three $8,000 sailplanes might assess a new member $1,000, with monthly dues of $25 or so. In such cases, membership is limited to a fairly small fixed number. The entry fee is refunded when a member leaves the club. Dues payments go toward hangar rent, maintenance, and insurance. For the serious pilot who can't spend $8,000 to $10,000 for a good sailplane but who feels $1,000 to be worthwhile, such clubs fill a need. Emphasis is placed on cross-country and competition soaring, and the planes are appropriately equipped with trailers and advanced instruments.

For the novice or the pleasure pilot who finds the price and proficiency requirements of a club like the above too forbidding, there's another type of group. General soaring clubs are rather more numerous than high-performance ones. Although they often have many sailplanes, and sometimes their own towplane as well, they tend more toward simple trainers and utility types. Their entry costs, dues, flying charges (if any), and proficiency requirements are all lower. Many such organizations not only permit but welcome zero-time beginners and provide them with flight training. Typical fees might be from $100 to $250 for entry, $10 per month dues, and perhaps $2 to $5 per hour for sailplane rental; instruction is often given free by a rated club member.

Clubs such as these are similar to the large clubs of Europe, although the latter are sometimes government-subsidized and frequently have a paid employee or two. In addition to offering a rewarding social experience, they represent the cheapest way to learn to soar, at the expense of time. If he's signed up to fly on a given day, a member should be present for the entire day to help with tasks like shifting sailplanes on the ground, helping to assemble or maintain them, cleaning canopies, and hooking up towplanes. This sort of work is fun, and by doing it the novice can learn a great deal about soaring before he ever gets behind the controls. Rules regarding advanced soaring or cross-country trips vary from club to club; many allow cross-country flights once certain proficiencies have been demonstrated, and some keep special gliders for that purpose. A few clubs —particularly in Europe, but in the United States as well—span the entire range of soaring, from the most basic training to the most exotic supership, allowing a member to move up as his skills (and sometimes his financial resources) increase.

Areas that offer good soaring conditions often have fairly large numbers of pilots and planes, and it's not uncommon for several clubs to form larger regional clubs or soaring councils. In many cases the primary function of such superclubs is to provide liaison among various local groups as well as a united front when dealing with local authorities of the FAA. Occasionally, these groups combine their resources to purchase land and facilities for their own soaring sites. Such groups often organize special large-scale activities, such as soaring competitions or encampments; many publish elaborate monthly journals that are more like magazines than are the mimeographed newsletters of the small clubs.

Occasionally, other interests bring soaring pilots into specialized groups. There have been German and Hungarian soaring clubs in the United States and clubs sponsored by firms (often an aircraft company) for their employees. One club in California specializes in the development of competition techniques for pilots and contest organizers. Its occasional contest workshops not only have produced some excellent competition pilots but also have evolved procedures that are now standard at world championship contests.

Greater love hath no man than that of a woman who will carefully wash down the wings of his sailplane before he goes off to fly.

Nearly every nation has a national aero club. In the United States, the National Aeronautic Association has chosen to delegate all soaring-activity responsibilities to the Soaring Society of America, a nonprofit national organization formed in 1937. The SSA provides liaison among the clubs, soaring sites, and commercial operators throughout the country; virtually every active pilot is a member. The SSA's Governmental Liaison Board helps the FAA to formulate its policies regarding motorless flight. One of the society's most important roles is the organization and regulation of soaring competition; the SSA sanctions and governs the twelve Regional Championships and one National Championship held each year and selects the members of the U.S. national soaring team sent to the biennial World Championships. As NAA and FAI representative, the SSA is also responsible for the administration of the U.S. section of the FAI International Soaring Achievement Award program, by which pilots can earn silver, gold, and diamond soaring badges. Finally, the society publishes an excellent monthly magazine, *Soaring*.

The Fédération Aéronautique Internationale was founded in 1905 to supervise and document the attempts that pilots already were then making to establish records in airplanes. Very soon, it began looking after balloon and glider records as well. Today, it makes record, proficiency-badge, and world-championship rules for all the aeronautical disciplines, including helicopters, model aircraft, aerobatics, and astronautics. The original nation members were the United States, Belgium, Germany, Spain, Great Britain, France, Italy, and Switzerland. Now fifty-nine nations are represented within the FAI.

This worldwide organization is headquartered in two small offices inside the Aero Club of France, in the center of Paris. The massive quantity of the work of the FAI is presided over by just two amiable and bilingual people. Surprisingly, this staff is enough, because the structure of the FAI relies on the expertise and energy of pilot enthusiasts all over the world to do a great deal of the work. This sensible arrangement ensures that the international rules and procedures of recording aeronautical achievements are made by people who are currently flying.

The FAI is made up of eleven commissions, one for each airborne sport, such as soaring, or activity, such as Air Education. Each commission is composed of an expert representative from each member country. The Soaring Society of America, for example, chooses whom it will send to represent the United States on the gliding commission—the Commission Internationale Vol à Voile. The CIVV then elects its own president and vice-presidents from among the national representatives by secret ballot. Coordination of the commission, general policy and finance are taken care of by the FAI Council, which is also made up of representatives of member nations. At the top of the federation's structure is the General Conference. This convention is held each year in a different country. There decisions made by the Council are ratified after debate among members of all the FAI nations.

As has been pointed out, the FAI office in Paris does not deal with applications for all the badges and records that are achieved. It gives a great deal of responsibility to national organizations, such as the SSA. It does, however, require confirmation of world-record claims, and occasionally will reject a claimed record. In these matters, time is important. While national aero clubs, such as the SSA, digest the heap of dirty, illegible scraps of paper that usually constitute the landing certificate and other

Climbing above California's San Joaquin Valley, a Schweizer 1-26 is towed to altitude before it sets off on a cross-country flight.

vital flight data that document the setting of a record, the pilot expecting to become famous must let the FAI know of his accomplishment within forty-eight hours.

Whether they are club pilots, fun fliers or supership owners, most pilots sooner or later feel the urge to try for the International Soaring Badges awarded by the FAI. There are three badges: silver, gold, and gold with diamonds, each successive award representing flight of greater difficulty. While the silver badge is fairly common, the gold is less so, and the gold with all three diamonds (there are separate tasks for each diamond) is still a major achievement. Although the badge requirements were set in the 1930s, the first three-diamond badge was not won until 1954, and there are only about fifteen hundred issued by now. Even so, pilots are already talking about an even stiffer challenge award, perhaps a badge of platinum or gold with emeralds, which would have a new requirement suited to the performance of today's supersailplanes.

The silver badge requires three tasks: a duration flight of five hours, a gain of altitude of at least one kilometer (3,281 feet) above the altitude at which the towplane was released, and a cross-country flight of fifty kilo-meters (about thirty-one miles). Not more than two tasks can be accom-plished on a single flight.

The duration flight, or "big sit," is fairly simple to accomplish in almost any trainer on a good soaring day. Fatigue, cramp, thirst, and boredom are the major hazards. To verify that the pilot was indeed aloft for the entire time, a sealed altitude recorder, or barograph, is carried. This device scribes a trace representing altitude over time on a smoked foil or on paper. After the flight, the trace is examined by an FAI official observer (another pilot who holds a silver badge or badge leg) and forwarded with the application to SSA headquarters for processing.

The barograph is also used to verify the altitude gain. Immediately after release, the glider pilot will dive off 200 feet or so of altitude to make a clearly perceptible "notch" on the barograph trace. This establishes a base altitude against which the flight's later high point can be measured.

With today's high-performance sailplanes, it would be simple to be towed to a high altitude, release, and glide fifty kilometers with no soaring skill needed whatsoever. Therefore, for the silver-badge flight, a rule

As the towplane and glider gather speed on takeoff, the lineman sprints to keep the wings level until the glider's ailerons become effective.

stipulates that the release altitude can be no more than 500 meters (about 1,600 feet) above the landing point. On longer flights, a sliding scale is applied to excess altitude to determine a distance penalty, which is subtracted from the actual distance. The badge itself consists of three white seagulls on a circular blue background, surrounded by a silver oak-leaf wreath.

The requirements for the gold badge are a five-hour flight (the one made for the silver badge counts here, if you like); an altitude gain of 3,000 meters (about 10,000 feet); and a distance flight of 300 kilometers (a little over 186 miles). Again, only two tasks can be accomplished on one flight.

Once you've got the gold badge, the three diamonds are earned individually. One requires an altitude gain of 5,000 meters (about 16,000 feet); one calls for a distance flight of 500 kilometers (about 312 miles); and one calls for a flight of 300 kilometers on a closed course (either to a goal 150 kilometers distant and return, or around a triangle). Turnpoints are verified either by ground observers or by photographs taken from the glider.

The barograph is carried on all flights. Its presence is self-explanatory for the altitude legs, but it is required for verification that the distance flights were accomplished with no intermediate landing and to determine the altitude/distance penalty, if any. Upon landing at the end of a distance attempt, the pilot must secure two witnesses and obtain their signatures on a landing card that is part of the badge leg application, a form which also is used to define the turnpoints for out-and-return or triangle flights before takeoff.

What's left to do once you have all the diamonds? For some, there's a thrill in attempting to set new records, using homologation procedures very similar to those used for badge legs. For others, the lure of head-to-head soaring competition is very strong.

6 FIRST TOW
THROUGH SOLO

At the start, all flying is the same. It is an imposing mystery which to a novice is full of boundless difficulties. Instructors all seem at first a little cold, a little indifferent, because they shrug off your hints about what you are feeling—a sense of awe, anxiety, uncertainty. The question "Can I really do it?" lies in your heart like an ice-cold iron ball.

The odd thing about it, the thing that takes some people more time and some less to learn, is that very little *doing* is required. The airplane is a bird that nearly knows how to fly by itself; you only have to give it a little help. The best flying students perhaps would be children. Unself-conscious and freighted with few preconceptions, they make quick connections between their actions and the results, and they soon learn the virtually automatic use of controls, which is the first requisite of good flying.

For an adult trying to learn a new skill like flying, there is no frustration like that of grasping again and again at an elusive trick—that of landing at ground level, for instance, rather than below or above it, only to have the trick of it slip away again and again, incomprehensibly. Nor is there any satisfaction like that of finally *getting it*, of feeling the trick grow in you and of finally being able to fly without *thinking*.

If you come to soaring without any previous flying experience, you have to make your way through the same obstacle course as must any other pilot. If you already have experience in powered airplanes, learning is much simpler, but there are still new sensations to handle and a new feel for a different kind of aircraft.

You sit in the front seat. The instructor sits close behind you, invisible, a voice and sometimes a sudden, independent willfulness of the controls. Someone connects the towline to your hook, checks it, and then signals that it is okay. The towplane takes up the slack in the line; the instructor tells you to waggle the rudder with your feet. There is a tug and a steady pull, and you are moving.

94

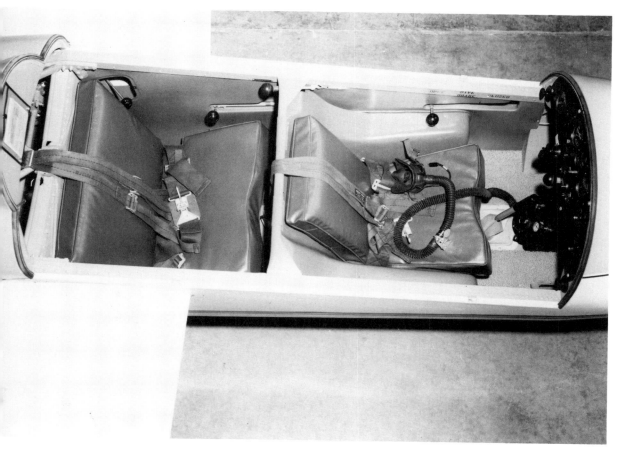

The cockpit of the Schweizer 2-32 trainer quickly gets to feel like home.

Even experienced pilots need nursing through the first tow. There is something unusual about being towed, a narrowness of focus that is at first hard to get used to. You have to learn the position to take behind the tow plane and how to stay there.

Usually, you can hear the towplane out there ahead of you. The nearer sounds are the muffled caress of the air on the skin of the airplane, an undulating whistle in the cabin vents, the occasional odd creak or pop of flexing wood or metal, and your instructor's voice.

If you have never flown before, the instructor will handle the sailplane during the first tow. You will climb to two thousand feet, and then he will have you pull the handle that releases the towline; he will bank you gently away to the right and then level the wings and give you control of the sailplane.

You soon will find that there is nothing to it. The motions are the ones you expect—stick right for a right bank, stick back to raise the nose, and so on—and you immediately get the knack of banking into a turn and then holding the bank with a little opposite aileron. At first you feel precarious, still harboring the suspicion that the whole works might go to pieces if you make a false move, but soon you learn that almost no balance or concentration is necessary to fly an airplane—much less than to ride a bicycle. If you let go of the stick the sailplane goes on straight ahead, mild and forgiving, quite capable of smooth and steady flight without your help.

You practice turns, at first, very gentle ones with aileron only, then bringing in the foot pedals that control the rudder and trying to keep the turn coordinated.

Sailplane trainers are mostly rough and ready but rather crude machines. They come down rapidly; you learn what you learn in small installments and while taking many tows. The result is that, unless there is a lot of free lift hanging around, you get much practice at being towed and at landing and comparatively little at flying—which is as it should be, since merely flying is very easy to learn.

Even just flying, though, has its problems. Speed control is one of them; centering the yawstring is another. The sailplane is equipped with a control, usually a movable lever or handle, that adjusts its trim. Trim

The takeoff and tow are among the most challenging aspects of flying a sailplane—even airline pilots sometimes have a hard time with them—yet the techniques are readily grasped. The sailplane lifts off while the tow plane is still rolling, and the glider pilot must be sure to stay out of the propwash to maintain stable flight. He will therefore fly "high tow" just above or "low tow" just below the propwash, coordinating his turns with those of the powered aircraft, until release.

determines the speed at which the ship will fly with your hands off the stick. To depart from the trim speed, some pressure on the control stick is necessary: a forward push to speed up, a backward pull to slow down. If you want to slow down or speed up briefly, you do so by means of the stick, but if you want to increase your speed or decrease it for an indefinite period, you usually first attain the desired speed by means of the stick and then adjust the trim until the stick pressure is gone. If you let go of the stick, the airplane then continues at the same speed.

The difficulty in speed control is usually overcontrol: you want to fly the airplane all the time, and so you constantly wiggle the stick around, chasing the airspeed needle up and down the dial. Your instructor urges you to hold the stick with two fingers, to ease it from side to side with light pressures and to relax your viselike grip. It takes time to learn to let go.

The yawstring, unfortunately, presents another problem. You have to work with it all the time, and when you let your attention stray from it, except in straight-and-level flight, it promptly wanders off on its own.

The yawstring is a piece of light yarn three or four inches long that is taped to the center of the windshield with its free end trailing backward along the sailplane's centerline. It is very sensitive to the direction of the air flowing over it, and it informs you when the airplane is not really aimed in the direction you want it to go.

It may never have occurred to you that this could be a problem. How could the airplane go anywhere except where it is aimed? Sailplanes, unfortunately, are notorious for pointing almost anywhere except where they are supposed to go. The problem arises from the fact that an airplane turns by banking and that the bank is produced by deflecting the ailerons —hinged portions of the aft edge of the wings, near the tips. An aileron deflected downward lifts its wing upward; upward deflection lowers the wing. A downward-deflected aileron produces more resistance to the air than does an upward-deflected one and so tends to retard its wing somewhat. Put the two factors together and you find that the wing on the outside of the turn seems to want to go slower than the wing on the inside. Consequently, the nose of the airplane is drawn outward and points wide of the desired direction of flight.

You are supplied with a pair of rudder pedals to overcome this tendency. The purpose of an airplane's rudder, unlike that of a boat, is not to turn the airplane; it is only to make comparatively small adjustments in the alignment of the fuselage with the line of flight. Right pedal swings the nose to the right. In a right turn, then, the left (upper) wing tends to pull backward, and you overcome this force by right rudder, which keeps the nose of the airplane pointed the way you want to go. When you turn the plane correctly, the yawstring trails straight back; if you make, say, a right turn without the rudder, the yawstring trails off to the left. The yawstring cue, therefore, is to press the rudder pedal on the side vacated by the yawstring.

The procedure of using the rudder to overcome the so-called adverse yaw of a turning airplane is referred to as coordination, and it is hard to learn. You notice, after a while, that when your turns are coordinated, you feel that you are sitting upright in the seat. When your turns are not coordinated you feel that you are leaning one way or the other. When this realization has sunk in, you can control a sailplane without a yawstring.

As soon as you can maneuver, stay more or less coordinated most of the time, and keep your speed where you want it, you'll be introduced to stalls. Stalls, as pilots tell drivers daily, have nothing to do with the engine. They involve the wing. An engineless airplane can stall just as can a powered one. When you get an airplane slowed down too much, its wing is no longer able to supply the lift necessary to sustain it. There is a particular point at which lift drops off and drag rises sharply, producing a peculiar buffeting, a gentle dropping of the nose, an unsteadiness in the wings, and a queasiness in the stomach. Some people never get used to stalls; they approach them with trepidation and rejoice to leave them behind, mainly because of the feeling that somewhere in that pasture there lurks a bull. The bull is the spin, or "tailspin," as it used to be called. Spins are entered from stalls, sometimes inadvertently and especially when the stall is inadvertent in the first place. It is because of the possibility of stalling inadvertently that you practice stalls.

Spins at one time were part of the curriculum for the power-pilot's license. They are still standard fare for sailplane pilots because sailplanes fly slowly in turbulent air and are hard to keep coordinated, which means that they have an uncommonly high exposure to conditions that lead to spins.

Very likely, your instructor will show you a spin or two so that if you ever enter a spin you will be able to recover. The sailplane is slowed to the stall, nose high. The sigh of the wind drops off to near silence. Just as the first signs of the stall appear, the instructor at once pulls the control stick back hard and pushes one rudder pedal full forward. Immediately the wing on the side of the forward rudder pedal seems to back up and fall downward; the fuselage seems to cartwheel sideways and there is momentarily the impression of being a little past the vertical, with the ground looming overhead. Then rapid rotation sets in, in what appears the first time to be a vertical nosedive. So long as the stick is held back and the rudder is held forward, the spin continues; the rate of rotation is constant, as is the nose-down angle. After the desired number of turns has been made, the recovery is simply a matter of momentarily pressing the opposite rudder pedal, moving the stick forward, and neutralizing the controls, and then pulling out of the dive.

The first few times one spins an airplane, it is a vastly exciting, sickening, thrilling, or terrifying experience. The movements are not violent, and the body is not subjected to powerful G forces or to dizzying rates of rotation, but there is something about spinning in empty space and staring straight down at a wheeling, ascending earth that is unforgettable.

The one aspect of sailplane flying that can exceed powered flying in difficulty is landing. In a powered airplane you control the approach with the engine, and if you blow it entirely, you can always go around for another try. In a sailplane there are no go-arounds; if you start to land, you end up landing, for better or for worse.

In lieu of engines for glide-path control, sailplanes have airbrakes or "spoilers," the latter so called because they spoil some of the lift of the wing. They are usually operated by a lever in the side of the cockpit and equipped with a lock to keep them closed when you don't want them. They make available a range of glide angles for landing. There are many ways of using them, and there is no best way. The easiest system for a beginner is to extend the spoilers partially during the landing approach so as to establish a rate of descent intermediate between the flattest glide and a fully braked plummet. He must then assess his progress as he approaches the field and increase or reduce his angle of glide accordingly.

At first, such a simple thing as arriving at the end of the runway at or near the ground can give you fits. It is a complicated version of pulling up very close to the curb without scuffing your whitewalls.

The landing pattern starts opposite the center of the landing strip, which is usually a grass area several hundred feet long, at a height of 500 feet above the field. Since one always lands as much into the wind as the alignment of the runway permits, the beginning of the pattern is flown downwind. You extend the spoilers to an intermediate position and fly straight ahead until the airport is about thirty degrees behind your wing. At this point you should be 300 to 400 feet above the ground; if you aren't, you make a small adjustment in the spoilers. You now make a ninety-degree turn toward the runway. You will lose a fair amount of height in the turn, so if you were slightly high at the end of the downwind leg, you might forego a change in spoiler position until you are established on the base leg.

On base leg, you are flying crosswind, perhaps 200 to 300 yards downwind of the touchdown point. You are now halfway through the approach, and so your height above touchdown ought to be around 250 feet, or a bit less than that.

As you approach the extended centerline of the landing strip, you roll into a final turn of ninety degrees until you are aligned with the runway. You are now on final approach. You forget about numbers and let your senses take over. The trick of the final approach is in judging the glide angle by eye. It is easy to do, once you know the cues. You must fix your attention on a point about fifty to one hundred feet short of the desired touchdown point and look at it steadily for several seconds. You will see a familiar optical phenomenon: all points in the visual field appear to be moving away from the central point; that point is the one toward which you are moving. Remember the old science-fiction films that had a few yards of footage in which the viewer appeared to be moving through a great field of stars that flew slowly outward toward the edge of the screen, tumbled off onto the curtain, rippled, and disappeared? The view from the pilot's seat will look the same, except that in lieu of stars you will see bushes, dogs, outhouses, and airplanes, all retreating from a central point.

What concerns you even more is the *vertical* center of movement. You must locate it and make it coincide with a point a little short of the intended touchdown point. The technique that is usually recommended is to see if the aiming point is moving upward or downward in the windshield; this indicates if it is above or below the center of the diverging points. If it is moving upward in the windshield, you are aiming short; if it is moving downward, you are aiming long. You adjust your glide angle—not the pitch angle of the sailplane, mind you, but the angle of descent, since it is direction of movement and not alignment in space that you are observing—to bring the aiming point to a standstill in the windshield. This may sound difficult, but it really isn't. Imagine how a verbal description of precisely how to bring a car to rest beside a curb would sound. In practice, all you are doing is looking at the aiming point and flying toward it; the rest becomes automatic.

When you are twenty or so feet above the ground and about to reach

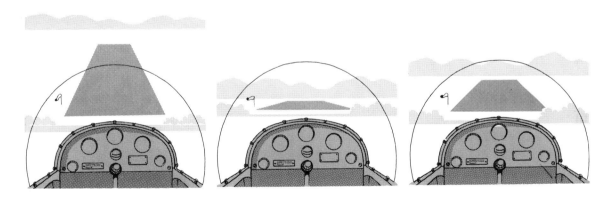

New pilots are taught to adjust their landing approaches by the look of the runway as they near it. If the runway looks steep, as at left, the plane is approaching high and at a steep angle. A shallow runway (center) means that the sailplane is perhaps too low to reach it, unless it is carrying sufficient speed. The "picture" from the windshield at right indicates that a good approach has been set up.

the aiming point, you begin the flare. To flare an airplane, you raise the nose slightly so as to arrest its descent gradually. Gliders land in a rather level pitch attitude, unlike powered airplanes, which land nose high. For a power pilot, therefore, the thing to study is how not to flare the sailplane too much.

When the wheel touches the ground, which it does with a startling rumble, you extend the spoilers completely, keep the wings level with the ailerons, and, in most trainers, push the nose down onto a skid, which brings you to a rapid halt with a horrible grating sound.

Learning to land is a long process. It takes a while, for instance, for judgment of the position of the aiming point to become automatic, though you may realize quickly what is involved. Talking about it with your instructor helps; if you spend a lot of time thinking about it on the ground, you may have less trouble with it in the air.

When you have learned the essentials of flight, you must practice. A student pilot's license, which permits you to fly solo and which is sufficient for most gliding, takes only a few hours—ten or fewer, usually fewer —to obtain. To get a private soaring license takes at least seven hours of solo flight. At first, the costs are high, because you always fly with the instructor and because you use frequent tows. When you have been flying a while, you learn to recognize and take advantage of lift and can stay up longer. Out alone on a good day, you may find yourself able to stay aloft as long as you like, always in sight of the field, but working your way from thermal to thermal or along upslopes and shear lines. No matter how aimlessly you circle about, the time is not wasted; it is making the job of flying more and more automatic and enlarging your acquaintance with the eccentricities of heated air.

It is maddening at first to see other sailplanes circling in a stack, rising away from you. One moment you are looking down on them and a little later all you see is their undersides against the sky. You fly toward where they are and circle beneath them, but except for an occasional bump or a few seconds of deceptive lift, you cannot clamber up after them. Your instructor can; he flies purposefully along toward a promising place, you feel a whooshing surge, he steadies the wings and then an instant later banks and pulls up, shedding speed and shooting upward. Then

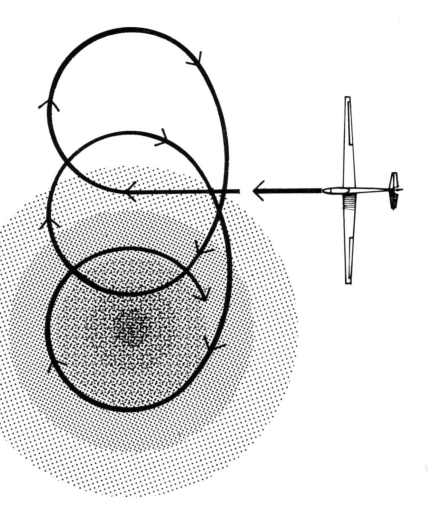

Finding and taking advantage of a thermal is in large part a matter of exploration. As the pilot detects a sudden surge of lift, he circles about 270 degrees to penetrate the column of rising air. Yet another turn may be necessary to reach the core of the thermal.

you are circling and, sure enough, the instruments show a steady climb.

Then *you* hook a thermal, then another one, and pretty soon, without exactly knowing how, you are picking up thermals and staying with them. If you think about it, you begin to see the patterns emerging, and you recognize the logic of the rules, at first so puzzling, that your instructor offered you. Finally, you become aware of a thermal as a palpable presence whose location with respect to you becomes ever clearer. You are playing blind man's buff with a ghost, but eventually, even this game becomes easy.

The rules of thumb with which you start are simple but at first seem to have no direct relation to the real world. You fly along until you hit lift. If your right wing rises, the lift is on your right; you hold the sailplane level and fly on for a couple of seconds to penetrate the thermal, and then simultaneously turn into the lift and pull up in a swoop to dissipate speed (thermaling speed is lower than interthermal gliding speed), finally establishing yourself in a thirty- to forty-degree bank. You then watch your vertical speed indicator. Assuming that you have connected with the thermal at all, and you may at first find it difficult to do so, you will probably find that during one part of your circuit you are getting good lift and during another part less lift, or no lift, or sink. This means that your circle is not concentric with the thermal, which is presumed—rather arbitrarily—to be round. You note the heading on which you got the best lift, continue turning for a little less than three-quarters of a circle, and then roll out to fly straight for a couple of seconds. Then you start circling again. Alternatively, you can find your heading of worst lift, continue turning another sixty degrees or so, then fly straight for two seconds and then recommence turning. If you spend almost all of your circle out of lift and only a small segment in it, you can try a figure-eight maneuver, rolling into the opposite turn as you pass through the area of lift.

These rules become clearer when you sketch them on paper, if you assume that the diameter of a thermal is about twice the diameter of the circle described by the turning aircraft. The idea, essentially, is that since the strongest lift is found near the core of the thermal, and the weakest lift, or even sink, is found around its perimeter, you want to move your turning circle around until you are getting steady lift at all times, and the inside wing is always trying to move up.

Looking intently ahead in his front seat, the student watches the towrope go taut and feels the trainer begin to respond to the controls. Solo is not far away.

Since you can't depend on a magnetic compass to give you meaningful heading information in a turn, you refer instead to the sun and to geographical features for a sense of when and where the lift is hitting you, and how much farther you should turn before rolling out to shift your circle. Even this is initially difficult: your eyes are mostly on the airspeed and vertical speed instruments; the landscape is going around and around in a dizzying whirl; you have to look around frequently to check for other traffic; the sun glares in your eyes; your movements in the cockpit are confined; everything seems to be turning wildly. But with practice you iron it out; you forget the rules, and you find yourself becoming as aware of the location of the thermal you are working as you may be of the position of other people in a room with you even when you turn away from them for a moment. You keep turning, not thinking in terms of numbers of degrees but of yourself turning away from a chimney of rising air, which you *feel* pass behind you and then come round beside you. When you are nearly facing it, you level out and move your circle over; then you roll back into your turn and see what you have in the way of lift. Now your invisible companion may seem to have moved off in a different direction, so you make another small correction. Sometimes you take your cue from a moment of sink that marks the edge of the thermal. As you hit it, you sense that the core is beyond the center of your circle, and you shift the whole show toward it.

When you have made friends with enough thermals to become confident that if there is lift to be found, you will find and harness it, you are ready to put your new skill to the test of a cross-country trip. Now there will be something at stake: a bit of pride, if that matters to you, and, at any rate, the possible inconvenience of a long retrieve if you don't manage to stay up long enough to make the round trip. There should be no problem. You have been staying up for hours in the vicinity of your home field, wandering around at will. Now all you have to do is wander off out of reach of your home field and then wander back. There's not much difference, but the psychological step is immense. You can make your first cross-country trip with an instructor or you can go it alone. Most people go it alone. You no longer really need an instructor; you know enough now to face the unknown on equal terms.

7 SCAN THE SKY
AND
READ THE EARTH

Any glider pilot must try to find lift; on a cross-country trip, he must find his way as well. Navigation is usually the less difficult chore of the two. Sailplanes make enough progress cross-country to permit a leisurely perusal of the terrain and landmarks except during the most frantic searches for lift. It is rare, after ten minutes of flight, to be out of sight of the place you were ten minutes before. The pilot of a powered airplane, if he is navigating by pilotage—that is, by reference to the ground—stands a fair chance of getting lost if he lets ten or fifteen minutes pass without taking a fix on his position. The pilot of a sailplane, on the other hand, is not likely to have the same trouble. He is usually very much aware of the ground beneath him because he uses it for position and wind-direction reference in his search for lift; he thinks constantly in terms of the amount of progress he has made away from his starting point and toward his destination. In certain circumstances, position becomes an obsession for him.

It is still possible, however, for him to get lost. Sailplane flights can last for hours and hours, covering hundreds of miles, often over unfamiliar terrain. Sometimes sailplanes fly in cloud for long periods, emerging after being blown along with the cloud for miles downwind. In slope and ridge soaring, the pilot works in such close proximity to the terrain, sometimes literally brushing the mountainside foliage with his wingtip, that the sectional terrain charts normally used for aerial navigation are worthless. Hills and mountains can be confusing; one valley looks like another, and at the altitudes used in slope soaring, it is rarely possible to see enough landmarks to make a positive identification of position. Finally, when the pilot is working weak lift late in the day, close to the ground and on the verge of picking a farmer's field in which to land, he is too busy to refer to a chart.

110

The rules for all kinds of aerial pilotage—powered airplanes, gliders, balloons—are similar and involve a combination of map reading and dead reckoning, an ominous name for a branch of grade-school mathematics. A novice pilot is encouraged to plan his flights in terms of landmarks or checkpoints at short intervals, preferably so spaced that as he passes one, the next one can be seen. By noting the heading necessary to make good a desired track along the ground and the time it takes him to get from one landmark to the next, the pilot can deduce his drift angle, which is caused by wind blowing across his track, and his groundspeed. He is further encouraged to calculate the heading and time to the next checkpoint and to compare his answer with the reality. The purpose of all these notations and calculations is to instill in the student a belief that if you go at a certain speed in a certain direction for a certain length of time, you are bound to end up in a certain spot, and that spot may be predicted reliably. This is dead reckoning—the name stands for deductive reckoning—and it was a technique also used by travelers on land and sea until the invention of modern navigational equipment.

Once a pilot is out of school, his pilotage and dead-reckoning skills can become rusty if he grows complacent, with the result that he eventually finds himself lost.

The tactic recommended in the conventional literature at this point is to pick up the radio mike, call some likely ground station, and confess your predicament, a proceeding that falls short of manly self-reliance but is preferable to flying around aimlessly until you run out of gas and crash. For several reasons, the confession of helplessness is less useful to the sailplane pilot than to the power pilot. In most cases, the power pilot can be told how to steer back onto course and can follow the directions, as long as he still has fuel with which to stay aloft. The soaring pilot must constantly go where he can find lift. For him, time is also a crucial item to be husbanded. Radioing for help could simply be too time-consuming for him, so the sailplane pilot, when he gets himself into a predicament, usually must get himself out of it.

The best landmarks are the unmistakable ones: large lakes, isolated mountain peaks, tank farms, meteor craters, Air Force bases, and similiar features. Needless to say, these are fairly uncommon, and pilots generally

The way a road bends or the presence of a pond can say much to a pilot as he navigates and keeps his eyes open for good forced-landing spots.

settle for second best: distinctive jogs or convergences of highways and railroads, towns with drive-in theaters or with oval tracks located at certain positions on their perimeters, small airfields, meandering rivers, small lakes preferably equipped with dams or islands. It is remarkably easy, especially for a beginner, to mistake one town for another, especially when he may be holding the map wrong-way-round or when all the towns in some featureless prairie were formed from the same causes and grew with the same shapes. There are plenty of places in any flat rural area where absolutely no recognizable landmark can be identified from a height of less than a mile or so above the ground, where all the roads were laid out with a ruler and all the streams with a string.

It is at such a point that dead reckoning is expected to help. The pilot is supposed to have noted his time of passage over his most recent checkpoint and to have kept at least a mental record of his general heading and the amount of time he has spent circling. He puts this information together with his known (more or less) groundspeed and concludes that he must be somewhere around *here* (indicating a large, featureless circle on the map). At this point he has several choices. If the lift is good, he can continue on his way, hoping to recognize something eventually; he can try to work in the general direction of some landmark that, if he stumbles upon it, he cannot fail to recognize. If the lift is getting weak, he can prepare to determine his position by inquiry of the farmer in whose field he will eventually land. Since sailplanes have the happy faculty of being able to land safely in small fields, being lost in comfortable terrain is no cause for a great deal of alarm.

What would be more alarming would be to find oneself lost in rough terrain. This would be the height of imprudence, since when a pilot sees himself moving into difficult terrain, he should take particular care to be sure of his location and of his escape routes if lift should fail. Lost in such a place, one can only work toward smoother, flatter ground or back whence one came, or, if need be, take the consequences of carelessness in the form of damage to the glider and/or its pilot.

Working mountain currents has a somewhat different quality; maps are pretty useless, and better information may usually be had from other pilots who are familiar with the area and the probable locations of lift.

Finding one's way along the slopes of a single large mountain is easy, since the mountain itself provides an immutable clue to the airplane's position. Working slope and ridge lift in a complex of mountains and valleys, on the other hand, may be more perplexing, though here again the sailplane's slow progress is a blessing: it spends so much time in one general locale and works the slopes so intimately, that the pilot knows his way back just as a hiker can retrace his path by the familiarity of the ground he has recently covered.

Some people show a greater natural talent for navigating than do others. Some have a hard time getting the simplest concepts through their heads, such as that a certain arrangement of landmarks on the ground does not coincide with a similar but different, say mirrored, arrangement on the map. In time, and with practice, everyone learns to navigate, because it is not that difficult. Like adding, navigating by pilotage is a skill of limited demands.

Finding lift is not quite so simple, and is much more important. The workings of the atmosphere are not perfectly known, and the varieties of its behavior are still partly uncatalogued. They combine and recombine in endless permutations, and every lesson and formula for finding lift must end with the disclaimer that regardless of the rules, lift is where you find it. The responsibility for finding it is thus shifted from the laws of nature back to the pilot, where it belongs if soaring is to be a sport rather than merely a task for a pocket calculator.

Lift is usually divided into three categories: thermal, slope, and wave. The classification is accurate, though it omits what might be called random lift—lift that arises independently of clear-cut causes, from air-mass movement, or as a result merely of the general shearing and mixing of the air. Such lift is constantly encountered and is usually either shoehorned into one of the three conventional categories, or else merely described as lift or zero sink.

The names of the three main categories describe them well. Thermal lift consists of heated air that rises because it is lighter than the surrounding air. Slope lift occurs along the slopes of hills and mountains, where the wind, unable to blow directly through the obstacle, rises to pass over it. Wave lift is a little less obvious, but, once understood, its mechanism is also quite familiar and natural. It consists of standing waves downwind of large obstacles to the wind's movement. We see standing waves commonly enough. The center of the wake of a motorboat often contains a ripple that seems to be pulled along behind the boat, with water and foam moving rapidly *through* it; and water in a stream passing over a log or submerged stone often goes through a series of sinusoidal ripples continuing for some distance downstream. The wave system is called a standing wave because the wave remains stationary and the material of which it consists—air or water—passes *through* it.

Thermals are the commonest source of lift for the majority of sailplane pilots. They normally occur only in daytime and mostly in summer, beginning to form in the late morning hours or around noon and weakening and fading from the later afternoon on through the evening. In typical rural areas, thermals rise from portions of the ground that the sun warms more rapidly than the surrounding areas: highways, fields of stubble, groups of buildings are examples. In desert areas, their sources are less obvious, but like the bubbles rising from the bottom of a pot of boiling water, they form where they do because they do not form elsewhere.

If a thermal were visible, it would appear as a column perhaps one thousand feet across, with a series of more or less defined bubbles rising along it like smoke rings. The air in the rings rotates parallel to the axis of the column, so that air on the inside of the ring is moving upward and that about the outside is moving downward. Since the entire ring is rising, the downward movement of air around its perimeter may be only relative, or it may be absolute—that is, the air may be moving downward with respect only to the core of the thermal, or with respect to the entire surrounding air mass in which the thermal is embedded. At any rate, it is a common observation upon entering a thermal that one first encounters sink, followed by an upward push. The sailplane at first tends to slow down in sink, and then to speed up as it enters lift, so the thermal signals itself as an initial quieting and perhaps a sense of dropping gently, followed by a whoosh or thump and the sound of increasing airspeed.

Since the thermal is invisible, the pilot must locate its center by trial and error. Normally, he is flying straight and at a fairly high speed when the thermal is encountered. The only clue he gets about its location may

The life cycle of a cumulus cloud: As the earth heats, warm currents cause condensation and a boiling upward of the moist air, which then may be caught by the wind and be blown away.

be a tendency for one wing to rise more than the other, which indicates that the strong part of the thermal is on the side of the rising wing. His response is to level the wings, continue straight for a second or two in order to penetrate well into the thermal, and then to pull up while banking toward the core. Since interthermal cruising speed is higher than thermaling speed, the pullup gives him a surge of climb called a stick thermal. If his instrumentation is sufficiently sophisticated, it will distinguish between climb due to pullup and climb due to the thermal, omitting the former; but if not, he must allow for the stick thermal when interpreting his rate-of-climb instrument. The pilot continues circling in a bank of thirty or forty degrees. Now, either he will continue to climb, or lack of climb will tell him that he has missed the thermal. If he climbs, but only unsteadily, feeling lift at certain parts of his circle but not at others, he will roll out of the turn for one or two seconds on a heading calculated to move his circle toward the core of the thermal. He then rolls back into a turn and continues to assess the lift and the need for another correction. Occasionally, if he feels he is well to one side of the core, he may roll into the opposite bank at a strategic moment and begin circling on the other side of a figure eight.

Once he is satisfactorily established within the thermal, all he needs to do to stay there is to circle regularly, since the sailplane and the thermal are being carried along on the same wind. If the pilot circles with sufficient precision, his position in the thermal will not change.

Thermals do not rise forever. How they are capped depends on atmospheric conditions, but in general, on a good summer day, "fair-weather cumulus," puffy white clouds distributed randomly about the blue sky will form at the tops of thermals where the moist warm air rises into a level of air cool enough to promote condensation into cloud. These clouds, whose myriad shapes lend themselves to identification with animals and monsters, seem like so many puffs of cotton from the ground. On close inspection, however, they are seen to be in constant, boiling movement, either growing up rapidly, lingering there and churning, or spilling their vapor into disappearing wisps and shrinking away. The process of building and shrinking can be rapid, and a stable cloud of long life is not the rule. The soaring pilot therefore must learn to distinguish between the

Cloud streets are sought after by pilots, for they assure continuous lift.

The pilot often has to choose whether to seek new lift, if he has lost it, or to land. As he heads for his airport, he will notice the cumulus clouds ahead. They are good indicators of a thermal—the ridge to his left—which might also provide lift, or the grass fire, which could be the best lift-giver of all.

waxing clouds that flag the tops of vigorous new thermals and the waning ones whose thermals are either weakening or may already have vanished.

Lift is strong below a developing cu (pronounced "cue"), weaker just beneath the cloudbase, and increasingly strong inside the cloud itself. Since the top of a strong cu may be at the 15,000- or 20,000-foot level, pilots who are proficient in and licensed for blind flying by instruments can thermal right up through the clouds. They quit when cold—turbulence, icing or lack of oxygen force them to. They then level their wings and penetrate straight ahead on the desired heading until they break out of the side of the cloud.

The heights of cloudbases vary from region to region. In rolling farm country, like that of England, much of Europe, and the Mississippi Valley and southern United States, they are often quite low, at 2,500 to 3,000 feet above the ground, making cross-country soaring difficult for beginners. Over the rough terrain of Arizona and Utah, cloudbase is often 5,000 to 10,000 feet above the terrain, or up to 18,000 feet above sea level—a height from which great distances can be achieved before another thermal need be found and worked. That is a blessing, since powerful high-altitude thermals are more widely spaced than weaker low-altitude ones. As a rule, the space between thermals is five times their height. (The advantages of high-altitude soaring are not only in the distances achieved but also in the fact that, in thin, high-altitude air, an aircraft can move along at a higher speed, for the same amount of drag, than in the dense air close to sea level.)

The thermaling pilot flies with an eye on his airspeed indicator, on his yawstring, and on his variometer. When the variometer tells him that the strength of the thermal is diminishing, he must decide to leave it; precisely when he leaves it depends on the strength or frequency of thermals he has encountered hitherto and expects to encounter henceforth. If the day is strong, he will leave a thermal when it is still giving him good lift, because he is confident that another one will be easy to find and because speed or distance, not time spent thermaling, is the scoring criterion in competition. On weak days, he will stay with a thermal longer because its lift is precious and he may not soon find another with which to replace it.

Good thermaling conditions can go awry. Sometimes thermals appear in well-defined lines called streets. It is possible to fly along a street

The combination of a sea breeze and a ridge can yield a whole day of relaxed, pleasurable soaring, as at Torrey Pines, California.

without circling and without losing height. This is fine, but streets and dense groups of cu may congeal into an overcast, precluding solar heating of the ground and turning off the lift altogether. Sometimes, air mass or shear lift continues to exist under an overcast sky, since the air cannot simply stop in its tracks but continues to roil about for some time after the first cause of its motion has been removed. In general, however, excessive thickening of the cloud cover is considered a bad sign.

Thermals may be present where there are no clouds, particularly in dry air and desert areas; in fact, they may be very powerful in such places, rising at one thousand feet per minute or more. On the other hand, they may be weak and erratic, when indications seem to point to the opposite condition. The soaring adage is worth repeating: Lift is where you find it.

Thermal lift disappears in a sufficiently strong wind, because the normal convective patterns of the atmosphere are broken up. A strong wind is essential to the two other categories of lift: slope and wave. Slope lift can exist in a breeze of any strength, but it becomes increasingly difficult to work as the wind becomes lighter. One of the familiar locations for slope soaring is Torrey Pines, near San Diego, California, where the sea breeze blows against a line of vertical cliffs over three hundred feet high. The abruptness of the cliff's contour enables a relatively light wind to hold a sailplane aloft, though landings on the beach are common, probably more so now since part of it recently became a nude beach. On more normal slopes of forty-five degrees or so, a good fresh breeze is needed, and even so, one must fly alarmingly close to the slope in order to make the best of the lift. The closeness—a wingspan or less—takes getting used to, though missing the mountain is no harder than missing other automobiles in freeway traffic. All turns are made away from the hillside, of course, so that the track of the sailplane as it tacks back and forth resembles a figure eight with one side flattened against the hill.

When a slope-soaring sailplane pilot reaches the top of the hill, he first of all does not go down the other side, since this would subject him to sink at least as strong as, and certainly much more turbulent than, the lift that got him there. He can rarely climb much above the ridge, but he may move along it, just to the upwind side of the top, still very close to the ground, or he can set out across the valley looking for thermals or slope lift elsewhere. In strong conditions, slope lift can cause rapid climbs, along with a sensation of speed and of maneuvering in a vivid three-dimensional frame of reference that is missing in thermal soaring. It also may afford a chance to wave at backpackers or skiers—or to be rescued by them.

In mountainous areas, beginners may work many a slope before they ever stumble onto a thermal. In a few, they may be exposed early to one of soaring's peak experiences: flying in wave. Wave, however, is rather heady fare for a beginner.

Wave lift exists on a whole range of scales, and though the most famous and oft-mentioned waves are the most powerful and visible ones, smaller and less reliable waves are to be found on occasion anywhere that a mountain ridge pokes up in the way of a strong wind.

Usually, when it is quite weak, wave is invisible, and pilots stumble upon it all unexpecting. Normally, however, certain distinctive cloud formations give indications of its presence. The classic wave situation requires a mountain barrier athwart a strong wind that increases in velocity with altitude, as most winds do. In the textbook case, a layer of clouds called the cap cloud or *foehnwall* lies upon the mountains. Just to the lee side of the mountains is a clear area, the *foehngap*, where air spilling over the mountains drops into the valley below, sometimes kicking up a dust storm as it goes. Several miles farther downwind, the air blowing across the valley kicks back upward, setting in motion an enormous ethereal rolling pin, the rotor cloud, which stands in one spot resembling a rather turbid cumulus. Above the rotor cloud stand in successive layers oval, flattened clouds, characterized by a peculiar humped shape which vividly adumbrates the flow of air upward into the leading edge of the cloud, over the hump, below which rolls the rotor cloud, and then downward, out of the trailing edge. When these clouds have a peculiarly smooth, lenslike appearance, often resembling a flying saucer hanging in the air, they are called lenticular, from a Latin word meaning, not lens, as is often said (the Romans did not have lenses), but "little lentil."

The lenticulars commonly stand in long lines parallel to the mountains and across the wind, and when the wave is well developed, the first line is echoed by others at regular intervals of ten to twenty miles downwind.

The energies at work in wave clouds are gargantuan and seem contrived to inspire fear in men. The wave itself contains mighty lift and sink—well over one thousand feet per minute—of such an absolutely eerie smoothness that the sailplane seems rigidly encased in the air as though in a plastic paperweight. The rotor cloud, on the other hand, contains turbulence that has been known to demolish a sailplane in an instant, leaving the startled pilot to open his parachute amid a rain of plywood, nuts, and bolts. Wave lift goes on into the stratosphere. The current absolute world altitude record for a sailplane, 46,267 feet, was made by Paul Bikle in a medium-performance craft in the Tehachapi Wave, the southernmost part of the Sierra Wave of California, in 1961. He was still climbing at 500 feet per minute and estimated that he could have gone up at least to 50,000 feet, when the $-60°$ C. cold and his knowledge of the human body's inability to retain oxygen at such a height caused him to turn back.

The beauty of a wave for the soaring pilot is its generosity; it rewards the effort he must expend to stay in the areas of best lift with climbs of phenomenal steadiness and duration. It is more common to leave a wave by mistake or design than to have it run out of steam. The wave also has the kindness most of the time to signal its exact position visibly. It sets up a formidable barrier in the form of the rotor cloud and requires of the pilot an unusual attention to physiological factors, such as lack of oxygen and cold. Wave flying centers are prepared to cope with these demands by making available the necessary equipment, clothing, and long tows through or around the rotor. A pressurized sailplane is currently being readied for an assault on the absolute altitude record, and its theoretical capabilities promise to bring the 60,000-foot level into reach. No birds fly in that region; hardly any airplanes do either.

In local soaring, with no goals, tasks, or records in view, the types of lift likely to be encountered are well known. Every airport has its surrounding terrain, its prevailing wind, its typical seasonal weather, and any place where pilots have soared for any length of time has its well-known "house thermal," or dependable slope or ridge. Since local soaring hugs the upwind side of the airport, because a retreat to the field from downwind is several times more difficult than one with the wind behind,

Wave clouds over Bishop, California. Discovery of the wave added a new dimension to soaring flight.

the choice of sources and types of lift on a given day is even more limited. When the field is busy, circling sailplanes will have thermals and upcurrents marked like so many neon signs. Cross-country soaring, on the other hand, makes much greater demands on the ability and ingenuity of the pilot. He may depart in thermals, make a late-afternoon save on a slope or ridge, hook another thermal, and even stumble upon a mild wave to give him height for his final glide.

In cross-country flying, especially in competition, it is a rare flight that does not have its bleak moments, its last-minute save, its slow crawl back to altitude on an expiring thermal. Pilots take what they can get, balancing the chances of finding lift ahead or to one side of their desired track against the time lost in a deviation. They are ever aware of the wind's direction and force. They watch the shadows of clouds on the ground as well as the clouds themselves, distinguishing between the crisp whiteness of a building cumulus and the somewhat more ragged and coarse appearance of one that is over the hump. They sense the warmth and humidity of the air within a thermal, and it sometimes gives them a clue as to its size or place of origin. Terrain features suggest where shear lines may exist; for instance, when wind flows down two valleys that converge, Y-fashion, into one, and the converging streams of air meet and roll upward into a line of lift along the center of the leg of the Y. Edges of fog banks or masses of smog sometimes tip them off to the presence of a miniature front with its rising warm air. In desert areas, powerful thermals are often marked by dust and debris, like tiny tornadoes, rising from the ground sometimes to heights of hundreds of feet. In a pinch, smoke from a factory stack, a burning field, or a dump or stream rising from a cooling tower may supply enough lift by which to continue a flight. The pilot knows of the tilt of thermals and the way in which one can be turned off when the shadow of its own cumulus cap or that of a neighboring thermal falls on its source.

Sometimes the pilot will find himself flying along in general lift of dubious origin; sometimes it will not be necessary to circle in thermals, but only to pull up while passing through them. Some thermals will be too small to work; the circling birds, which are often recommended as signposts of lift, are not wholly reliable, not only because they too make mistakes, but also because they can circle in thermals much more slender than a sailplane can, or may as easily be signaling the presence of carrion as of lift. Sometimes, whole areas will unexpectedly go dead; sometimes, areas like the open ocean, which normally can be expected to offer only sink, will offer the only lift to be found anywhere.

The ability to deal with the variety and unpredictability of lift is something the sailplane pilot must develop through thousands of hours of soaring. It is like dealing with people; rules and slogans are well enough, but in the particular case, something else, a certain feel for what the other person feels, is necessary. The rules about where and how to look for lift and what to do with it when you find it are good mechanical devices for setting beginners on the right track and helping them to avoid the most obvious and discouraging mistakes. But once the novice is on his way, only experience will teach him to read the book of the earth and sky—a book for which no comprehensive Rosetta stone has yet been found.

8

THE SPAN OF THEIR BEAUTY

There are several ways in which a machine can be said to be beautiful. Its appearance as it performs or remains at rest can please one's aesthetic sense. The sheer efficiency it displays can bring a lump to the throat of one who is engineeringly inclined. And we have often heard people say about automobiles, boats, bicycles, and other machines that certain models "handle beautifully."

Sailplanes are no exception. One of their greatest sources of attraction is their beauty in flight. Even trainers, which tend to look less streamlined than high-performance ships, become exquisitely graceful when aloft, or even on takeoff. All sailplanes, when flown with coordination and intelligence, seem to float at ease within their element. Even on the ground, a sailplane's lines and construction can profoundly impress a knowledgeable aircraft fan.

Get two glider pilots together and before long, they will be comparing their favorite ships, describing pleasures they have enjoyed at the controls. Some sailplane models suffer reputations for poor performance—they are called "dogs"—but others are almost universally praised by pilots as highly desirable and satisfying craft. Here are a relative few examples of the latter.

SCHWEIZER 2–32   When the Schweizer Aircraft Company introduced the 2–32, this sailplane was billed as the best two-place ship in the world. Even today, its good performance—34-to-1 glide ratio—smooth handling and roomy, comfortable cockpit have earned it a reputation for being the "Cadillac of Sailplanes." In keeping with its Cadillac image, the 2–32 is solid and rather heavy. Those who take it cross-country should eschew the tiny, rutted fields where some of the single-place ships can land and should retain a large, well-fed ground crew. Heavily-instrumented 2–32s have been used for meteorological research work, and the airframe

130

has been used as the base for several interesting powered aircraft, including a low-level reconnaissance plane, a high-altitude drone, and a ship designed to fly around the world nonstop.

CAPRONI-VIZZOLA A-21   The advent of the Caproni-Vizzola A-21 marks a resurgence of interest in the high-performance two-place sailplane. Such aircraft have been ignored by designers since the creation of the Focke-Wulf Kranich (Crane) during the immediate postwar era. The Caproni's three-piece aluminum wing spans sixty-seven feet and features a combination of camber-changing flaps and spoilers for both in-flight and landing control. The fiberglass forward fuselage is shaped to allow side-by-side seating with little or no drag penalty over the less comfortable and companionable tandem arrangement, and the aluminum tail boom and tail surfaces help to reduce weight. With performance claimed at 43 to 1, the Caproni is in the same class with the highest-performing single-place machines. For those who wish to have the ultimate plane—and can afford it—the Caproni is available with a 220-pound-thrust turbojet engine, which makes it independent of towplanes or retrieve crew without reducing its soaring performance.

SCHWEIZER 1–26   If any particular sailplane is the mainstay of the American soaring movement, it must be the 1–26. This sailplane is the prime example of Schweizer's goal of providing low-cost, simple aircraft to the widest possible range of pilots: it's available in kit form as well as ready-to-fly off the Schweizer assembly line. Successive models of the 1–26 have featured various design improvements, but the basic 40-foot wingspan, 325 to 350 pounds of empty weight, and 23-to-1 performance remain unchanged. As a result, competition among 1–26s comes close to sailboat class racing in the evenness of the matchups. The machines are essentially the same, so pilot skill is everything, and several 1–26 competitors have gone on to higher laurels in other classes on the basis of what they learned in such close head-to-head flying. More than 750 1–26s have been built; used ones therefore are often available and change hands for amounts starting at $3,500 (fully equipped). Most American pilots make their first duration and cross-country flights in the 1–26; a hardy few have gone on to make all three diamonds in it.

SCHLEICHER KA. 6   Wooden sailplanes made their first appearance long before World War II and they reached their highest eminence in the immediate prewar and postwar eras. Development of the Schleicher Ka. 6 was begun by the German firm of Alexander Schleicher in the early 1950s. The series has survived to the present with the introduction of the Ka. 6E, designed by Rudolf Kaiser. The Ka. 6E features an improved airfoil, a lowered fuselage, and an all-flying horizontal stabilizer. Still *the* classic standard-class sailplane, the Ka. 6 series has delightful handling and performance, adequate for diamond flights. It's a favorite of European clubs, and of private owners here and abroad. Used ones appear on the market in the $5,000-and-up bracket.

SCHWEIZER 1–34   In an effort to produce a sailplane of higher performance than the 1–26 or 1–23, and to provide an American design for standard-class competition, Schweizer used experience gained with the 2–32 to design and produce the all-metal 1–34. Despite its fairly high price, the 1–34 has been well accepted. Its performance is roughly on a par with that of the Ka. 6E—it has a 34-to-1 glide ratio—and its strong construction makes it an excellent cross-country machine for a soaring club or school. The 1–34 is quite docile and easy to fly; a pilot with 1–26 experience will find the 1–34 the logical next step in the sailplane hierarchy.

GLASFLÜGEL H201 LIBELLE   The dainty and graceful Libelle (dragonfly) was one of the first German fiberglass sailplanes to be available in the United States and remains a favorite here, not only because of its very good performance but also its small size and light weight. The first generations of the Libelle were open-class sailplanes, sporting camber-changing flaps and a drag parachute for landings. A demand for standard-class machines—as well as Glasflügel's decision to produce a new open-class sailplane—led to the current H201 Standard Libelle, which has a somewhat thicker flapless wing, water ballast, and large dive brakes. Both types are in great demand; count on used-Libelle prices somewhere in the $10,000 bracket, with new-ship prices, depending on the position of the dollar, around $12,000 to $13,000.

SCHEMPP-HIRTH STANDARD CIRRUS   The popularity of standard-class competition has led several firms to design fiberglass sailplanes especially for the purpose. The Standard Cirrus is a typical "glass standard," incorporating water ballast and dive brakes. Performance of this sailplane —and of the other glass standards, such as the Schleicher AS–W15 or the Schneider LS-1—is very similar to that of the Libelle, as are its new and used prices. Some of the glass standards have reputations for very sensitive handling and high landing speeds. Current class rule changes allow large-span flaps, which can be used for camber change in flight and which can be deflected almost ninety degrees for slow landing approaches.

SCHWEIZER 1–35   The 1–35 marks a major departure for Schweizer: it is their first all-out competition machine since the 1–21 of the 1950s. The 1–35 indicates how strongly the Schweizers feel that their long-term program of simple and rugged trainers and club machines has established a wide enough pilot base to justify manufacturing a high-performance competition machine at least as good as the glass standards with a similar base price of around $12,000. The 1–35 joins the all-metal Laister Nugget as America's only production competition sailplanes. The 1–35 is designed to the latest standard-class rules of the FAI, which allow it to have large-span flaps for better low-speed handling in thermals and for very steep landing approaches.

DIAMANT 18   The Diamant was developed from a university student project by Flug-und-Fahrzeugwerke Altenrhein, a Swiss firm that builds aircraft and railroad cars. The prototype was a standard-class machine that used Ka. 6 (later, Libelle) wings; production models use 16½- or 18-meter wings designed for the aircraft. Minimum frontal area is achieved by placing the pilot almost supine under a very long canopy. With the Phoebus and Cirrus, the Diamant represents the first generation of fiberglass open-class sailplanes.

GLASFLÜGEL H604 "JUMBO"   This very large and expensive sail-plane characterizes the second generation of superships, which are generally easier to fly. Basically an enlarged and improved development of the 17-meter Kestrel, the 22-meter 604 has been used in competition and in attacking world speed and distance records. Other German firms have developed similar superships from earlier open-class designs. Schempp-Hirth's Cirrus series evolved into the Nimbus II, while the AS-W12 gave rise to the AS-W17. A new supership can cost as much as $30,000.

SCHREDER HP-14   Richard Schreder, of Bryan, Ohio, has been one of the mainstays in America of building sailplanes oneself. Indeed, until very recently, the only way to obtain a high-performance sailplane in the United States was either to import one or to build it oneself. The open-class HP-14 is only one in a series of more or less successful Schreder designs, some of which have captured speed records. With performance on a par with the early fiberglass open-class sailplanes, the HP-14 is well worth the effort involved in building it. It offers large-span flaps (a frequent Schreder design characteristic) and retractable landing gear. Those who dislike the V-tail (another typical Schrederism) can construct a T-tailed version.

9 SOARING AMERICA

No other sport is as markedly affected by the spectacular features of terrain and climate that distinguish the regions of the United States as is soaring. Nor is there a country so blessed with varied terrain features and climatic conditions conducive to different kinds of soaring enjoyment as is the United States. Nor is there a more exciting and aesthetically rewarding way of becoming familiar with a region's landforms and weather than from the air, and particularly from the cockpit of a sailplane. Not surprisingly, Americans in both the East and the West have been quick to count these blessings and take advantage of them.

In a sense, there are almost two separate soaring movements in the United States, so great can the differences be between eastern and western conditions. American soaring got its start in the Northeast, in conditions that very closely approximated those in Germany, where the sport was being most intensively developed. It was several years before the inevitable westward spread began, but when that happened, an entire new dimension was added to the sport.

It is not entirely simple to define East and West in terms of soaring conditions, since these are literally as fickle as the weather. Nonetheless, there are typical weather patterns that we have come to associate with particular areas. So-called western conditions usually obtain in the area from the Pacific coast to the eastern borders of Kansas, Nebraska, and the Dakotas. Farther south, the dividing line starts to slant somewhat westward, passing through Oklahoma and Texas at about the longitude of Dallas, and then slants farther west toward the Big Bend country along the Mexican border.

East of that line, the terrain is usually thickly covered with vegetation, and the air is often moist. The temperatures are more moderate than in the West, and the thermals are often capped by fleecy cumulus clouds. The air below the clouds is frequently hazy.

146

In the center of the United States, the Great Plains dominate both terrain and weather. While the coasts are subject to the action of marine air, the plains are often under patterns of dry continental air pushing southward from the prairies of Canada or northward from Mexico. In the southern region, this is sometimes mixed—occasionally with spectacular results—with moist, warm air from the Gulf of Mexico. The unbroken sweep of the plains allows patterns to move along relatively unaffected by terrain. Sometimes cloud streets, or rows of thermals, form, enabling pilots to fly tens or even hundreds of miles without circling.

As we move farther west, the terrain, while remaining flat, begins to rise. This has an important effect upon soaring conditions: given the same air mass, updrafts will begin to form above high ground at lower temperatures than over low terrain. Thus, as we approach the Rockies, we sometimes find spectacularly good soaring conditions above the high plains of Colorado and New Mexico, even on days when the low plains offer only mediocre conditions. As the terrain becomes more mountainous, the conditions can become even stronger; sites such as Marfa, in the rugged hill country of southwestern Texas, near El Paso, have left Easterners and Europeans alternately elated and flabbergasted over the kind of soaring to be found there.

Europeans may feel more at home in the Rockies, since much of the soaring in the alpine regions of Colorado is quite similar to that found in the Swiss, German, and Austrian Alps. Of course, these mountains are not nearly as densely populated as their European counterparts. A German might land in a hayfield and find a farmhouse after a short walk, but an American landing in the Rockies might end up in a mountain meadow from which he will have to hike for two or three days to find civilization.

West of the Rockies, some of the world's most popular soaring grounds are found in the more or less contiguous Sonora and Mojave deserts. The Sonora is in Arizona and Utah, and the Mojave is in California and Nevada. This large tongue of desert runs all the way up into southeastern Oregon, Idaho, and even a bit of Washington. Farther west, we again encounter mountains, California's majestic Sierra Nevada, home of the famous Sierra Wave during the winter, and its northerly extension, the Cascade Range.

Swooping close to slopes to catch updrafts, as at Mt. San Jacinto, California, can yield some of the most thrilling soaring experiences a pilot can have.

Finally, in the relatively narrow strip between these ranges and the Pacific, we find the inland valleys of southern California and the San Francisco Bay area, where marine influences again make themselves very directly felt.

Generally, thermals in the West are larger and stronger than those in the East, particularly at the desert and mountain sites. This is a mixed blessing, however; since thermals tend to occur roughly five times as far apart as they are high, those in the West can be as far as fifteen or even twenty miles apart on a strong day. Thus, while it's easier to "get high and stay high" in the West, the consequences of getting low are more serious. It's harder to make a "save" and the often rough terrain can make landing out quite a difficult proposition.

Moreover, while the powerful thermals of the West move immense volumes of air upward, somewhere nearby the air is coming down just as hard. The sink between thermals can be disheartening indeed, particularly when it's several miles to the next source of lift.

This contrast with the gentler but more consistent conditions of the East even led, at one time, to the construction of special sailplanes for use in the plains and mountain states. While the typical European or eastern American sailplane was built for lightness and best possible climb performance, western planes were developed to possess both high weight and aerodynamic cleanliness. The object in creating this new generation of American ships was to produce sailplanes with the ability to achieve maximum "penetration," or the ability to cruise between thermals at high speeds without significant loss of performance, thus enabling the pilot to spend the shortest possible time in areas of sink. While climb performance suffered by comparison, the strength of the updrafts made this an acceptable compromise. More recent designs combine the best features of both the "floaters" and the "lead sled" designs.

Southern California is one of the most active soaring areas in the nation, owing both to the good conditions and to the large numbers of local enthusiasts, many of whom are attached in one way or another to the aerospace industry. Soaring has been going on for quite a while on the Coast. Hawley Bowlus soared Pt. Loma, near San Diego, in the 1920s and even had a soaring school there. The historic Torrey Pines site on the cliffs

El Mirage Field, California: one of the nation's biggest soaring centers.

of La Jolla is still very active, drawing not only sailplanes but radio-control model soarers and, most recently, the hang-glider contingent. The so-called Inland Empire—the valleys behind the Coast Range between San Diego and Los Angeles—has a few sites for good year-round local soaring.

California's real soaring heartland is the Mojave Desert, which begins behind the coastal and transverse ranges that rim the Los Angeles Basin and continues into Nevada and Arizona. This is a high desert—about three thousand feet above sea level in most areas—so relatively moderate temperatures are sufficient for good soaring. Several famous soaring sites are fairly closely grouped, including Crystalaire (Pearlblossom), Rosamond, Tehachapi, and especially El Mirage, a former Army Air Force base located next to a seven-mile-long dry lake. The lake bed offers an excellent surface for automobile tows, for the towing cable can be as long as 3,000 feet; the 4,000-foot runways of the airfield accommodate the tow-planes. El Mirage has been the scene of numerous national and regional meets, and many techniques developed there have been adopted around the world. On summer days, the mountains surrounding Los Angeles are

readily accessible after one has topped the first thermal (eighteen miles), and they offer very good soaring. In the winter, they produce wave conditions that are sometimes more easily reached from Crystalaire, which lies in the foothills. Both sites are ideal jumping-off places for flights northward into the Owens Valley along the east side of the Sierras and on northward to Reno or Lake Tahoe as well as eastward toward Phoenix or northeast toward Las Vegas or Salt Lake City.

The Central Valley of California, while flat and therefore ideal for landings, is usually covered by a layer of trapped air so stagnant that even birds are hard-put to fly through it. The valley is bounded on the east, however, by the Sierras, which offer strong thermals in the summer and powerful wave conditions in the winter; they're accessible from Tehachapi in the south and Bishop in the east, and from Minden, Nevada, and Truckee, California, both of which are near Lake Tahoe.

The San Francisco Bay area has some sites as well. Fremont, on the bay's east side, nearby Sky Sailing and Livermore, one valley farther east, offer good local soaring. Sky Sailing is a particularly good example of a field at which informality, camaraderie, and generosity mark the atmosphere. The field is located adjacent to a highway, and on weekends especially passersby stop to watch the gliders take off and land. Sometimes people who stop to get their very first look at a sailplane out of sheer curiosity find themselves actually flying in one, for the payment of a mere five-dollar fee.

Calistoga, about seventy-five miles north in the wine country, offers good local and occasional wave soaring in some of the lovelier scenery of the state. Farther north, the Portland, Oregon, area harbors a few soaring clubs, but the real activity in the Northwest comes from groups based in and around Seattle, another hub of aerospace activity. The Seattle area itself is rather miserable for soaring—as well as for most other activities that do not require large amounts of fog and rain—and many of the clubs operate from fields like Wenatchee, Pasco, or Ephrata.

Once one leaves the coast, soaring sites become a bit scarce until one nears the Rockies. There is an active operation (commercial) at Sun Valley, Idaho, which offers mountain soaring to rival that of the Alps. Clubs are beginning to explore the vastnesses of Wyoming and Montana. Activity picks up in Utah, however, and Arizona rivals California as a soaring state. There are numerous clubs in and around the Phoenix area; Estrella Sailport, lost in the desert between Phoenix and Tucson and operated by a pair of colorful Hungarian émigrés, offers excellent conditions and has hosted the national 1-26-class championships. Prescott does not have an active commercial operator, but it is often visited by clubs for soaring encampments.

New Mexico is also light on commercial operators because of the relatively thin population of the state, but it offers excellent soaring conditions to be utilized by local clubs and occasional visitors. Hobbs, in the south-central portion of the state, has an immense, old airbase used for various meets and contests. In the northern portion of New Mexico, the high plateaus around Albuquerque and Santa Fe provide fine conditions. The even higher plateau running from Taos into southern Colorado may yet be the scene of world-speed-record achievements. Various pilots have made excellent flights there, and it's an area likely to be more exploited in the future.

If California is the original home of desert soaring, Colorado might well be considered the home of American mountain soaring. The most active area centers around Colorado Springs and includes Black Forest Gliderport and the very active glider club of the United States Air Force Academy. During the summer, flights tend to head eastward into the plains; in the winter, the Pikes Peak Wave attracts altitude flights with such consistency that earning an altitude diamond at Black Forest is considered a bit unsportsmanlike. A bit farther north, Boulder offers similar conditions. Within the Rockies, rather than at their eastern edge, are soaring operations at Aspen and club operations at other fields for temporary weekends and encampments.

Great Plains soaring actually got its start south of the Plains, in Texas, another highly active soaring state. Western Texas, in particular, offers terrifyingly strong conditions such as terrain that makes one quail at the very thought of starting out. However, competent pilots soon learn to handle these givens safely and enjoyably. Marfa, in the southwest corner, was the site of the 1970 World Soaring Championships. To the east, the Midland-Odessa area is the base of some of the most famous soaring pilots now flying and a frequent starting point for northbound world-record flights and attempts. The first flight to exceed 1,000 kilometers, Al Parker's 647-mile trip to Kimball, Nebraska, started there, as did Wally Scott and Ben Greene's 717-mile dual flight made later. The Texas plains stop a bit short of Dallas, which is already somewhat more eastern in character and vegetation, but a good day makes them accessible from that area as well. Flights from the Marfa-Odessa area don't always head north; some have gone west, deep into Arizona. One flight, which was broken off to land at Gila Bend (it was a declared-goal flight) might well have carried on to the Pacific coast itself.

Oklahoma and Kansas show a very gradual transition from desert to prairie, although soaring conditions remain generally the same; often, the prairie air masses produce enough moisture for cumulus clouds to mark thermals, while pilots of the really dry regions must often contend with "blue" thermals, which have no visible signs. Liberal, Kansas, in the southwest corner of the state, has hosted national championships, with flights ranging far into Oklahoma, Texas, and Colorado. The eastern part of Kansas, again verging on eastern conditions, is another center of soaring activity, owing to the concentration of general-aviation manufacturers at Wichita.

The Great Plains offer some of the pleasantest soaring known. Long lines of thermals form on good days, and pilots can fly along the cloud streets with fair confidence of finding another thermal when they need it. This is why cruising speeds in this area are often higher than those in areas like Marfa, where the actual thermals may be stronger. It is consistency as well as strength that determines the quality of the conditions. There are a few soaring clubs in Nebraska and even fewer in the Dakotas, but the plains conditions continue well on into Canada, and it is conjectured that future flights of great distance may start at Odessa or somewhere similar early in the day and continue northward into Alberta or Saskatchewan.

East of the plains, the terrain gradually becomes wetter and lower as it descends almost imperceptibly into the Mississippi Valley, where the East begins.

The East and Midwest once were the "Heartland of American Soaring." The emergence of the West as a major soaring area has changed all that, but the area east of the Mississippi has a great deal to offer both to the competition and record-seeking pilot and the pleasure flier. It remains the cradle of the motorless-flight movement in America.

There is a close resemblance between certain northeastern areas—notably upstate New York—and the valleys of central Germany, in which soaring had its first powerful impetus. Thus, when the first German pilots to visit the United States in the late 1920s chose the areas they wanted to soar in, they naturally selected terrain similar to areas with which they were familiar in Europe—they chose such areas as Elmira, New York, and the sand dunes and beaches of Cape Cod, Massachusetts. Since then, these eastern areas have retained a tradition of keen interest in soaring. The current world open-class champion, George B. Moffat, Jr., is a product of that tradition. His home base is Wurtsboro, New York, not far from Elmira.

The entire eastern area of the United States is dominated by the Appalachian chain and its various extensions. The coastal plain to the east of the mountains offers relatively little in the way of soaring, owing largely to its usually being covered with stable marine air, although occasional shear lines can form out of interaction of the maritime air mass with air coming from the hills inland. Away from the coast and into the hills, however, conditions improve rapidly. We soon come to terrain very similar to the classic soaring areas of central Europe: ranges or rows of hills, often wooded, separated by relatively narrow valleys, often cultivated.

Terrain like this can provide several sorts of lift. The fields of the valley floor areas often provide quite respectable thermals; the air is frequently moist enough to give rise to impressive displays of cumulus cloud, sometimes making thermal spotting simpler than in the dry, blue air of the deserts. Thermals often form along the ridges, either because the sloping ground is more nearly perpendicular to the sun's rays or because the still air on the lee side of a ridge can be heated more effectively. With open fields in the valley bottoms fairly nearby, a pilot can venture relatively close to the ridgetops in search of ridge or thermal lift, a luxury denied his western compatriot.

While the consequences of landing out in the East may be less serious than they could be in the West, staying aloft may often require more finesse in the East. Competition and cross-country flying place an even greater premium on the pilot's situation-analyzing and decision-making abilities. Many a western pilot, on his first trip to an eastern soaring meet, has impatiently abandoned a 400-foot-per-minute thermal that had other pilots ecstatic because he believed that there had to be "stronger stuff around," not realizing that he had left the best lift of the day. Task speeds are slower in the East, and some of the heavier sailplanes used in the desert and plains states are not as popular in the East as are the lightly loaded sailplanes that can remain aloft in the weakest thermals.

Navigation can be a problem in the East, too. Low altitudes and frequently hazy air combine to make it hard for a pilot to orient himself after crossing a ridge separating two small valleys essentially identical in appearance.

At various places along the Appalachians, the rolling hills that are prevalent in most areas give way to mountains; these, in turn, give rise to such phenomena as mountain waves. An example of the strength of such conditions is the summit of New Hampshire's Mount Washington, where surface winds have been clocked at over two hundred miles per hour. In West Virginia, near Morgantown, during the middle and late summer the mountainous terrain and moist, unstable air masses often combine to produce some of the most monstrous thunderstorms on the planet. While these are usually too violent to be considered as safe sources of lift, prefrontal squall lines sometimes move through the area and can provide a genuine boost to the pilot lucky enough to be in the right place at the right time.

A terrain feature that has remained virtually unused until the advent of high-performance sailplanes in recent years has been long ridge systems, particularly in the Alleghenies, which stretch from Pennsylvania well into Virginia. These ridges run for many miles without a break, usually in parallel rows; when wind conditions are favorable, ridge lift exists along the tops and windward sides for hundreds of miles.

The advantage of such lift for long-distance or out-and-return flights is obvious: with the lift remaining in long bands at known locations, the pilots need not spend time circling in thermals or searching for lift. Instead, the pilot can cruise along the ridges at the best possible speed, using his valuable and limited time aloft to make distance rather than gain altitude.

The great disadvantage in this kind of flying is low altitude. Ridge lift often requires that the pilot remain very close to the ridge, frequently less than a wingspan from the treetops. This places him in a very sticky situation should the wind change and leave him too low to glide to a safe landing spot.

High-performance sailplanes improve this situation in several ways. Such a plane needs far less height over the ridge to be able to flee to a valley-bottom field, to jump gaps in the ridge, or to penetrate upwind to a parallel ridge system. Moreover, with their lower sink rates, the high-performance aircraft can sometimes gain more altitude over the ridges. Nevertheless, the strongest lift is very close to the ground along a ridge. The records set by the select group known as the Allegheny Ridge Runners include out-and-return flights of more than seven hundred miles. Such flights require constant instantaneous and correct decision making

A Schweizer 1-35 flying over Chemung County Airport, at Elmira, New York. At the right, in the crook of the two runways, is the Schweizer Aircraft factory.

as well as an intimate knowledge of the terrain. Such abilities come only with years of experience and exhaustive exploration of the route of flight. Pilots who try for long ridge flights—there are only a handful—have committed to memory every possible landing spot or source of lift along the route, and they usually plan their flights with minute-by-minute checkpoints. Such flights indeed may be the most nerve-wracking soaring can offer: eight or nine hours in the cockpit; never more than a few hundred feet above the terrain; and the pilot saddled constantly with the knowledge that there is literally no margin for error.

Most eastern soaring is done from a relatively few prominent airports. Elmira, New York, remains the most prominent of these, in no small part for historic reasons already mentioned in this chapter and elsewhere in this book.

Elmira is situated just north of the Pennsylvania border. Its setting in the valley of the Chemung River is ideal for good soaring, as German pilots such as Wolf Hirth discovered. In the early days, a glider field was established at Harris Hill, on a bluff overlooking the Elmira suburb of Horseheads. The WPA built hangars, shops, lodging, and even a swimming pool at Harris Hill, which became the official field for the United States National Soaring Championships.

The present-day visitor to Elmira will find an active club operation on "The Hill," which now has a strip large enough for airplane tow. In the valley below, at Chemung County Airport, the Schweizer factory operates one of the largest and most successful soaring schools in the world. Cross-country flights can take the adventurous pilot south from Elmira into Pennsylvania, west toward the shores of lake Erie, or north into the lovely wine-growing Finger Lakes area.

Unlike Elmira, Wurtsboro, New York, is definitely not a place where a glider pilot may find himself sharing airspace with an airliner. Wurtsboro is a typical fun-soaring site, as well as a place for serious learning. It is surrounded by gently rolling terrain that doesn't offer much lift for cross-country flying, being thickly wooded, although the better pilots at the field fly cross-country regularly. The major activity there involves people wanting to learn to soar. The atmosphere is relaxed, even idyllic.

Sugarbush, Vermont, is almost unique in the soaring world. It's a resort community—a very rich one. The ski area that forms its nucleus is very social. The airport is set among a forest of pines, and the surrounding country is quite rugged; the soaring conditions there can be spectacular by Eastern standards. The field is often the base for fierce regional competition. Luxury is a keynote here, with excellent inns and restaurants easily available. It's a good spot to learn how to soar.

The Appendix to this book can tell you the locations of many other soaring sites, West and East. Their variety is great; their charm is extraordinary; their distinctly American flavor is unmistakable, for the people who frequent them possess the individualism, friendliness, determination, and generosity that many people still regard as typically American traits.

10 SOARING ABROAD

Because soaring is an intensely international sport, a trip abroad often can mean staying in touch with its pleasures, not only by flying but by getting to know other soaring pilots, their fields, their ships, their particular soaring world. A trip to Europe could also include a look at some of the famous locales where soaring began, a look at the hills and skies as they may have been seen by the early pioneers. A visitor can visualize the great slow gliders of the past floating overhead and can understand better the passions and the achievements of the men who flew them. Close on the heels of such thoughts naturally follows a desire to be airborne oneself, to fly new gliders, to seek out new experiences.

As in the United States, the weather in Europe from north to south is highly varied, but it is varied essentially according to latitude; for example, much of Europe does not have particularly hot summers, but the days are long—in Finland, some twenty hours long in June—so there are more soaring hours in a day than at first might be expected.

A tour of the gliding centers of Europe easily could occupy a whole summer. A pilot can learn much about Europe and its culture by studying the landscape as he lazes about the sky. And on the ground, he is likely to do far better than most tourists because he will eat, drink, and be entertained in the homes of local glider pilots. His silver or gold pin will assure him of a welcome wherever there are sailplanes.

Frankfurt, West Germany, is an ideal place to start a soaring vacation because Germany offers excellent soaring conditions along with a particularly rich soaring history. The first calling point should be the Wasserkuppe and its Museum of the History of Gliding. The museum contains early gliders and drawings of gliders along with letters written by famous pioneers of the sport. The Wasserkuppe mountain is now only a training school, and it is easy for visitors to fly there. Simple accommodations and

162

food are available on the site, and there is a hotel at Poppenhausen, in the valley near the Schleicher factory. This is the home of the AS-K and AS-W series of gliders. New Schleicher gliders can be seen being test-flown above the Wasserkuppe.

In North Germany, the gliding school on the sandy soil of Oerlinghausen, near Bielefeld, does more flying in a year than any other gliding facility in the world—forty thousand launches of gliders alone. There are some twenty-four sailplanes, airplanes, and motor gliders available for cross-country and ridge soaring or instruction. Full board is available at the airfield.

The Hornberg, near Göppingen in southwest Germany, has been a soaring center since the 1930s. As is usual with German schools, the range of flying and available aircraft is wide. Accommodations are provided in houses owned by the school.

In Bavaria, near the Austrian border, is Unterwossen. The gliding school is in the northern Alps and specializes in cross-country flying. Guest houses and hotels nearby provide beds, food, and drink.

Each June, a motor-glider competition is held at Burg Feuerstein. Things are quite casually run: if you want to win the meet, you fly each day's contest task, but if your interest is less serious, you may enter on some days and fly as you wish on others. If your interest is purely technical, you can arrive at Burg Feuerstein with your motor glider and work on it in the heady scent of warm pine trees in the company of other enthusiasts. A large castle on the nearby hilltop has been converted to a hostel. You may stay there or in hotels down in the valley.

In Austria, which is predominantly an Alpine country, you can find fine mountain soaring. The center at Zell am See is organized for visitors. Not only is the soaring magnificent, but there is sailing and swimming in the lake in summer. In the winter wave-soaring season, skiing is possible. Visitors are given a license to fly for up to three months and can use the center's gliders after check flights are performed. A hotel and restaurant are on the airfield. Other centers in Austria are Nieder Oeblarn, near Aigen, and Turnau, near Maria Zell.

Italy's Varese is a small strip with a magnificent club house and good food. The Club has Bocian and AS-K 13 two-seaters and is obtaining six new Libelle gliders for solo flying. Flying in Italy means red tape; the wise visitor will apply to the club he wishes to visit *at least* four months in advance. All launches at Varese are by airtow. The climb-out is made over the lake; often, the pilot sees the mountains reflected in its mirror-smooth surface. Within easy airtow reach of the field is a fine forest-covered mountain that provides good slope soaring and a superb view of the Alps and the great Italian lakes. Waves of up to 5,000 meters can develop in winds from 300 degrees to 340 degrees. The months to visit Varese are March through June. Soaring for foreigners is also possible at the national centers of Rieti, Torino, and Bergamo.

Switzerland offers Samedan, in 1948 the site of the first World Championships after World War II. From here, magnificent soaring is possible above the peaks and glaciers of the high Alps. There are not many aircraft available for use by the visitor to Samedan and arrangements for rental should be made in advance. There is no gliding in the winter, but at this time, nearby St. Moritz provides all other forms of sport—mainly skiing.

Switzerland also offers Schänis, which lies Zurich-ward from Samedan, between the two long lakes of the Walensee and the Zurichsee. This is a center specifically developed for visitors. Many of them, in fact, come from nearby Germany to attempt their gold and diamond heights in wave. Such great heights are not easily obtained in their own country, partly because of the ban on cloud flying there. The best wave soaring at Schänis occurs in a *föhn* wind situation, mostly in November and February, when a south wind blows over the Alps. Schänis provides sleeping accommodations of dormitory standards, all meals, and a wide range of gliders for hire. K 7 and Blanik two-seaters are used for check flights, with K 8, K 6, and Cirrus—both standard and open-class versions—for soaring. July and August are the best months for 500-kilometer distance flights.

In France the traveler may go to Fayence, in the mountains near Cannes and sixteen miles from Grasse. This is a center that has become internationally famous. The airfield is on a plateau surrounded on three sides by hills, with the high Alps in sight twelve miles to the north. The instructors are totally involved with the center, being not only teachers but tow pilots: they do all the work on the aircraft. French flying discipline is strict, but no opportunities are lost in getting pilots airborne, even when the wave is working only at dawn. The center is equipped mainly with French gliders and has its own sleeping accommodations and restaurant. There are also hotels in the small town of Fayence, perched high on a hill two miles from the airfield.

Southern France also has centers at Vinon and St. Aubon, not far to the west and northeast, respectively, of Fayence, and La Montagne-Noir, which is southeast of Toulouse.

At Angers, northeast of Nantes, in the wide valley of the Loire, international competitions are held every July. Now called the Coupe d'Europe, their earlier name was Le Huit Jours d'Angers, which became rapidly mistranslated into "the eight days of danger."

Issoudun, southwest of Bourges, is right in the center of France and offers excellent cross-country possibilities in all directions. There are good aircraft and launching facilities, but accommodations must be found in local pensions.

Belgium and Holland have the reputation of being either flat or geographically uninteresting. They are neither, certainly as pertains to gliding. Their centers are in lovely, rolling countryside among national parks.

The Cirrus is one of the most popular sailplanes flown in Europe.

St. Hubert, in Belgium, caters to the visitor, with airtowing and a range of German sailplanes and motor gliders. These facilities, along with accommodations and food, are available all year, except in July and August, when the whole center is taken over for student flying. The manager speaks good English. The best time to visit is May and June.

Terlet, located at Arnhem, is the national center of Holland and provides much scope for 200- to 300-kilometer triangle soaring. As do many small European countries, Holland has problems with controlled airspace, but it welcomes glider pilots. National championships take place at Terlet, as does a great deal of general and instructor training. There are simple accommodations on the site, but the sailplanes for use by visitors are sophisticated and include five Libelles and two Standard Cirrus.

Leszno, Poland, is one of the most famous soaring centers in Europe. It has been the site of world-championship meets and is the training base for the many first-class Polish pilots, who have such a high reputation in world soaring. Leszno is south of Poznań, lying on a flat and seemingly endless sandy plain that stretches eight hundred kilometers across the countryside. From this base, many 500-kilometer triangles have been flown and also many distance records. This is a Mecca for some soaring pilots. There is a fine hotel block and restaurant. The school offers perhaps the most comprehensive training anywhere. Polish gliders—Bocian, Much, Pirat, Foka, Cobra, and Jantar—are used exclusively and are of excellent quality and performance. Aerobatics, cloud flying, and night airtowing are taught along with cross-country flying. Language can present a problem, but not an insuperable one. Permission is necessary to fly at Leszno, and application to go there should be made several months in advance. For young Poles, flying is free with training up to world-championship standards for those showing exceptional talent.

It is possible to travel by boat from Poland to Sweden, and from Poland, the next logical ports-of-call would be in Scandinavia. Eskilstuna, one hundred miles west of Stockholm, is the base from which the current Swedish soaring records—including the 500-kilometer triangle—have been broken. Although accommodations have to be found in hotels in the nearby town, the airfield offers a swimming pool and sauna as well as a large range of aircraft to fly. As the latitude of the countries visited increases, the soaring season shortens, and there is almost no glider flying in Sweden from October to April. In Norway gliding is possible only from June through August.

Notodden, more than five thousand feet high in the mountains and two hours' driving southwest of Oslo, is the place to go in Norway. It is scenically beautiful, offers very interesting thermal soaring in mountain conditions, and has an upcurrent locally called "The Comfort." This is a large quantity of silk-smooth lift that can be found in the evenings over a nearby large lake up to six thousand feet. It gets its name from the solace it gives to pilots who have failed to stay up during the day. Notodden is still developing as a center, under a new manager who speaks excellent English. Visitors are very welcome.

The Finnish countryside, with its forests and lakes, can provide the soaring visitor memorable flying in clear air. The main soaring centers are at Räyskälä and Nummela, in the southern part of the country, not too far from Helsinki. The 1976 World Championships will be held at Räyskälä. The season lasts from May through September, with the best days in June, providing up to ten hours of thermal soaring each day. Cloud bases are often higher than expected, sometimes up to nine thousand feet. Gliders available are the Blanik, K 8, K 6, and Vasama. There are some sixty to seventy gliding clubs in southern Finland, most of them near lakes with swimming, camping facilities, and saunas.

Denmark's Arnborg airfield, near Herning, brings one back to a climate that permits flying the year round. Bergfalke, Falke motor-glider, and K 6 machines are used, launched by winch or airtow. Two-hundred- to 300-kilometer triangles are practicable from the site, and in April through May, a favorable north-wind situation allows world-record distances down through Germany. A restaurant and simple accommodations are available on the airfield, and good motels are within walking distance.

A visit should be made to Britain's center at Lasham, an hour's drive southwest of London. Flying for visiting pilots is on a seven-day-a-week basis, with bedrooms and meals available on the field. High-performance sailplanes, such as the Kestrel, may be used by skilled pilots by arrangement. Check flights are given on Falke or K 13 machines, with solo flying in K 8s and Pilatus sailplanes. Other places to visit in Britain are the historic site of Dunstable Downs and the Scottish Gliding Union in Fife-shire, northeast of Edinburgh, where wave soaring to diamond height is possible.

Gliding in Europe is organized much more in clubs than in schools or glider-rental establishments. It therefore may seem odd to a non-European that although there are a number of gliders around that are not privately owned, it is difficult to find one that is available for flying by a visitor. The reason for this is that there is usually a large number of club members per glider. Particularly on weekends, they expect to have the priority on their own club aircraft. In northern Europe especially, where the weather is often poor for long periods on end, members have to take every opportunity they can get to fly.

Usually, club members are delighted to get visitors airborne, but a wise pilot from the United States will ask if there is a limit to the length of time allowed for local soaring; if there is, he will come down when that time is up.

Another difference about European flying is that some gliding sites have no special traffic pattern. The pilot is expected to use his eyes and common sense. At other sites, particularly mountainous ones, the pattern may be rigidly defined. Good pilots quickly lose their sense of pride and modestly ask questions about local conditions until they are sure they understand what is expected of them.

Soaring takes place in many countries other than those in Europe, but in many of them, facilities are not generally available to foreign visitors. This is not due to a lack of welcome, but simply to a lack of equipment.

In Australia, there is plenty of gliding. The scale and weather are similar to those of the western United States. Visitors should write to the Gliding Federation of Australia. Australia is fine for high-speed thermal flying, with 1,000-kilometer triangles being quite possible. New Zealand is more suited to slope and wave soaring. In South Island, Mount Cook produces wave systems equivalent to Bishop in the Sierra Nevadas. But big-wave flying is not always suited to the short-time visitor. In North Island, the Matta Matta Gliding Academy, which is located one hundred miles southeast of Auckland, offers seven-day-a-week flying in two-seater or solo aircraft. The Piako Gliding Club is on the same site, providing

A standard Austria soaring near the Gross Glockner, Austria's tallest mountain, near the Zell am See soaring school.

sleeping and eating facilities. The hills near Matta Matta—the Kaimai range—are extensive enough for slope soaring over silver distances and provide wave soaring in both north-northwest and south-southeast winds. At Ardmore, only twenty miles from Auckland, the visitor can fly Falke and other sophisticated planes from the general-aviation airfield.

In general, it is always better to write to the places you want to visit a month or so beforehand. National aero clubs or gliding associations usually have information leaflets about flying in their country available, along with the addresses of clubs or schools that take visitors from abroad. Such formal correspondence may be slow, so if you have a gliding friend in that country, it could be better to write to him direct. Countries in Europe vary widely as to the formalities required of visitors. These range from special permission from the state authorities to no more than the ability to sign a declaration of physical fitness, as is the case in Great Britain. Always take your license to soar with you. It is normal to have to join the club at which you fly, but short-term membership arrangements exist for visitors.

Gliding clubs usually expect a visitor to fly a check ride with an instructor. This should never be regarded as a slur on the visitor's skill, but as an insurance requirement. At some sites, particularly in mountainous regions, a visiting pilot should be only too grateful to have a familiarization flight with a local expert.

Here are addresses to which inquiries and requests for reservations may be sent:

GERMANY
    Wasserkuppe. Segelflugschule, Bei Poppenhausen, West Germany
    Oerlinghausen. Segelflugschule, Bei Bielefeld, North Germany
    Flugplatz Burg Feuerstein, Herr Stolle, Manager, Bei Ebermannstadt, N. Bavaria
AUSTRIA
    The Guide Achteltuer. A-5700, *Zell am See* flugplatz, Austria
ITALY
    AVAL, Calcinate del Pesce, *Varese*, 21100, N. Italy
SWITZERLAND
    Herr Risch, Manager, *Samedan* Airfield, bei
      St. Moritz, Unter Engadin, Switzerland

FRANCE
　　Association Aéronautique Provence, Côte D'Azur, 83440 *Fayence*
　　Aeroclub d'Issoudun, BP48, 36100, *Issoudun.*
　　Aeroclub de l'Ouest de la France, 21 Bd Foch, 49000, *Angers*
BELGIUM
　　The Director, Centre Nat. Vol à Voile, Aerodum. *St. Hubert*, Belgium
HOLLAND
　　The Manager, National Gliding Center, *Terlet*, Arnhem, Holland
POLAND
　　Leszno G4–100 Lotnisko, Poland
SWEDEN
　　Write to Club (Secretary) Box 53, 631 OZ, *Eskilstuna*, Sweden
FINLAND
　　Finnish Aeronautical Association, Malmin Lentoaseama, Finland. 0700 Helsink, 70
NORWAY
　　Norsk Aeroklub, Nedre Slottsgate 17, Oslo. 1
DENMARK
　　Svaevelflyvecenter, *Arnborg*, 7400 Herning, Denmark
BRITAIN
　　The Manager, *Lasham* Gliding Society, Lasham, Nr. Alton, Hampshire, England
　　The Manager, London Gliding Club, *Dunstable*, Bedfordshire, England
SCOTLAND
　　The Manager, *Scottish Gliding Union*, Nr. Kinross, Fifeshire, Scotland
NEW ZEALAND
　　Matta Matta Soaring Academy, Nr. Auckland, N.Z.
AUSTRALIA
　　The Manager, *Waikerie Gliding Club*, South Australia, Australia

11 GAMES PILOTS PLAY

For many pilots, the thrills of local soaring are entirely sufficient. For others of slightly more adventurous bent, cross-country or altitude flights, in which the pilot has no adversary other than the air itself, provide enough stimulation. For some, competition—and, more important, winning—are of paramount importance. In the most extreme cases, these pilots may regard soaring as a means to an end rather than as an end in itself. For them, soaring isn't even necessarily pleasant, but rather a grim struggle against time, space, and opponents. What's pleasant is winning.

The first soaring meets were just that—meetings of sailplane pilots at some soaring site to compare progress and exchange knowledge about new advances. The original criterion for a successful flight—survival—was soon refined to a desire for minimal damage to the aircraft. Pilots soon began speaking in heady terms of duration aloft.

As their confidence increased, pilots dared search for higher and higher hills for launching. This led to flights of sufficient distance to be scored, sometimes even requiring measurement of the distance on a map rather than the simple expedient of pacing off the distance from takeoff to touchdown.

As time went on, the forms of competition continued to evolve; some categories were added while others were dropped. Duration flying was the first to go, for it was soon discovered that at certain soaring sites, most pilots could stay aloft as long as they wanted. The contest became one of staying awake rather than one of flying skill. Altitude was also deemphasized on the grounds that in certain weather conditions, pilot skill played no more of a role than did luck and equipment.

In the meantime, pilots were gaining more skill in cross-country flying; simple distance competition was soon joined by flights to preselected goals, flights to a goal, and return and speed races.

Today's local, regional, national, and international soaring competitions, while more refined in execution, remain identical in spirit to those of the early years. With few exceptions, soaring competitions are not spectator sports. The absence of cheering crowds, in fact, seems to draw competitors and contest organizers closer together and to heighten the sense of an esoteric sport shared and loved.

Seen superficially, modern soaring contests seem to be divisible into two types of competition: speed and distance. On closer examination, all "tasks" (daily competition goals) are, in essence, speed tasks. Because there is only so much time for flying each day, and because the best soaring conditions often span only a few hours, it is necessary to fly fast in order to make as much distance as possible. The only difference is that speed tasks are set with specific goals—often a visit to some distant turnpoint and a return to the starting point—and departure and return times are carefully noted.

The simplest task, and the last holdover from the early days, is "free distance." The object is simple: take off and fly as far as you can. It's obvious that one will go farther with the wind than against it, unless circumstances dictate otherwise (for example, a takeoff at Los Angeles with an easterly wind); thus free distance sometimes is also called the "downwind dash." Ground crews dislike free distance, since they have to retrieve the sailplane after hours of chasing it, then haul it back during the still watches of the night so as to be back at the contest site in time for the next day's flying. Free distance is assigned rarely now that improved sailplane performance makes long flights likely; national and international contest rules dictate "rest days" if pilots exceed certain distances the day before. "Rest days" invariably have the best soaring weather of the entire contest. On the subsequent contest day, it always rains.

To allow distance flights without sending the sailplanes too far from home, other techniques have been developed. For example, a course can be called around one or more distant turnpoints; these are set by the contest committee after consultation with weathermen so that few, if any, pilots will complete the entire course. In many cases, pilots who *do* make it all the way around must then fly as far as possible along a given course, or perhaps start the original course a second time.

Above: Paul Bikle, one of competitive soaring's most important figures, posting turnpoints as a day's task is given. Below: As pilots don their parachutes and prepare for takeoff, they keep an eye on the sky to see if conditions may be changing.

The logical outgrowth of this method is today's most common distance task: "Distance in a Prescribed Area." It's also sometimes called "Bikle's Baseball," after its original inventor, Paul Bikle, or "Cat's Cradle," since it resembles a baseball diamond or cat's cradle when depicted on a map. Several turnpoints are designated, all of them spaced around the contest site at varying distances and directions. Pilots may depart from the contest site and fly to the turnpoints in any order, with the exception that one can't retrace one's course. Thus, if you fly from A to B, you'll have to visit C (or Q, for that matter) before you can return to A.

All such distance tasks have the advantage that pilots can fly great distances without getting too far from the home field, thus reducing retrieve problems and the risk of imposed rest days. "Cat's Cradle" has the additional advantage of stressing each pilot's individual soaring acumen, weather wisdom, tactics, and decision-making skills, since the choice of turnpoints is up to the pilot rather than the committee. Such skills are terribly important in competition. Some of the most successful pilots have been rather mediocre sailplane handlers from a stick-and-rudder aspect, but incredibly sharp estimators and deciders.

Take a closed (out-and-return or triangle) distance course, add some means of clocking sailplanes away and back, and you've got a speed task. Courses for these are usually chosen for a given day's weather, so that most of the competitors will make it around; those who don't are scored on a pro rata basis. Short (100-kilometer) speed tasks provide the most grueling competition, where the smallest mistakes will have the greatest effect on scores.

All of these tasks require a means of verifying the arrival of the contestants at the turnpoints as well as timing for speed tasks. The story of the development of these techniques reveals in microcosm not only the heights of ingenuity but, occasionally, the depths of treachery.

In the balmy days of yore, turnpoint verification was easy. Observers were stationed at the turnpoints. Since the gliders were never very high, it was simple to keep a lookout, then note the large competition numbers painted on the bottom of the wings. As performance improved, altitudes increased, and it became harder to read the numbers or to see the sailplanes at all. Something better was needed.

Although the observers had a hard time locating the pilots in the vastness of the sky, it was fairly easy for the pilots to locate the position of the turnpoint on the ground. The turnpoint crews were equipped with large cloth panels that could be laid out in various arrangements. These arrangements were changed from time to time by the crew; arriving pilots noted the time and the disposition of the panels on cards that they turned in at the end of the day's flight.

This system soon revealed weaknesses. If the turnpoint was in a prominent location, a pilot could spot it from miles away, especially with binoculars, and "cut the corner" to save time. In the western United States, cruising altitudes tend to be quite high, and it was often difficult to spot the panels at all. One pilot arrived over a turnpoint at seventeen thousand feet, then spiraled down to eight thousand (wasting time all the while, of course), searching vainly for panels until what he thought was a driveway suddenly picked itself up and turned ninety degrees. Something better was needed.

Various groups continued to search for better solutions. One answer was that of the Southern California Competition Club, or S3C, whose members ultimately were instrumental in evolving procedures used currently in World Championships. Their answer to the turnpoint problem was the "Bikle-Williams No-Cheat Turnpoint." This was an imposing pyramidal structure—a large tent, actually—of fabric and aluminum, set up in the center of a giant fabric X with 100-foot arms. Each side of the pyramid could be flipped to be either black or white, requiring the pilot to fly all the way around the monster to note all four sides on his time card.

Alas, this system, too, soon showed its weaknesses. By now, turnpoints were often so far from the contest sites that crews were taken to them each day by airplane. Even folded, the device was a hefty package, too large for many single-engine ships. It was cumbersome to erect, and in a strong breeze it displayed fairly respectable soaring performance. This was unfortunate for those pilots who arrived at the turnpoint during one of the periods in which the turnpoint crew was unwrapping the fabric from around some nearby tree or a passing diesel truck. Worst of all, it wasn't cheatproof. An unscrupulous crew (unfortunately, there are a few of these) could hasten to the turnpoint by road and observe the disposition of black and white panels, later communicating them to the (unscrupulous) pilot on some unused radio channel. Something better was needed.

The next advance was the immediate precursor of the present photo turnpoint technique. Pilots fitted their planes with Instamatic cameras mounted in the left side of the canopy. By aiming the left wingtip at the target, pilots could photograph turnpoints. No longer did crews have to be sent out with panels or pyramids. The contest committee simply could choose prominent, easily recognized landmarks as turnpoints.

While this represented a great improvement, there were still a few minor loopholes. The most obvious allowed the unscrupulous pilot to fly around the course the day before in a powered aircraft, snapping the photos at his leisure. Sealed films and cameras looked like the way to solve that, until another pilot came up with the airborne print-copier system. Moreover, since multiple attempts are permitted for speed tasks—you can start, change your mind if you think you're too slow, come back, and start again—pilots could start, shoot the first turn, restart, and proceed directly to the second turn from the starting point.

These problems were not insurmountable, though. In current practice, each sailplane carries two cameras (one is a backup). The cameras are loaded any time before takeoff; just before departure, a contest organizer makes a line on the canopy with a grease pencil directly in front of the lens. Since it's so close to the camera, it's not in focus, and the turnpiont can be shot "through" it; but it leaves a gray shadow across each exposure. The orientation of the line is changed each day to provide proof that the film hasn't been switched. Moreover, just before takeoff, the pilot must photograph a "task board" held at his wingtip by a ground crewman and bearing the date and the sailplane's contest number; this will be the first frame on the film and will bear the telltale shadow.

To avoid the multiple-start problem, a "start clock" panel is laid out at the contest site near the starting gate. Obviously, the time of each start will be recorded; if a pilot returns for a second start, he must photograph the clock panel, which changes at regular intervals. Each photo is shot with both cameras; at the end of the day, the films are turned in and one is developed. If it comes out, the second is discarded; if not, the second is available as a backup.

At the beginning of the day's race, the pilot snaps a shot of a board on which the date and his competition number are posted. This must be the first shot on his film. When over a prescribed turnpoint, he banks his ship sharply to photograph the spot.

Timing for speed tasks is, of course, critical. FAI rules have established a starting gate for such tasks: a square, one kilometer wide by one kilometer high. A simple optical sighting device ensures that the sailplane is within its limits at the moment that the start-line sight operator calls "Mark!" and notes the time. The finish gate is a kilometer wide but only three hundred meters in height; often the same sighting device is used for both. Pilots are in radio communication with the gate operators to warn them of impending starts and finishes ("Seven Hotel, one mile out . . .") and to be advised whether they were in the gate during the run ("Seven Hotel from Gate, good start . . .").

At present, most soaring meets are scored using a sliding-scale system. The best performance of each day's task receives 1,000 points, and others are scored accordingly. In speed tasks, those who don't make it all the way around the course are awarded distance points on a similar, but lower, scale. Thus, it behooves the speed contestant to finish, no matter how slowly; this comes back to points of tactics and strategy, since flying fast and spending as little time as possible climbing in thermals increases the risk of "flying into the ground" before crossing the finish line. Speed-task finishes are the only really spectacular sight at a soaring competition: when the pilot feels he's close enough to the finish—usually thirty miles or less—he'll start his "final glide," eschewing further thermals. He'll leave a slight height margin for safety, and as he nears the field and a finish is assured, this margin can be turned to speed. Finishing sailplanes cross the finish line a few feet off the ground at or near redline with a faint rush of air, then pull up into a gigantic chandelle around the field to arc gently back down for a landing.

Some of the most frantic activity at competitions takes place far from the field: the infamous "relight." If a contestant starts on a speed or distance task and, through error or mischance, is forced down before he's gotten too far out on course, he can "relight," that is, disassemble the sailplane, load it onto the trailer, drive back to the contest site, reassemble the sailplane, and try once more. Meets have been won and lost on relights; they're the acid test of a top-notch ground crew. Pilots often determine a "relight distance"—the distance beyond which a relight would no longer be feasible—before launch and send their crews out to that point

Hurry up and wait: Before takeoff, preparations such as filling the wings with water ballast (above) are often hurried and are just as often followed by periods of waiting for one's turn to fly (below).

before they take off. The crew then waits at that point until the pilot either makes it back to the home field or lands out.

If you're interested in competition flying, there are ways you can get your feet wet without having to compete against the aces and their super-ships. Local clubs often sponsor "fun" meets, with short-speed triangles or distance tasks. In southern California, the Southern California Competition Club tests its new ideas and refines old ones by holding "workshops," which are day-long mini-meets followed by critiques during which pilots and contest personnel can discuss and resolve problems.

Some of the fiercest competition in the United States occurs in the regional and national 1–26 championships. Although the Schweizer 1–26 has rather low performance qualities, there are almost seven hundred of them around. A meet in which everyone flies the same model sailplane makes pilot skill alone the determining factor; some winners of 1–26 meets have gone on to standard- or open-class competition.

The 1–26 may be the precursor of an inexpensive international competition class. At present, there are only two classes: standard and open. The standard class was originally conceived to provide the soaring public with a class of sailplane that would be relatively inexpensive, simple to fly and maintain, and still have good performance. Such expensive features as retractable landing gear or camber-changing flaps were not permitted; wingspan was set at fifteen meters (about forty-nine feet) and terminal-speed-limiting dive brakes were mandatory. Thus, if a standard pilot became disoriented in a cloud, he could descend with the brakes with no risk of overstressing the sailplane.

The classic "original standard" is the all-plywood Ka. 6, built by the firm of Alexander Schleicher in Germany. Various models of this graceful design have appeared; all offer delightful handling and performance sufficient for flights of three hundred miles or more. Other German designs soon followed, as did ships from Poland (Foka—"seal"), Holland (Sagitta —"arrow"), Finland (Vasama—"arrow"), and Australia (Arrow). An extremely graceful Brazilian design was christened "Urupema," which supposedly meant "arrow" in an Indian dialect, but a new translation later revealed that "Urupema" is actually a primitive mortar and pestle used to grind corn. Edmund Schneider in Australia failed to stick to the point

The Brazilian Urupema, a fine example of the current generation of super-streamlined sailplanes. Note the reclining position of the pilot.

of the name game by redesigning the ES–59 Arrow and calling the new version the ES–60 Boomerang.

Unfortunately, the original ideals of the standard class seem to have been lost. As open-class sailplanes became more and more sophisticated, the standard pilots became envious; as manufacture of fiberglass standards began, pilots pressed for and got rule changes permitting retractable gear, water ballast, and camber-changing flaps (if they also could be used as dive brakes). The result is that today's standards differ from opens primarily in their 15-meter wingspan limit. Performance and sophistication are very high; so is the price, with a good new standard delivered in the United States leaving little more than carfare from $15,000. Sentiment is now running strongly toward definition of a new "sport" class, which may be limited to 13 meters, fixed gear, and other simplicities to reduce costs. It will then probably be at least five years before we see rule changes permitting fantastically sophisticated "sport" sailplanes.

As the name implies, in the open class anything goes. Fiberglass sail-planes, which are now the rule, were, at their introduction in the early

1960s, the most exotic open-class sailplanes in the word. Open-class sail-planes are almost invariably larger than their standard brethren; in recent years, spans have averaged around 17 meters (56 feet), with a few 18- and 19-meter ships. The World Championships at Marfa, Texas, in 1970 marked the first competition appearance of "jumbo" sailplanes like the Schempp-Hirth Nimbus (22 meters) and the Glasflugel 604 (22½ meters); two years later, the Caproni 23-meter A-23 appeared at the world meet at Vrsac, Yugoslavia. This all-metal monster—it soon gained the sobriquet of "spaghetti wagon"—was the bane of ground crews. It was very heavy, and, after landing in the muddy fields of the area, tended to sink in up to its wingtips.

In addition to large size—the latest German version, the SB–10, has a span of 35 meters, well over 100 feet—open ships usually sport an array of performance-increasing devices and features. Retractable landing gear is the rule, of course; nowadays, almost all have flaps for changing wing camber to suit airspeed. The latest wrinkle is area-increasing (Fowler) flaps to change wing loading as well. Another frequently-used method of wing-loading change is the inclusion of several hundred pounds of dispos-able water ballast. This feature—also seen on later standard-class sail-planes—allows the pilot to take off with a heavy ship with which he can "penetrate," or cruise between thermals, at higher-than-normal speeds. Such extra performance is gained at the expense of climb speed, but during the strong part of the day this can be lived with. Later in the day, the ballast can be partially or completely dumped; the decision as to whether and when to dump is yet another of the fine tactical points that can win or lose a meet.

Electronic devices are also beginning to come into widespread use. Since many variometers are already electronic, it has proven quite simple to use them as data inputs to simple analogue computers that can tell the pilot such things as the most efficient speed for cruising, how high to climb in each thermal, and when to start the final glide. Many of these devices reflect amazing complexity and cost; it is reassuring to note that in the last World Championships in Australia, their presence or absence seemed to have little to do with the final standings.

It's hard to look at the future of competition unless we restrict ourselves

Above: A modern competition sailplane's panel is a storehouse of vital information. A recent addition is the Bohli compass, which provides pitch and roll guidance as well as direction—a valuable aid in cloud-flying. Below: At the finish of a race, spotters watch the ships barrel over the line at top speed.

to generalities, but there are a few directions in which things may go.

A change in the scoring systems may appear fairly soon; both pilots and scorers agree that the current "1,000-point-base" system is cumbersome, laborious, and susceptible to occasional inequities. A possible alternate, proposed independently at about the same time in England and the United States, would simply award a pilot two points for each competitor he beat and one for each that he tied. "Relative" scoring of this sort is vastly easier to compute than the old system; it also allows contest organizers to call smaller speed or distance tasks without tightening the point spread.

Another possibility is handicapping. This seems increasingly attractive for local and regional meets. There has been much grumbling in the ranks about the greater costs of competitive sailplanes; the supership of two years ago may well be eclipsed by the latest standards of today. Computing and assigning a "figure of merit" or handicap for each production sailplane type is a major task, but hardly an insurmountable one in this computer age. Software can be designed by which to refine the figures of a good handicapping system and to learn from its mistakes.

One area where competition will probably never change is in the necessity of immense amounts of work by the ground forces. A good-sized regional contest has a competition director, a task-selection committee, meteorologists, operations directors, tow pilots, scorers, timers, and so on —each of whom often has several people working for him. Almost all of the ground forces are usually pilots who would much rather be competing themselves, but running a contest has a curiously masochistic charm of its own.

Whatever the future of soaring may bring, it seems certain that competition will remain an important part. Sailplane pilots are individualists by nature, and any such group is certain to harbor members who feel they must test their mettle and skill against one another as well as against the sky itself.

12 THE MAN
WITHIN THE SHIP

Ski jumpers, football players, sprinters, auto racers, swimmers, jockeys, and other sportsmen are so attired, so positioned, or so equipped that they may address themselves to competition looking like heroes even before things come down to cases. Glider pilots would, at first glance, seem unlikely members of such a fraternity. Sailplanes lined up to start a race look peculiar. They rest low to the ground, tilted awkwardly on one centered wheel and the tip of a wing. Each pilot enters his craft like a cautious bather climbing into a tub of hot water, lowering himself into the cockpit delicately until only his head is visible. Often, his head is crowned by a shapeless, small white hat. Once aboard, the contestant checks his equipment, tidies things up, and sits waiting in his little tub until a transparent canopy is fitted over him and he is completely enclosed. Few glider pilots resemble athletes. The outward marks they carry as badges of their sport are carried in common with boat skippers, marksmen, and many artists: a sharpness of eye, a penetration of glance. During the soaring season, the transparency of the canopy exposes them constantly to an intensified sun (which is why they wear the shapeless white hats), so they often possess enviable tans or painful-looking sunburns, or both.

A glider must be walked delicately, like an invalid, to its starting position. The values of its lines are lost when fitted snugly against the ground, and its wings merely seem outrageously long for such a small machine. Even when the towplane taxis with a roar to its position ahead of the glider and the towrope is inserted into a hole in the sailplane's nose, betokening the imminence of flight, the sailplane itself still seems depressingly dormant.

Then something ironic and splendid happens. The two aircraft accelerate in unison down the runway, and well before the towplane leaves the

What in flight will be a superb machine is, on the ground, something helpless looking.

ground, the sailplane rises and its pilot disappears from view. As the ships climb away, the enormous wings, the wasplike fuselage, the low-slung profile become beautiful. Released and free, circling and gliding, the sailplane appears from the ground to be without any volition but its own easy response to the fluid air. Only when it lands and slows to the point where it must again tilt in undignified rest does the pilot come back into view. Unjustly, an impression of ludicrousness returns.

Unjustly, because without the combination of motion and *mind*, the sustaining logic of a sailplane is lost. Flying is seldom a matter of physical strength for a pilot. Almost always, a slight touch of hand or foot sustains controlled flight. Like the brain within the skull, the pilot within the ship brings thought to bear on the surrounding environment, enabling the machine to remain aloft. Soaring is competition between the pilot and gravity; the arena is the open air and the terrain beneath. Such competition demands force of mind, a solidly linked partnership of perception and intelligence. Add to that a test of skills against other pilots, and the battle becomes much more intense, calling for exceptional steadiness or the explosive daring of the inspired.

Wings flexed upward, rising well before the towplane, the ship becomes a harmony of line and directed intelligence.

In competitive soaring, the psychological factor is vital. How good a pilot is depends foremost on his makeup, especially when under stress. How well a pilot can intimidate his rivals into giving him the winning edge depends a great deal on the image of himself that he can impose upon them. One of the few truly amateur sports still extant, soaring does not boast a pantheon of manufactured heroes established by media ballyhoo. Reputations are built upon performance and demeanor.

The great pilots vary amazingly in their makeup. Some are cool and imperturbable; others are vitriolic, unpredictable. Some work out of sheer rationality; others apply a hefty amount of instinct. All of them are masters of their craft: they can read the weather, the terrain, the capabilities of their ships, the capabilities of each other with amazing precision. So fine are the differences among them that most contests seldom seem one-sided. Yet those who seem most consistently to rise to the top of the heap seem to carry within them characteristics and capabilities more finely honed, more reliable than those of their confreres.

They possess, for instance, dedication—the dedication of competitors

A.J. Smith, one of the most demanding of soaring competitors, and his Schleicher AS-W 12.

needing to win as well as the dedication of fliers needing to fly. Some of them are people of disparate backgrounds: teacher, doctor, engineer. Others fly to live as well as live to fly: one recent world champion is an airline pilot; many soaring competitors are professional power-pilots.

They possess, also, a sense of commitment, the drive to conquer not only the elements within which soaring must be done but the elements of human character that can undo a competitor. A pilot must be sharp, but sharpness in soaring competition is seldom if ever a matter of performing spectacularly and briefly as at a track meet, excepting an event such as the decathlon. The top soaring pilots are close enough in ability to be able to beat the others on any given day. In fact, it is possible for a pilot to win a meet without ever placing first. Far more important than flashes of brilliance is consistent excellence, with reasonably good luck thrown in, over a long period of time. Under such demands, sharpness means perception and intelligence unwaveringly directed, like a laser beam, free from distraction. Commitment provides that freedom.

To keep one's commitment in focus and to implement it demands the direction of energy and the husbanding of it, as well as capitalizing on whatever good things that fortune may throw one's way. This involves a sense of pace. On the ground or in the air, a champion pilot applies his physical and psychological energies so as to conserve them while using them to the full during a given moment. And he seeks to drain his competitors of their energy—what is called psyching-out. Some pilots, such as Goran Ax, of Sweden, are apparently immune to the tactics of creating apprehension in one's opponent, and merely laugh them away. America's George B. Moffat, Jr., is likely to use a psychological approach, himself assuming a passive-aggressive posture of aloofness in the face of crisis to establish an image of superiority. Some competitors lose their cool, as West Germany's Hans-Werner Grosse has been known to do, and reveal their own insecurity by ineffectively seeking to psyche-out other pilots.

How best to use one's energy becomes crucial over a long contest. Moffat, for instance, approached the 1974 World Championships with a plan. Instead of taking the meet on a day-by-day basis, hoping to do as well as he could each day, he would try to do extremely well the first four or five days; in so doing he would amass such a formidable lead that his opponents would have to expend inordinate amounts of energy to beat him, which would be counterproductive. Such a plan was tantamount to putting all his eggs in one basket, like a miler setting up a vicious pace for the first three laps, hoping to outdistance his rivals to the point where he could gut his way to a win, even while fading. Had the plan failed, Moffat would still have been willing to expend as much energy as it would take to win, hoping he would have the energy to do it or to make his opponents give out before he did. As it happened, the demanding plan worked, and he won handily.

Commitment begins with preparation long before the contest. In locales far from the contest, pilots and their associates go over every inch of their ships looking for ways of making them more aerodynamically efficient. Even at this stage, the differences that might spell conquest or defeat may subtly begin to appear. Some pilots are accomplished engineers, either through formal training or self-tutelage. Others, falling back upon their own experience with sailplanes or that of others, work by intuition. However the work is done, it usually takes place in less than heroic surroundings. Preparation begins in a shop, where the splendor of a sailplane can seem to be reduced to scattered junk as its keepers take it apart and refine it into perfection. If glory is fulfillment, then such an obscure place must resemble a vacuum. One can work days without noticing a change. Eventually, however, the fine differences appear. They provide a psychological boost to the pilot and, if they are made to appear conspicuous enough, they can be a discouragement to the competition.

Preparation also means flying, flying, flying—under all kinds of conditions. Some countries, such as Poland, hold camps for competing pilots. At the other end of the spectrum, the United States relies on head-to-head competition and individual practice to sharpen its representative pilots. As in all sports worthy of the name, the hours spent in actual competition are but a small fraction of the hours spent in practice.

Nevertheless, nothing can substitute for the benefits of actual experience. On whatever level he may fly—local airport contests, regional meets, national championships, world championships—the new pilot is at something of a disadvantage. At each level he finds himself competing against names he has come to revere. He has heard talk about them, has read about

Above: Dedication means a compulsive concern for making each detail of the ship perfect. Below: Decision time for George Moffat and his rivals as the weather changes and launch times are reconsidered.

them, has thought about them, and they seem separate from him, removed and superior. Most pilots need a few contests under their belts for the psychological leveling that will free them to do their best. On occasion, the daunting effect of inexperience is dissipated by other forces.

Helmut Reichmann, of West Germany, is an example. At the World Championships at Marfa, Texas, in 1970, Reichmann was an apparently minor contender in the standard-class competition. This was his first time in world competition. The strong weather conditions of Texas had instilled a spirit of convervatism in Reichmann's competitors, even the Americans. Reichmann simply saw things differently. While his rivals opted for lightness, he saw the Texas weather as calling for weight and he loaded approximately one hundred pounds of lead in his ship as ballast each meet day and won by just the margin of speed the added weight produced. He has always been a first-class pilot; at Marfa he added the strength of a divergent conviction. And he won, on his first time out.

Reichmann, however, is not a pilot to operate on mere impulse. He is methodical, as are most of the outstanding ones. Most of the best pilots dwell much on contingencies, on conditions that may or may not hold up, on the odds. At the beginning of the contest day, the task is announced and the weatherman predicts the conditions. On his charts, the situation seems neatly schematized, but the wise pilots know how wrong such prophecies can be. Their crews are already at work assembling the sailplanes and beginning such dull but vital tasks as wiping down the fiberglass surfaces. Meanwhile, each pilot much decide when he wants to take off. To do that, he must estimate what the best four or five gliding hours of the day will be.

A thorough pilot such as Moffat figures his time in reverse. Knowing the relationships between available lift and the probable speeds of his ship, he estimates how long it should take him to get around the assigned course under various conditions. Out of this comes a group of starting times that would give him the best conditions of the day, meaning that he would be on his way home when the day begins to cool and the lift subsides.

An early departure may have its advantages. Good pilots like to get what they call "markers" out on the course. These are other ships that will test various thermals, revealing the best ones for those who hang behind to observe. A pilot can make as many starts as he likes; that is, he can go through the area in the sky designated as the starting gate and then return for another start. The best pilots are usually followed by lesser ones, who figure that the stars will lead them to the good thermals. The stars, therefore, work out strategies to fool their followers, making more than one start before setting off in earnest.

Sometimes, getting launched can involve fun and games. During one meet, Richard Schreder suddenly set the whole field aflutter by unexpectedly dashing to his ship and taking off. A covey of pilots switched their launch times and followed, thinking that Schreder had discovered something important. He had done it just for fun.

Before the launch, preparations are very careful. Water is loaded into the wings for ballast; charts, computers, and pencils are loaded in side pockets of the cockpit; things to nibble and things to sip (through hospital-like plastic tubes) are put in place; the parachute is donned; oxygen equipment is added—when there is room for it; turnpoint cameras are checked; instruments, seat position, play of stick and pedals are checked. The ritual of readying takes place in an atmosphere of barely concealed nervousness. At last, the pilot lowers himself into the cockpit—and waits.

When one's time to fly comes, it comes in a flurry of activity: the shouted instructions of the starter, the roar of the towplane, the shouted encouragement of well-wishers, and the sudden rush of air as the glider builds to flying speed. Once airborne and free, having released at 2,000 feet, a pilot may climb to a comfortable altitude and simply fly around, settling in, watching the competition, enjoying the show before making his move or the first of several starting moves. Moffat is a master of this, taking delight in the practice. Yet at the world meet at Waikerie in 1974, where Moffat won his second world title, things became rather nerve-racking. On the first day, as several planes maneuvered to start, circling for altitude, there was heard on the common radio frequency the anguished voice of Hans-Werner Grosse: "George Moffat is dropping water all over me! I am covered with water—George Moffat, I will never forgive you. Unbelievable!" The trouble was that Moffat had decided to dump some of his water ballast. Unaware that he was still losing water, he had returned to a thermal above Grosse.

Hans-Werner Grosse (left)
of West Germany.

The first thermal of the day is extremely important. The most effective operation of a sailplane takes place between 3,500 and 5,000 feet above the ground. The first thermal should be strong enough to take the sailplane well into this operating band if the proper speed is to be established. Finding thermals is partly a matter of luck, although there are indicators to help one find them. Puffs of cumulus are a big help, as are certain kinds of terrain. And, of course, there are the "markers." Watching them can be very instructive.

Watching you can be instructive for others, too, so the better pilots find ways to make themselves invisible. A sailplane's slim lines tend to make it invisible in any case, especially since the machines are painted white. In a bank, the surfaces of the long wings, however, are exposed to the sun; it takes but one gleam to mark a plane's position for experienced pilots. Pilots learn to find a time to make themselves visible just long enough to draw their followers into a foolish move.

Moffat, for instance, draws his pursuers into cloud, when cloud-flying is permitted, as it was at Vrsac, Yugoslavia, at the world championships there in 1972. Moffat would climb out of sight into the murk, giving the

Just beneath the cloud ceiling, a ship keeps to its course, searching for the next rising column of air, trading altitude for speed and distance.

impression that he had found significant lift. Once out of sight, he would climb a hundred feet, level out, and leave the cloud, while his less sagacious trackers kept climbing after altitudinal gold that didn't exist. Moffat actually disdains climbing in cloud unless its lift is at least 50 percent better than that outside, for cloud flying demands adjustments that can cancel the advantages of what lift there is.

True thermals, on the other hand, are a joy, for they provide money in the bank, the energy source for speed. A good pilot knows almost by instinct how to make the most of a thermal. By the seat of his pants he can tell if he has hit one, and by his instruments he determines how best to use it. That's when conditions are good. Just as often, there aren't many indicators of lift; the pilot just plows along, hoping for the best, particularly when there are no puffy clouds to mark columns of rising air. In "blue thermals," the pilot simply hits something and seizes his opportunity. On such days, luck is particularly important.

Whatever the conditions, there is a constant checking out of alternatives, a constant calculating and recalculating. On glides between thermals, the ship is kept at a pitch attitude designed to give the best airspeed commensurate with the best lift under the circumstances. The work is that of trading off: altitude for speed, time for lift, speed for lift for time. So the pilot calculates: "Below 1,500 feet the lift is small, so every 1,500 feet, there had better be a thermal. That distance will consume four minutes. Okay, this thermal is small, and I want the best 20 percent, no average ones, they're not worth it, no speed. I'm down to around 3,000 feet and nothing good has come up. The thermals are there, I know they're there. Let's give up another 500 and go for the big one."

It is there, in that point of decision, that the pilot seeks out his best allies and takes his biggest chances.

If things go well, they may do so in the form of cloud streets that enable him to retain lift without sinking. On occasion, birds may reveal sources of lift as they thermal, although their assistance can be as legendary as it is real. There are times when a glider pilot will find birds coming to join his thermal because he has found something better than theirs. Things may also go well in the form of man-made lift. There is nothing like a good grass fire for sending a glider pilot skyward. Fires lit in recently harvested fields are perfect, and many a pilot has his stories about whooshing aloft at 2,000 feet per minute, accompanied by cinders, smoke, and his heart in his mouth as he escapes falling into the flames, rising instead swiftly upward on the gathering heat.

Unseen thermals, grass fires, uncertain cloud bases—these and other factors ensure that the gamble is always present. In mountainous country, a pilot may be sinking to within fifty feet of a ridge. What to do? "Very simple," says George B. Moffat, Jr., "If you get over the hills, you get another fifty kilometers. You just go over or you don't go over. As anyone flying knows, there are a lot of go and no-go decisions. When you wake up in the morning, you have a certain number of chances to live through the day. Certain things you do will decrease those chances; certain things will increase them. I doubt if flying an airplane ever increased them very much." Except that Moffat has thousands of hours aloft in aircraft to look back upon. Apparently, he does things right.

During the flight, the pilot is alone and yet is not. Below him is his crew, driving sometimes furiously to a point he has asked them to reach, or parked somewhere, waiting for word. Essentially, they have but one reason for being there: to retrieve him. Their very existence is a token of his possible failure, until and unless he can say the welcome "Ground, go home."

He is alone, and yet not. They are attuned to his voice and can tell if he is happy or worried. He speaks briefly over the radio, but his terse words carry his elation or frustration. The frustration can be torture for all, pilot and crew. One can be in a thermal, rising, and wonder if there isn't a better one a hundred yards distant. It is discouraging to make a long climb in a mediocre thermal and discover, too late, where the real thermal was all the time. Or one can make one circle too many in a thermal—consuming twenty-five or thirty seconds—and know one has lost time that cannot be regained. Any number of miscalculations can bring gloom into the cockpit. And the crew senses it.

The crew can retrieve, but the crew cannot relieve the pilot of his problems. Especially in desert areas, a pilot can give in to too much tension, for fear of landing in rough or isolated country is not an easy thing to shrug off. Even cool pilots notice that their efficiency falls off under such circumstances. As Moffat points out, "I don't think you consciously say, 'If I do that, it's going to risk my neck.' Your judgment is not as good as it should be; too many extraneous factors are bothering what you should be thinking about."

Thermaling can be extremely tense when time is of the essence. The ship must be kept straight for just so long, perhaps two seconds, on entering the thermal and then be zapped over into a 45-degree bank to catch the column of rising air near the core. A thermal lost is usually lost for good, because there is often sink surrounding it, meaning that it could be costly to try to recapture it. One resigns oneself and resumes the search.

When time is of the essence—in fact, when being aloft is of the essence—another tool may be available: team flying. The point of team flying is to provide one's colleagues with as much useful information as possible about conditions—cloud bases, degree of lift and sink, storm problems. Team flying is not new to soaring competition, and, in fact, can be highly regimented. Some teams—Poland is a salient example—assign some pilots to be sacrificial goats to test conditions and others to be heroes, the recipients of the experimental data. At Waikerie, the Americans hardly went that far—such a system would not suit itself to a group of individualists—but they did institute a system of cooperation that helped them considerably. The system was a simple grid and color code, which was necessary because other teams would monitor the U.S. frequency of 125.05 mHz. A report such as "blue-seven, black-six" would mean, for instance, that the lift was 700 feet per minute and the effective cloud base was at 6,000 feet. In the case of first thermals, such information was golden, for the pilots could tell if what they were working was better, the same as, or worse than the norm, and they could perhaps make their way to where the lifting was easy.

Team flying was always a valuable tool, but it is never more so than on the final leg of a task, when the right combination of altitude and speed are crucial. Nothing is as frustrating to a pilot than to think he has the finish line made, only to find himself forced to land before getting there.

One day at Waikerie in 1974, Moffat's was one of several ships that had rounded the second turnpoint at low altitude. The homeward track paralleled that of the standard-class ships. Moffat was flying open. He was

Ben Greene, veteran world-championship-meet contestant.

forced to grab a weak thermal at 1,500 feet, a 200-foot-per-minute thermal
that was all that seemed to be around and that could do little but slow him
and drain away points. He was accompanied by a number of ships, including that of Hans Holighaus, his friend and rival from West Germany.
Moffat was checking with his teammate, Ben Greene, who was ahead of
him by about eight miles. Greene suddenly reported a new thermal that
was yielding about 600 feet a minute. After a few more questions and
answers, Moffat struck out after the thermal and caught it only 1,000 feet
above the ground. Immediately, he started rising. He used the altitude to
win the day by six or seven minutes. Later, Holighaus approached him
and said, "George, you fly risky. You shouldn't have left that thermal."
He seemed very concerned. He became furious when Moffat revealed that
he had learned about the winning thermal from a teammate. Holighaus
had had a teammate in that thermal, too, but his teammate had not passed
the word.

However cool and precise he may be, every competition pilot knows
that he must take some chances. There is no part of a race that calls for

more chance taking than the finish. As in any race, the dash for home can fulfill or undo all the good things done during the rest of the event. Unlike a runner, who can pound out the remainder of his energy on the final straightaway, or the racing driver who can stand on it and to hell with the engine, the soaring pilot must remain cool, calculating, and, to an amazing degree, patient. There is nothing different that he can do physically except ignore the effects of hours of sitting in the small cockpit—the fatigue, the heat, the tension. Physical risks there will be, but it will be only his mind, the qualities of his ship, and the conditions of the air through which he must fly that will affect the outcome.

The pilot must calculate how high to climb to cover the remaining distance at best speed. He has a computer to help him figure it out: At twenty miles out and cloud base at 5,000 feet, with 300-feet-per-minute lift, 5,000 feet of altitude will give, say, a glide ratio of 20:1; 4,000 will give 30:1; 4,500, 25:1. He figures the wind and the strength of the thermals and then chooses the speed that, if held constantly, will give him the best ratio for his needs.

The process seems cut and dried, but the checkpoints one has carefully marked suddenly aren't there; the airport is moving farther up the windshield, meaning that the plane isn't gliding well enough to reach it. A thermal shows up and the pilot has to decide whether to spend time gaining lift or risk diving for the finish line. And there is the question of how much to leave the direct flight path for the search for lift.

This struggle may last a long time, as much as seventy miles' worth of time. Pilots have made the finish line with only ten feet to spare; others have missed it by as much. The ideal is to cross the finish line virtually on the ground, diving to about fifty feet above the terrain and zooming to completion in ground effect. More often, the pilot approaches the line while trying not to be lifted by time-consuming, nuisance thermals. He does this nervously riding out the shaking of a ship flying beyond its "redline speed," the speed at which the airplane's structural integrity is threatened.

"Finish lines: only a masochist could love them," Moffat says, with a chuckle and a shake of his head. Pilots do crazy things at finish lines, such as barreling in at three feet of altitude, which is fine, but then doing crop-duster chandelles into the wind to land, often above the heads of the spectators, whom they also may drench by dramatically dropping their water ballast. At the finish line there is always the threat of collision both in the air and on the runway. With such congestion, the dangers of which are compounded by the effects of fatigue, most pilots are glad to get down in one piece.

We are used to thinking of sports champions as men of clout, such as the Alis, the Aarons, the Howes—men who can put muscle behind their skill. Soaring has its men of clout, too, but they have chosen a more abstracted sport, in which they practice their craft isolated in their ships, more in contact with the seemingly empty air than with any other physical entity. They put reflexes behind their performance and the powers of analysis behind their turnings. Like the brain within the skull, the man within the ship exerts a force upon his surroundings that is all the more surprising for the fact that he is able to do it at all—and with such authority.

EPILOGUE/THE VIEW AHEAD

In this book we have sought to convey the scope and vitality of the sport of soaring. We have, in various ways, pointed out that where there is soaring there is action—excitement, relaxation, beauty, and virtually limitless challenges. For pilots ranging from beginning students to world champions, there are thrills of adventure and thrills of achievement. We have also sought to portray soaring's vital past, in which feats of engineering, imagination, and sheer courage were accomplished almost as a matter of course. Soaring is perhaps the most salient example of man's determination to fly. It was the departure point for the evolution of heavier-than-air craft, and its future could, in some ways, outstrip the evolution of powered airplanes.

Soaring has long been a growth industry. That may seem strange at first, particularly to the nonsoarer, but a second look at the growth of the sport can be convincing. Since 1966, the number of active glider pilots has increased by an average of 15 percent from year to year. There are now more than 13,000 glider pilots in the United States, and the number is expected to continue to increase. Designers and manufacturers have increased the number of models and the number of units available, and plan to continue to do so. Hang-gliding, which once seemed to be a small offshoot from the mainstream of soaring, has become popular enough to suggest that it is more than a passing fad.

The number of fields at which soaring takes place has also increased, and from these fields have come increased numbers of competitors. Soaring competition, in turn, has become more and more sophisticated and has attracted more and more interest.

Why has this been happening? As we've suggested earlier in this book, soaring has retained the qualities of intensely personal flight more than any other form of flying, and it has retained an attractiveness that many other forms of recreation have lost. In no small part, that attractiveness is a result of the people who participate in the sport, for they have not allowed the sport to become impersonal and seemingly hostile to newcomers.

And there is that wonderful, almost mystical resemblance of the flight of sailplanes to the flight of birds, a resemblance deepened by the ever-closer similarity between sailplane design and the makeup of birds.

Those who soar, therefore, justifiably expect more and more people to join them in their special domain. Many say that as urban life becomes increasingly constrained, people will seek the freedom that soaring offers. Others say that the relative inexpensiveness of this form of flying will be the vital factor. Whatever the reason, there is an overwhelming expectation within the soaring community that many more people will be getting into the sport—and there is plenty of room for them.

Soaring has a particularly keen attraction for people of imagination. The future, therefore, no doubt contains innovations in aircraft and equipment design that will make the sport even more attractive. At present, the hang-glider movement is just beginning to build momentum, but some of the most creative minds in soaring—or gliding, since hang-gliding has not yet become a true soaring activity—are working to provide ultra-light flying machines with capabilities that only sailplanes have today. One of their goals is to create a glider light enough and strong enough to be foot-launched from a hill or tower and then operated as a true sailplane, with a full capacity to thermal. Several designs for such a machine are on the drawing boards. It is probably just a matter of time before a foot-launched sailplane, with an enclosed cockpit and other amenities of a true sailplane, will be designed, produced, and flown.

At the other end of the spectrum, even larger superships than those now flying are inevitable. There is a gleam in many a soaring pilot's eye at the dream of flying coast-to-coast. We expect new ships to make transcontinental motorless flight possible within a decade, at least. Similarly, the instrumentation that these and other sailplanes will need will also be forthcoming.

Given such advances, all sorts of records will be broken, again and again. Such a machine as the pressurized Alcor is bound to push the altitude figures higher and higher. What we are talking about, really, are aircraft with much of the sophistication of powered planes but without a reliance on fuel power to stay aloft. It is already the case that a sailplane flight can last much longer than a similar flight in terms of distance or altitude by a powered airplane. The endurance factor has become the pilot, not the power. New designs are also likely to improve speed records.

And we can probably expect the towplane, the towcar, and the winch to be less in demand as motorgliders become more popular. Actually, the motorglider may prove to be the most practical of aircraft, for it would be a boon to pilots to have to burn fuel only so as to attain needed altitude and to maintain it. To have an airplane with both a motor and an excellent gliding—even a soaring—capability would be ideal.

Other advances, many born of unexpected inspiration, others of unexpected need, no doubt lie before us. If the history of soaring indicates anything, it indicates that the creative minds within this field are amazingly adaptable. Their object is to create machines that do what is tantamount to the miraculous. They work as if there were no limitations to ingenuity or possibility. The result has been aircraft of extraordinary capabilities.

It is extraordinary, for example, that sailplanes have been used to investigate the intricate and deadly characteristics of thunderstorms. It is extraordinary that sailplanes have flown for hundreds of miles. It is extraordinary that what began as flying by hop, skip, and jump without a motor has become flight that can last literally as long as a pilot is able to stay with it, still without a motor. Most extraordinary of all, perhaps, is the fact that what soaring has evolved into is an activity that makes man one of the most efficient flying animals of all, rivaling the best of the birds. And this is done with no significant pollution of the environment. Silently, burning no fuel, sailplanes work with the atmosphere, a study in pure flight. No wonder people of good heart and creative mind are drawn to it.

APPENDICES

Most of the following information has been compiled by the Soaring Society of America and is reprinted here from the SSA's *1973 Soaring Directory* by permission of the society.

GLOSSARY OF SOARING TERMS

AGL—Above ground level (altitude).

Anabatic wind—The rising air close to the surface of a sun-facing slope.

ASL—Above sea level (altitude).

Aspect ratio—The ratio of the glider's span to the mean chord of its wings. High aspect ratio in a glider is associated with a high glide ratio, other factors being equal. The mean chord is the mean distance from the leading edge to the trailing edge of the wing.

Auxiliary-powered glider or sailplane—Glider or sailplane equipped with auxiliary power plant, allowing sustained flight or reduced rate of sink, but usually not allowing unassisted takeoff or climb.

Chandelle—A flight maneuver in which an aircraft turns sharply and climbs, closely approaching a stall condition but using its momentum to maintain its rate of climb.

Convection—Buoyant air rising through relatively cooler air. Thermals are associated with convection.

Cumulonimbus—Cumulus cloud that has started to produce rain.

Cumulus—Cloud formed by thermals. They are sometimes referred to as "cus."

Dive brakes—Devices whose prime purpose is to create drag; most dive brakes also reduce lift.

Federal Aviation Administration (FAA)—The governing body of civil aviation in the U.S. Its responsibility in the field of soaring includes the airworthiness of gliders, licensing of pilots and gliders, air traffic rules, and other matters.

Floater—A glider with low wing loading, low minimum speed, and low rate of sink. The opposite of a lead sled.

Foehn gap—In a mountain wave system marked by clouds, the foehn gap is an area of blue sky between the mountain's cap clouds and the lenticular cloud over the first lee wave.

216

Foehn wind—A warm dry wind blowing down the slope of a mountain. The chinook, of the Rocky Mountains, is one of many local names given to foehn winds.

Glide—Sustained forward flight in which speed is maintained by descending in the surrounding air.

Glider—A motorless, winged, heavier-than-air aircraft. (See "Sailplane.")

Hang-Glider—An ultralight glider, generally weighing from 30 to 100 pounds, from which the pilot hangs or is suspended, using his legs for takeoff and landing.

High tow (normal tow)—In aero tow, the position of the glider slightly above the towplane's wake. It is not high with respect to the towplane itself.

Katabatic wind—The downslope or drainage wind caused by radiation cooling of a shaded slope. It is similar in form to the anabatic wind, lying close to the slope.

Lapse rate—In the atmosphere, the rate of change of temperature with altitude.

L/D (spoken L over D)—Lift divided by drag. This significant ratio is numerically the same as the glide ratio and varies with forward speed.

Lead sled—Slang for the high-performance sailplane with high wing-loading. It achieves a fast, flat glide at a sacrifice of some thermaling ability in weak conditions.

Lee wave—The effect of a steady wind flowing over a large land feature such as a mountain range. The air descends down the lee slope and then rises, forming waves and providing substantial lift for sailplanes. Also referred to as the wave.

Lenticular cloud (lennie)—The characteristic cloud of a lee wave.

Lift—(1) Upward currents strong enough to carry a glider up. (2) Loosely, the supporting force of a wing. More accurately, the force acting perpendicularly to the path of flight of an airfoil.

Low tow—In aero tow, the position of the glider slightly below the towplane's wake.

MacCready speed ring—A rotatable bezel around the variometer which shows the speed to fly between thermals for the fastest cross-country speed.

Minimum sink speed—The indicated airspeed at which the glider loses altitude most slowly. Minimum sink speed will be found at the crest of the performance curve a few mph above stalling speed and moderately below best glide speed.

Motorglider—Glider or sailplane equipped with power plant, usually allowing unassisted takeoff; also powered sailplane or self-launched sailplane.

N—letter designating the United States, appearing on SSA's A, B, and C pins, the FAI Silver and Gold Badge pins, and used as the first character of FAA aircraft registration numbers.

Open-class gliders—Unrestricted, within the competitive definition of the term glider.

Overdevelopment—An increase in the extent of cumulus cloud cover which significantly reduces the sun's heating of the earth, slowing or even stopping thermal activity.

Penetrate—To make progress against an adverse wind. Good penetration requires that the glider have a good glide ratio in the upper speed range.

Powered sailplane—Sailplane equipped with power plant, usually allowing unassisted takeoff.

Redline speed—The highest speed at which an aircraft can fly and not endanger its structural integrity. The speed is indicated by a red line on the airspeed indicator and is referred to as the never-exceed speed.

Release—The device for, or the act of, disengaging the towrope.

Ridge soaring—Soaring flight utilizing the lift provided by wind flowing up the slope of a ridge. Also referred to as slope soaring.

Rotor—The swirling circulation under a lee wave. The rotor is sometimes marked by ragged wispy clouds and is an area of severe turbulence.

Sailplane—A glider designed especially for soaring.

Sea breeze front—The zone of convergence between warm inland air and the moist cool air from over the ocean.

Self-launched glider—Ultralight glider or hang-glider capable of being launched solely by the pilot, the pilot usually using his legs for takeoff and landing.

Self-launched sailplane—Sailplane equipped with power plant, enabling unassisted takeoff. Also motorglider or powered sailplane.

Shear line—The plane of separation between air masses moving at different speeds or in different directions. The shear may be vertical, horizontal, or inclined.

Sink—Descending currents in which the glider loses altitude faster than in still air.

Soar—To fly without engine power, maintaining or gaining altitude by using rising air.

Spoilers—Devices that disturb the airflow across the wing to spoil the lift and increase drag.

Stable air—An atmosphere with a lapse rate such that a parcel of air which is displaced up or down will tend to return to its original level.

Stall—A flight condition in which the air passing over and under the wing of an aircraft stops providing sufficient lift to hold the aircraft's altitude. A stall is induced by increasing the wing's angle of attack to a point at which lift degenerates and dies.

Standard Class glider—A class of sailplane established by OSTIV and adopted by FAI, originally aimed at moderate cost, ease of operation, good performance, and good flying qualities, 15-meter span.

Thermal—Air heated by the underlying surface rising through surrounding cooler air. Thermals may also be triggered when unstable air is lifted by other means, for example, by cold fronts. Thermaling is climbing in a thermal.

Total energy variometer—A variometer which has been compensated so as to respond only to changes in the total energy of the sailplane; thus a change in airspeed due to stick deflection does not register as lift or sink on the variometer.

Triggering time and temperature—The time and temperature at which usable thermals begin.

Ultralight—Lightweight aircraft, having a wing loading of less than three pounds per square foot, including hang-gliders and man-powered aircraft.

Variometer—A sensitive and fast-responding instrument showing rate of climb or descent. The basic instrument of soaring.

Weak link—A section of rope of a breaking strength specified by the FAA that is incorporated into stronger towropes and cables as a safety device for both towplane and sailplane.

Wind shadow—An area of calm in the lee of windbreaks such as hills, buildings, and rows of trees. Such spots, when sunny, are likely sources of thermals on windy days.

Wind Velocity Gradient—The horizontal wind shear close to the ground caused by the frictional effect of the terrain.

Wing loading—A measure of aerodynamic efficiency. It is obtained by dividing the gross weight of the aircraft by the gross wing area.

Yawstring—A few inches of yarn tied to the top of the pitot-static head of a trainer, or similar mast on other gliders. When it blows to one side it indicates a slip or a skid. When a yawstring is taped to the canopy, the dividing airflow around the canopy results in wildly exaggerated yawstring action.

AMERICAN SOARING SCHOOLS AND COMMERCIAL SAILPLANE OPERATORS

The following is a summary of the known places that offer instruction and rental of sailplanes on a commercial basis. Mailing addresses, if different, are in parentheses.

ARIZONA

ARIZONA SOARING, INC. Estrella Sailport, 24 Mi. SSW of Phoenix, 6 1/2 mi. W of Maricopa (P.O. Box 27427, Tempe, Arizona 85282). Ph. (602) 568–2318. Sailplanes: 1–26 (4), 2–33 (3), 2–32, 1–34 (2). Open daily.

TURF SOARING SCHOOL. Turf Airport, 1 1/2 mi. E of Interstate 17 on West Bell Road (P.O. Box 94, Phoenix, Arizona 85001). Ph. (602) 942–7781. Sailplanes: 2–33 (3), 1–26B, 1–26D (2). 1–34R, 2–22CK, Blanik. Open daily except Christmas.

CALIFORNIA

ARONSON'S AIR SERVICE, INC. Rosamond Airport, 2 1/2 mi. W on Hwy. 14 (P.O. Box J, Rosamond, California 93560). Ph. (805) 948–3016 & 252–2200. Sailplanes: 1–26, 1–34, 2–33 (2), 2–32. Open daily.

BORDERLAND AIR SPORTS CENTER. Field on Otay Lakes Rd., 15 mi. SE of Chula Vista, California (4627 Vista St., San Diego, CA 92116). Ph. (714) 426–2055 & 283–8915. Sailplanes: 2–33 (3). Open weekends & holidays.

CALISTOGA SOARING CENTER. Calistoga Airpark (1546 Lincoln Ave., Calistoga, California 94515). Ph. (707) 942–5592. Sailplanes: 2–33 (4), 2–32, 1–26D. Open daily.

EL MIRAGE SOARING CENTER. El Mirage Field, 12 mi. W of Adelanto (R.R. 1, Box 101, Adelanto, California 92301). Ph. (714) 388–4309. Sailplanes: 1–26, 2–32, 2–33 (3). Open Wed.–Sun., all holidays except Thanksgiving & Christmas.

GREAT WESTERN SOARING SCHOOL. Crystal Airport, 4 mi. E of Pearblossom (Box 148, Pearblossom, California 93553). Ph. (805) 944–2920. Sailplanes: 1–26E (4), 2–33A (9), 1–34 (3), 2–32 (2). Open daily, except Thanksgiving & Christmas.

HAMM'S FLYING SERVICE. Hemet-Ryan Airport (20916 Thunderbird Rd., Apple Valley, California 92307). Ph. (714) 247–6560 & 658–6577. Sailplanes: Blanik, 1–26. Open daily.

HOLIDAY HAVEN SOARING, INC. Holiday Haven Airport, 1 1/2 mi. SE of Tehachapi on Highline Rd. Between Steuber & Dennison Rds. (P.O. Box 631, Tehachapi, California 93561). Ph. (805) 822–3456. Sailplanes: 1–26, 2–33 (2), 1–34, 2–32. Open daily.

PANOCHE SOARING SITE. Panoche Airport, 40 mi. SE of Hollister, 60 mi. W of Fresno (P.O. Box 45, Paicines, California 95043). Ph. (408) 628–3589. Sailplanes: 2–22E, 1–26D. Open daily, check rides & dual on weekends only.

SAILPLANE ENTERPRISES OF HEMET. Hemet-Ryan airport, W of Hemet on Hwy. 74 (P.O. Box 1650, Hemet, California 92343). Ph. (213) 658–6577. Sailplanes: 2–32, 2–33 (3), 1–26 (2), 1–34, Blanik. Open daily.

SKYLARK GLIDERPORT. Skylark Field, SE end of Lake Elsinore, off Hwy. 71 (24111 Palmek Circle, El Toro, California 92630). Ph. (714) 837–0200 & 674–9909. Sailplanes: 1–34 (2), 1–26D, 1–26E, 2–33 (5). Open Wed.–Mon.

SKY SAILING AIRPORT. Sky Sailing Airport, 25 mi. S of Oakland (44999 Christy St., Fremont, California 94538). Ph. (415) 656–9900. Sailplanes: 2–33 (8), 1–26 (3), 2–32. Open daily.

THUNDERBIRD SOARING. 1501 Dixon Road, Fremont (10342 Lochner Dr., San Jose, California 95127). Ph. (415) 263–0463.

TURNER AVIATION (MOJAVE SOARING CENTER). Mojave Airport, 1 mi. E of Mojave (P.O. Box 13, Mojave, California 93501). Ph. (805) 824–4344. Sailplanes: 2–33, 1–26, 1–34. Open daily.

VACAVILLE SOARING, INC. Vacaville Airport, 3 mi. S of Vacaville on Hwy. 80 (P.O. Box 176, Vacaville, California 95688). Ph. (707) 448–4610. Sailplanes: 2–32, 2–33A, 2–33, 1–26D. Open daily.

WONDER VALLEY SOARING SCHOOL. Wonder Valley Dude Ranch Airport, E of Fresno on Hwy. 180 to Elwood Road, (543 E. Scott Ave., Fresno, California 93710). Ph. (209) 229–9155. Sailplanes: 2–33 (2), 1–26. Open weekends.

COLORADO

GLIDERS OF ASPEN, INC. Aspen Airport, 5 mi. W of Aspen on Hwy. 82 (Box 175, Aspen, Colorado 81611). Ph. (303) 925–3418. Sailplanes: 2–33, Blanik (2), Rhoenlerche. Open daily June 1–October 31.

WAVE FLIGHTS, INC. Black Forest Gliderport, 7 mi. NE from Academy Blvd. on Templeton Gap (9990 Gliderport Rd., Colorado Springs, Colorado 80908). Ph. (303) 495–4144. Sailplanes: 2–33A (4), 2–32 (2), 1–34, 1–26E, 1–26D. Open daily.

WAVERLY WEST SOARING RANCH, INC. Waverly West Soaring Ranch, 12 mi. N of Fort Collins (P.O. Box 1055, Fort Collins, Colorado 80521). Ph. (303) 484–5606. Sailplanes: 1–26, 2–33A (2), 2–32, 1–34. Open Tuesday–Sunday.

CONNECTICUT

RALPH J. E. BOEHM.   (153 Bushy Hill Rd., Simsbury, Connecticut 06070).

FLORIDA

LENOX FLIGHT SCHOOL.   Plant City Air Park, 7 mi. W of Plant City on Hwy. 92 (P.O. Box 706, Dover, Florida 33527). Ph. (813) 752–7074. Sailplanes: 2–22C, 2–33A, 1–26 (3). Open Wednesday–Monday.

NATIONAL AVIATION ACADEMY.   St. Petersburg–Clearwater International Airport (c/o Delta Aircraft Corp., Airport Branch Post Office, St. Petersburg, Florida 33732). Ph. (813) 531–3545. Sailplane: 2–33. Open daily by appt.

SOARING SEMINOLES, INC.   Flying Seminole Ranch, 10 mi. NE of Orlando on Hwy. 419 (Rt. 1, Box 475, Oviedo, Florida 32765). Ph. (305) 365–3201. Sailplanes: 2–22E, 2–33 (2), 1–26C, 1–26B. Open daily.

GEORGIA

ATLANTA SAILPLANES, INC.   Woodward Field, 5.6 mi. W of Griffin, GA, on GA Hwy. 362 (P.O. Box 25, Williamson, Georgia 30292). Ph. (404) 227–8282. Sailplanes: 1–34, 2–33 (3), 1–26E (2), 1–32. Open daily.

HAWAII

HONOLULU SOARING.   Dillingham Gliderport, 40 mi. N of Waikiki (Rt. 1, Box 673-B, Waialua, Hawaii 96791). Ph. (808) 637–9579. Sailplanes: 2–32 (2), 1–34. Open daily.

IDAHO

SAWTOOTH SOARING.   Hailey Airport, 11 mi. S of Sun Valley (Box 1302, Ketchum, Idaho 83340). Ph. (208) 726–4834. Sailplane: Blanik. Open daily, December–March & June–October.

SUN VALLEY SOARING FLIGHTS.   Hailey Airport, 11 mi. S of Sun Valley (P.O. Box 248, Sun Valley, Idaho 83353). Ph. (208) 726–3703. Sailplane: AS-K 13. Open by appt.

INDIANA

CALLAHAN AVIATION, INC.   Kendallville Airport, 2 mi. N of Kendallville & 15 mi. N of Ft. Wayne (R.R. 1, Kendallville Municipal Airport, Kendallville, Indiana 46755). Ph. (219) 347–1066. Sailplanes: Blanik, LK-10A. Open daily.

KANSAS

AIR CAPITAL SOARING ENTERPRISES.   Wichita Gliderport, 1 1/2 mi. E of Greenwich Rd. on 45th Street No. (c/o Fay Edwards, 753 N. Gow, Wichita, Kansas 67203). Phones: (316) 733–2107 & 942–6196. Sailplanes: Blanik, Pilatus B4.

LOUISIANA

LOUISIANA SOARING CENTER, INC.   Greater St. Tammany Airport, Abita Springs, 3 mi. E of Abita Springs on Hwy. 36 (P.O. Box 1173, Covington, Louisiana 70433). Ph. (504) 892–1629. Sailplane: 2–33A. Open weekends, weekdays by appt.

MASSACHUSETTS

BERKSHIRE SAILFLIGHTS, INC.   Harriman Airport, between No. Adams & Williamstown on Rt. 2 (P.O. Box 1022, No. Adams, Massachusetts 01247). Ph. (413) 664–6188. Sailplanes: 2–33, 1–26. Open daily.

INTERSTATE AVIATION, INC.   Hiller-Barre Airport, 5 mi. S of Barre, off Rt. 32 (Hiller-Barre Airport, Barre, Massachusetts 01005). Ph. (617) 885–5880. Sailplanes: 2–33 (2), 1–26. Open daily.

SAILAIRE CORP.   Gardner Municipal Airport, 1 1/2 mi. S of Rt. 2–A in Gardner (Box 466, Airport Road, Gardner, Massachusetts 01440). Ph. (617) 632–3939. Sailplanes: 2–33 (2), LP–49. Open daily.

YANKEE AVIATION, INC. (GLIDING CLUB OF BOSTON).   Plymouth Municipal Airport, 4 mi. W of Plymouth on Rt. 44 (Plymouth Airport, Plymouth, Massachusetts 02360). Ph. (617) 746–7337.   Sailplanes: 2–33   (2),   Blanik   (4),   2–32,   1–26.   Open daily.

MICHIGAN

FRANKFORT AVIATION CO.   Frankfort Airport, 1 1/2 mi. SE of Frankfort (Frankfort Airport, Frankfort, Michigan 49635). Ph. (616) 352–9941. Sailplane: 2–33A. Open daily.

J. W. BENZ SOARING.   Ionia County Airport, 3 mi. S of Ionia on Hwy. 66 (260 East Main, Saranac, Michigan 48881). Ph. (616) 642–9019 & 527–9070. Sailplanes: 2–33A (2), 1–26E. Open April 1–December 1, weekends, evenings & some weekdays.

CLOUD BASE SOARING.   Lenawee County Airport, 3 1/2 mi. SW of Adrian, Michigan, near intersection of Hwy. 223 & 52 (23840 Roanoke, Oak Park, MI 48237). Ph. (313) 399–9877 & 263–9853. Sailplanes: Blanik (2), Pilatus B–4. Open April–November, weekends & by appointment.

MISSISSIPPI

ERNST FLYING SERVICE.   Ernst Strip, 1 mi. S of Webb, MS (Box 298, Webb, Mississippi 38966). Ph. (601) 375–8741 & 375–8740. Sailplanes: Blanik, LK–10 (2). Open March–October.

MISSOURI

ST. CHARLES FLYING SERVICE.   St. Charles Airport, St. Charles, Missouri 63301. Ph. (314) 946–6066.

NEBRASKA

KENT. S. BUCKLEY.   (117 No. Jefferson, Papillion, Nebraska 68046).

NEVADA

EDWARD BLALOCK.   Stead Airport, 7 mi. N of Reno on Hwy. 395 (c/o Desert Research Institute, Reno, Nevada 89507). Ph. (702) 972–1676 weekdays 8–5. Sailplanes: AS†K 13, Bergfalke 2–55. Open weekends.

LAS VEGAS GLIDER CENTER.   Sky Harbor Airport, 16 mi. S of Las Vegas (500 E. Hwy. 41, Las Vegas, Nevada 89119). Ph. (702) 739–6623. Sailplanes: Blanik (2), 2–33, 2–22, 1–26 (2). Open daily.

NEW HAMPSHIRE

FRANCONIA SOARING CENTER.   Franconia Airport, 3 mi. S of Franconia, on Rt. 116 (Box 278, Franconia, New Hampshire 03580). Ph. (603) 823–5684. Sailplanes: 2–32, 2–33A (3), 1–26E (2). Open daily April 15–November 1.

NORTHEASTERN LIGHT AIRCRAFT, INC.   Northeastern Gliderport, Brady Ave., 1 mi. SW of Salem, New Hampshire (P.O. Box 425, Methune, Massachusetts 01844). Ph. (617) 688–6019. Sailplanes: 1–26, 2–33, 2–32. Open daily May 1–November 1.

NEW JERSEY

BLAIRSTOWN SOARING SERVICE.   Blairstown Airport, 4 mi. W of Blairstown on Rt. 94/Lambert Rd. (R.D. 2, Box 23, Blairstown, New Jersey 07825). Sailplane: 2–22. Open April–December.

NEW YORK

HUDSON VALLEY AIRCRAFT CO., INC.   Randall Airport (Box 296, Randall Airport, Middletown, New York 10940). Ph. (914) 343–8883. Sailplanes: 2–33A, 1–26E. Open April–December.

SCHWEIZER SOARING SCHOOL. Chemung County Airport, between Elmira & Corning (Box 147, Elmira, New York 14902). Ph. (607) 739–3821, ext. 10. Sailplanes: 2–32, 2–33 (5), 1–26E (4), 1–34A. Open daily, May 1–October 31.

THERMAL RIDGE SOARING, INC. Canastota Municipal Airport, 16 mi. E of Syracuse, on Rt. 5 (115 Kittell Road, Fayetteville, New York 13066). Ph. (315) 446–3790. Sailplane: 2–33A. Open weekends & evenings.

WURTSBORO SCHOOL OF AVIATION. Wurtsboro Airport, 2 mi. N on U.S. Rt. 209 (Wurtsboro Airport, Wurtsboro, New York 12790). Ph. (914) 888–2791. Sailplanes: 2–33A (6), 1–26 (2), 1–34. Open daily March 1–December 31.

OHIO

BRYAN SOARING CLUB. Williams County Airport, 1 1/2 mi. E of Bryan (Box 488, Bryan, Ohio 43506). Ph. (419) 636–1340. Sailplane: Ka. 7. Open daily May–October.

CANTON AVIATION CENTER, INC. Martin Field, 3 mi. NE of Canton, off Old Rt. 62 (5367 Center Dr. NE, No. Canton, Ohio 44730). Ph. (216) 452–3189. Sailplane: 2–22. Open weekends May–October.

CARDINAL AVIATION. Columbiana Airport, E. Liverpool, Ohio (P.O. Box 2106, Calcutta, Ohio 43920). Ph. (216) 386–3761. Sailplanes: 1–34, 2–33, 1–26 (2). Open daily.

SOARING SOCIETY OF DAYTON, INC. Soaring Society of Dayton Gliderport, 3 1/2 mi. S of Waynesville (P.O. Box 581, Dayton, Ohio 45419). Ph. (513) 299–1943. Sailplanes: 1–26, 2–22, 2–33, 2–32, 1–34. Open weekends, daily June–September.

OREGON

CASCADE SOARING, INC. Worden Dry Lake, 19 mi. S of Worden on Hwy. 97 on CA & OR state line (P.O. Box 1117, Klamath Falls, Oregon 97601). Ph. (503) 884–4296. Sailplanes: 1–26C, 2–33, 2–22E, TG–2. Open May–October.

EAGEL FLIGHT CENTER. Eagle Airport, North Plains, Oregon, 20 mi. W of Portland on Hwy. 26 (Portland-Hillsboro Airport, Hillsboro, Oregon 97123). Ph. (503) 648–7151. Sailplanes: 2–33A (4), 1–34, 1–26B. Open Wed.–Sun. April–November.

PENNSYLVANIA

BIRCHWOOD-POCONO-AIRPARK. Birchwood-Pocono-Airpark, follow Birchwood signs from Rt. 447 in Analomink or from Rt. 611 in Tannersville (R.D. 3, East Strouds-burg, Pennsylvania 18301). Ph. (717) 629–0222. Sailplanes: 1–26, 2–33, 2–32. Open daily.

ERWINNA AVIATION. Van Sant Airport, 12 mi. N of Doylestown, PA off Rt. 611 (Van Sant Airport, Box 31, Erwinna, Pennsylvania 18920). Ph. (215) 847–5230. Sailplanes: 2–33A (3), 1–34, 1–26, Blanik, Pilatus B–4. Open daily.

KUTZTOWN AVIATION SERVICE, INC. Kutztown Airport, 1 mi. W of Kutztown (Rt. 1, Box 1, Kutztown, Pennsylvania 19530). Ph. (215) 683–3821. Sailplanes: 2–33, 1–26. Open daily, January–November.

MARTIN VOELK. Gettysburg-Charnita Airport, 2 mi. SE of Fairfield (Gettysburg-Charnita Airport, R.D. 2, Box 153, Fairfield, Pennsylvania 17320). Ph. (717) 642–5392. Sailplanes: Rhoenlerche, 2–33. Open weekends & weekdays by appt.

SOUTH CAROLINA

BERMUDA HIGH SOARING SCHOOL, INC. Chester Cty. Airport, 6 mi. N of Chester (P.O. Box 134, Chester, South Carolina 29706). Ph. (803) 385–6061 & 385–5253. Sailplanes: 2–22E (2), 2–33 (2), 1–26E (2), 1–34 (2). Open daily.

TENNESSEE

EAGLEVILLE SOARING SCHOOL. Puckett Field, 4 mi. S of Eagleville on Hwy. 41–E (1331 Currey Rd., Nashville, Tennessee 37217). Ph. (615) 832–7417 & 274–6341. Sailplanes: Ka. 13, Ka. 8B, Ka. 6CR, Ka. 6E, TG–3A (3). Open daily.

TEXAS

ANDREWS ENTERPRISES. Oliver Farm Airport, 4 mi. NW of Meacham Field (1904 Wills Lane, Keller, Texas 76248). Ph. (817) 281–6266 & 237–1619. Sailplanes: 2–22 (2), 2–32, 1–26 (2). Open weekends (weekdays by appt.).

HOUSTON SOARING CENTER. Clover Field, 10 mi. S of Houston (8727 Dover, Houston, Texas 77017). Ph. (713) 643–4412 & 482–2055. Sailplanes: 2–33 (3), Blanik, 1–26, 1–26E, 1–26D. Open weekends, weekdays by appt.

SOUTHWEST SOARING, INC. Rockwall Municipal Airport, 16 mi. E of Dallas (Box 665, Rockwall, Texas 75087). Ph. (214) 722–8819. Sailplanes: 2–33 (2), 1–26 (2), 1–23. Open daily, except Christmas.

TEXAS SOARING CENTER, INC. San Marcos Municipal Airport, 3 mi. E of San Marcos on Hwy. 21 (P.O. Box 1271, San Marcos, Texas 78666). Ph. (512) 392–7730. Sailplanes: 2–33 (2), 1–26 (2). Open Wed.–Mon.

UTAH

HEBER VALLEY FLYING SERVICE, INC. Heber Valley Municipal Airport, 1 mi. S of Heber City on Hwy. 189 (R.R. 1, Box 333, Heber City, Utah 84032). Ph. (801) 654–1483 & 654–2061. Sailplanes: 2–33, 1–26. Open daily.

K & E SKYSAILING. Nephi Municipal Airport, 87 mi. S of Salt Lake City on Hwy. 9 (1871 Severn Dr., Salt Lake City, Utah 84117). Ph. (801) 623–9917. Sailplane: 2–32.

NORTHERN NEVADA AVIATION. (c/o Brent Jones, Wendover, Utah 84083.)

VALLEY AIRMOTIVE CORP.   Logan-Cache Airport, 4 mi. N & 1 mi. W of Logan (Logan-Cache Airport, P.O. Box 281, Logan, Utah 84321). Ph. (801) 752–5131. Sailplane: 2–22C. Open daily.

VERMONT

PRECISION VALLEY SOARING.   Hartness Airport, No. Springfield (Buker Airways, Hartness Airport, North Springfield, Vermont 22151). Ph. (802) 866–2285. Sailplanes: 2–22C, 1–26. Open weekends & by appt. SSA BUSINESS MEMBER.

SUGARBUSH AIR SERVICE (SUGARBUSH SOARING).   Warren-Sugarbush Airport, 2 mi. E of Rt. 100 (Warren-Sugarbush Airport, Waitsfield, Vermont 05673). Ph. (802) 496–2290. Sailplanes: 1–26 (2), 1–34, 2–33 (2), 2–32 (2). Open daily, April 15–November 30.

VIRGINIA

CAPITAL AREA SOARING SCHOOL, INC.   Warrenton Air Park, 2 mi. S of Warrenton on Rt. 29 (R.D. 2, Warrenton, Virginia 22186). Ph. (301) 559–5140 & (703) 347–2433. Sailplanes: 2–33 (3), 1–26. Open Wednesdays & weekends.

L. B. GLIDERPORT.   L. B. Gliderport, 5 mi. S of Lexington, 3/4 mi. off U.S. 11 (RFD 4, L. B. Gliderport, Lexington, Virginia 24450). Ph. (703) 463–2701. Sailplanes: 1–23, 1–26, 2–33. Open daily by appt.

WASHINGTON

RICHLAND FLYING SERVICE, INC.   Richland Airport, 2 mi. NW from Richland (P.O. Box 639, Richland, Washington 99352). Ph. (509) 946–5176. Sailplane: LK–10A. Open daily.

SOARING UNLIMITED, INC.   Bayview Airport, 1 1/2 mi. NW of Mt. Vernon (P.O. Box 548, Kirkland, Washington 98033). Ph. (206) 454–2514. Sailplanes: 2–33, 1–26, 1–34. Open daily.

WISCONSIN

SYLVANIA AIRPORT, INC.   Sylvania Airport, 3 mi. W of Sturtevant (Rt. 1, Box 316, Sturtevant, Wisconsin 53177). Ph. (414) 886–2517. Sailplane: 2–22. Open daily.

WEST BEND FLYING SERVICE.   West Bend Municipal Airport, 2 1/2 mi. E of West Bend on Hwy. 33 (Box 409, West Bend, Wisconsin 53095). Ph. (414) 334–5603. Sailplanes: 1–26, 2–22E, 2–33. Open daily.

WYOMING

LOW AVIATION.   Wenz Field, 6 mi. S of Pinedale (Box 213, Pinedale, Wyoming 82941). Ph. (307) 367–4446 & 367–2280. Sailplane: Ka. 7. Open by appt.

AMERICAN SOARING CLUBS AND ORGANIZATIONS

The first two lines of each listing give the club name; address; phone; sailplanes; number of members; maximum number of members allowed or open to new members; initial fee to join; monthly dues.

ALABAMA

BIRMINGHAM SOARING SOCIETY, INC.   c/o James C. Lewis, 2101 Magnolia Avenue, Suite 501, Birmingham, Alabama 35205; (205) 324–9559; 2–33; 21; open; $50; $10.
Meetings: 1st or 2nd Tues. ea. mo., 7:30 P.M. Call for location.
Soaring Site: Talladega Airport, approx. 45 mi. E of Birmingham, AL
Contacts: Richard James, 3653 Crestside Rd., Birmingham, AL 35223; (205) 967–2036.
John P. Ward, 2425 Regent Lane, Birmingham, AL 35226; (205) 822–2605.

HUNTSVILLE SOARING CLUB.   c/o Bill Rueland, 2506 Apen Ave., Huntsville, Alabama 35810; (205) 859–1186; Ka. 7; 9; 20; $500; $10.
Meetings: Stanford Research Institute, 306 Wynn Dr., Huntsville. Call for date & time.
Soaring Site: Epps, 10 mi. NW of Huntsville, AL.

SOARING CLUB IN DALE COUNTY, INC.   Drawer "W," Ozark, Alabama 36360; (205) 774–5705; 2–22C, 1–26A, Ka. 6CR; 20; open; $25; $5; SSA chapter.
Soaring Site: Headland Municipal Airport, 1 mi. E of Headland, AL.

ALASKA

ALASKA SOARING ASSN.   c/o Sherwood Hall, Box 1166, Fairbanks, Alaska 99707; (907) 452–4275; TG–3A; 18; open; —; —; SSA chapter.
Contacts: Dennis Rice, c/o RCA Alascom, 629 "E" St., Anchorage, AK 99501.
Wolfgang Falke, 918–7th Ave. Fairbanks, AK 99701; (907) 452–4275.

ARTIC SOARING, INC.   c/o Jim Messick, 5360 East 41st, Anchorage, Alaska 99504; (907) 333–9847; 2–22; 20; open; $50, $10; SSA chapter.
Meetings: 3rd Thurs. ea. mo., 8:00 P.M., 5360 East 41st, Anchorage, AK.
Soaring Site: Palmer Airfield, 45 mi. NE of Anchorage, AK.
Contacts: Dennis Rice, c/o RCA Alascom, 629 "E" St., Anchorage, AK 99501.
James R. Siddle, 1721 Diomede, Anchorage, AK 99504; (907) 333–7115.

ARIZONA

ARIZONA SOARING ASSN., INC.   P.O. Box 11214, Phoenix, AZ 85017; —; 1–26D; 45; open; $12 annually; SSA chapter.
  Meetings: 4th Mon. ea. mo., 8:00 P.M., 3500 N. Central Ave., Phoenix, AZ.
  Soaring Site: Estrella Airport, 40 mi. S of Phoenix; Turf Airport, 10 mi. W of Phoenix.
  Contacts: Ruth Petry, 1626 W. Hazelwood, Phoenix, AZ 85015; (602) 274–3968.
     Paul Dickerson, 8444 E. Keim Dr., Scottsdale, AZ 85253; (602) 948–9292.

TUCSON SOARING CLUB, INC.   P.O. Box 3983, Tucson, Arizona 85711; (602) 623–1124; 2–33, 1–26, Blanik, LP–49; 100; open; $200; $16; SSA chapter.
  Meetings: 3rd Wed. ea. mo., 8:00 P.M. Call for location.
  Soaring Site: Ryan Field, 12 mi. WSW of Tucson, AZ.

YUMA SOARING ASSN.   P.O. Box 4755, Yuma, Arizona 85364; —; 2–22C, 1–26; 16; open; $200; $10; SSA chapter.
  Meetings: 3rd Tues. ea. mo., 8:00 P.M., Sunkist Office, Star Dust Hotel complex.
  Soaring Site: Fishers Landing, 30 mi. N of Yuma, off Hwy. 95.
  Contacts: Ken Swanson, 1910–9th Ave., Yuma, AZ 85364; (602) 726–5599.
     Jim Gillaspie, 3030 Arizona Ave., Yuma, AZ 85364; (602) 726–5599.

ARKANSAS

THERMAL HAWKS OF ARKANSAS, INC.   c/o Marion Burton, 8001 Evergreen Road., Little Rock, Arkansas 72207; (501) 225–2783; 2–22E; 9; open; —; —.
  Contact: Victor Menefee, 4923 Hawthorne Rd, Little Rock, AR 72207; (501) 666–0776.

CALIFORNIA

ACADEMIC SOARING CLUB.   c/o George Lessard, 11135 Yardley Place, Loma Linda, CA 92354; (714) 796–1070; —; 25; open; $5; $5–$10.
  Meetings: Sun., 7:30 P.M., 11135 Yardley Place, Loma Linda, CA.
  Soaring Site: Hemet-Ryan Airport, 1 1/2 mi. W of Hemet, CA.
  Contacts: Len Motz, 1471 Massachusetts #D, Riverside, CA 92507; (714) 686–0966.
     Jim Watrous, 140 Big Springs #15, Riverside, CA 92507; (714) 686–7539.

AIR EXPLORER SQUADRON 8.   c/o W. L. Urie, 10369 Marklein, Mission Hills, CA 91340; (213) 365–6114; —; 35; open; $3; $1.
  Meetings: 1st & 3rd Wed. ea. mo., 7:30 P.M., Lockheed Cafeteria, Woodley & Saticoy, Van Nuys, CA.
  Soaring Site: Rosamond Airport, 2 mi. W of Rosamond, CA.
  Contacts: Mike Miller, 10467 Des Moines, Northridge, CA 91324; (213) 360–0565.
     Bill Defress, 6502 Capistrano, Canoga Park, CA 91304; (213) 346–7199.

AIR SAILING, INC.   c/o George D. Asdel, Sec.-Treas., 794 Midvale Lane, San Jose, CA 95123.

A nonprofit organization developing a gliderport north of Reno, Nev. Membership open to anyone in the U.S. Annual dues, $25.00.

AMES SOARING CLUB, INC.   c/o George Evans, 3746 Heppner Lane, San Jose, CA 95123; (408) 266–2099; 1–26, 1–23, K 7; 20; 30; $150 ($75/under 18 yrs.); $10; SSA chapter.
Meetings: Call for date & location.
Soaring Site: Hummingbird Haven, Livermore, CA, 4 mi. E of Livermore, Patterson
              Pass & Greenfield Roads.
Contacts: Alexander Zuckermann, 1211 Evelyn Ave., Berkeley, CA 94706; (415) 527–
          1301.
          Ulf Gustafsson, 1950 Sacramento St., San Francisco, CA 94109; (415) 885–
          2103.

ANTELOPE VALLEY SOARING CLUB.   c/o El Mirage Soaring Center, El Mirage Airport, Adelanto, CA 92301; —; 2–32, 1–26B, 1–23E; 35; 35; $75; $7; $7.50; SSA chapter.
Meetings: 1st Sat. ea. mo., evenings, location as announced.
Soaring Site: Ann Enevoldson, 38621 Desert View Dr., Palmdale, CA 93550; (805)
          947–0698.
          Phil Anderson, 10380 Cunningham Ave., Westminster, CA 92683; (714)
          839–5428.

ASSOCIATED GLIDER CLUBS OF SOUTHERN CALIFORNIA, LTD.   P.O. Box 3301, San Diego, CA 92103; (714) 232–3301; 2–22C, 2–22E, 2–33, 1–26 (3); 235; open; $110; $10.
Soaring Site: Torrey Pines & Skylark Field.
Contacts: Harry Baldwin, 3490 Lockwood Dr., San Diego, CA 92123; (714) 278–8718.
          Dr. A. J. Owens, 3007 Melbourne Dr., San Diego, CA 92123; (714) 277–7717.

ATLAS FLYERS SOARING CLUB.   c/o Ken Hornbrook, 633 Norumbega Dr., Monrovia, CA (213) 359–5027; 1–23, TG–3A; 20–30; $85; $15; SSA chapter.
Meetings: 1st Wed. ea. mo., 8:00 P.M., Straw Hat Pizza Palace, 1208 N. Citrus, Covina,
          CA.
Soaring Site: El Mirage Soaring Center.
Contacts: Jacques Miller, 268 Pleasant St., Pasadena, CA 91106; (213) 449–2055.
          Bill Jennings, 645 Almirante Dr., West Covina, CA 91791; (213) 332–8285.

BAY AREA SOARING ASSOCIATES, INC.   c/o Hal Lawrence Inc., 227 Town & Country Village, Palo Alto, CA 94301; (415) 326–2000; 2–32 (2), Cirrus, 1–34; 37; 48; $250; $24; SSA chapter.
Meetings: Last Wed. ea. mo., 6:00 P.M., Towne Oak Restaurant, Sunnyvale, CA.
Soaring Site: Sky Sailing Airport, 30 mi. SE of San Francisco, 10 mi. N of San Jose.
Contacts: Don Burke, 1612 Manzanita Dr., Belmont, CA 94002; (415) 591–6618.
          I. H. Moore, 21040 Canyon View Dr., Saratoga, CA 95070; (408) 867–1975.

CALCONDORS SOARING CLUB, INC.   P.O. Box 663, Sunnyvale, CA 94088; —; 1–26B, Slingsby T–53B; 18; 30; $350; $20.
Meetings: 2nd Thurs. ea. mo., 7:30 P.M., Lockheed Corp., Bldg. 160, Conference Rm.
          Sunnyvale, CA.

Soaring Site: Sky Sailing, 1/2 mi. W. of Hwy. 17, Fremont, CA.
Contacts: Don Hurd, 1479 Petal Way, San Jose, CA 95129; (408) 257–9367.
      Doug Gray, 106 Monroe #18, Santa Clara, CA 95050; (408) 966–2815.

THE CALIFORNIANS SOARING CLUB. c/o Rudi Roeger, 3234 Rohrer Dr., Lafayette, CA 94549; (415) 284–1937; Ka–8B, AS–K13; 12; $250.
Soaring Site: Sky Sailing Airport; Calistoga Airport.

CENTRAL CALIFORNIA SOARING CLUB. c/o Gary Kemp, 741 Josephine, Corcoran, CA 93212; (209) 992–4874; 2–22; 10; open; $100; $10.
Meetings: 1st Sat. ea. mo., 10:00 A.M., Tulare Airpark, Pilots Lounge, Tulare, CA.
Soaring Site: Tulare Airpark, 3 mi. S of Tulare on Hwy. 99.
Contact: Bill Saltzman, 814 Gem, Tulare, CA 93274; (209) 686–6172.

CHICO SOARING ASSN., INC. c/o Gordon Casamajor, P.O. Box 46, Chico, CA 95926; (916) 342–8971; 2–22E, 1–26, AS–K13; 30; open; $200; $12.50.
Meetings: 2nd Wed. ea. mo., 7:30 P.M. Call for location.
Soaring Site: Chico Municipal Airport, Chico, CA.
Contacts: Harold Haas, 240 Mulberry Ave., Red Bluff, CA 96080; (916) 527–2289.
      Richard Pugh, P.O. Box 1110, Red Bluff, CA 96080.

CHINA LAKE SOARING CLUB, INC. c/o R. Lubben, Rt. 2, Box 42, Ridgecrest, CA. 93555; —; 2–22; 15; 16; $30; $2; SSA chapter.
Soaring Site: Inyokern Airport, Inyokern, CA.
Contacts: Dwight Dennis, 77 Bard Rm. 1, China Lake, CA 93555.
      Roger Harley, 206–B Ellis, China Lake, CA 93555.

CYPRESS SOARING, INC. c/o Francis Railey, P.O. Box 694, Cypress, CA 90630; (714) 527–3115; 2–22E, 1–26C; 14; 20; $50; $15; SSA chapter.
Meetings: 3rd Wed. ea mo., 6:00 P.M., Tech. Ed. II Bldg., Cypress College, Cypress.
Soaring Site: Hemet-Ryan Airport, 2 mi. W of Hemet, CA on Hwy. 74.
Contacts: Dean Bilyeu, 619 Scott Lane, Anaheim, CA 92804; (714) 826–6181.
      R. R. Bush, 4426 Stanbridge Ave., Long Beach, CA 90808; (213) 429–9011.

DOUGLAS SOARING CLUB, INC. c/o F. K. Nieuwenhuijs, 5224 Rockland Ave., Los Angeles, CA 90041; (213) 254–8275; 2–32, 1–34, 1–26; 27; 30; $75; $12–$18; SSA chapter.
Meetings: 3rd Thurs. ea. mo., 8:00 P.M., McDonnell Douglas Cafeteria, 29th St. & Ocean Park Blvd., Santa Monica, CA.
Soaring Site: El Mirage Field, El Mirage, CA.
Contacts: Lavona Jo Adams, 4935 W. 121st St., Hawthorne, CA 90250; (213) 644–1552.
      Ray Schor, 1569 Helen Dr., Los Angeles, CA 90063; (213) 261–0902.

EAST BAY SOARING CLUB, INC. G. F. Knapp, 770 McClay Rd., Novato, CA 94947; (415) 897–6495; 2–33, 1–26A; 21; 30; $300; $15.
Meetings: Annual. Call for date, time & location.
Soaring Site: Calistoga Airport, Calistoga, CA.
Contacts: Don Mythen, 2600 McDonald Ave., Richmond, CA 94804; (415) 233–7317.
      Dale Thompson, 443 Fieldcrest Dr., Richmond, CA 94803; (415) 223–4259.

ELSINORE VALLEY SOARING CLUB, INC.   c/o H. M. Schurmeier, 1950 Midwick, Altadena, CA 91001; (213) 798–2388; Blanik, HP–14; 16; 16; $800; $15; SSA chapter.
Meetings: Call for date, time & location.
Soaring Site: Skylark Gliderport, Elsinore, CA.
Contacts: Murray Freeman, 11151 Kensington Rd., Rossmoor, CA 90720; (213) 431–9826.

HIGH DESERT SOARING ASSN., INC.   c/o Dave Tapper, 44038–D Beech Ave., Lancaster, CA 93534; (805) 942–6931; 2–33, 1–23; 15; $750; $8.50; SSA chapter.
Meetings: None.
Soaring Site: El Mirage Field, 10 mi. NW of Adelanto, CA.
Contacts: Bruce Peterson, 863 W. Holquin St., Lancaster, CA 93534; (805) 942–1273.
        Jack Cowen, 5653 Columbus Ave., Van Nuys, CA 91401; (213) 780–0729.

INLAND EMPIRE SOARING ASSN., INC.   c/o James Towell, 263 Estudillo, San Jacinto, CA 92383; (714) 654–4024; 1–26, LP–49; 14; open; —; —; SSA chapter.
Meetings: Call for date, time & location.
Soaring Site: Hemet-Ryan Airport, 3 mi. W of Hemet, CA.
Contacts: Jerry Tubbs, 306 N. Torrens, Anaheim, CA 92806; (714) 637–9428.
        Jim MacNamara, 1475 Coral Dr., Laguna Beach, CA 92651; (714) 494–3937.

NORTH BAY SOARING ASSN., INC.   c/o George Congdon, 100 Sunny Oak Dr., San Rafael, California 94903; (415) 479–0944; Ka. 7; 15; open; $300; $1; SSA chapter.
Meetings: Wed. ea. mo., 8:00 P.M., Sonoma Skypark Airport. Call for date.
Soaring Site: Sonoma Skypark Airport, 1 mi. N on 8th St., from Napa Hwy.
Contacts: Stanley Montagne, 1305 Kaehler St., Novato, CA 94947; (415) 892–2007.
        Andrew Tagliafico, 4020 Chanate Rd., Santa Rosa, CA 95404.

NORTHERN CALIFORNIA SOARING ASSN.   P.O. Box 338, Livermore, CA 94550; (415) 447–4110; None; 50; open; $60; None.
Meetings: Annually, call for date, time & location.
Soaring Site: Hummingbird Haven Gliderport, 4 1/2 mi. E of Livermore, CA.
Contacts: Ulf Gustafsson, 1950 Sacramento St., San Francisco, CA 94109; (415) 885–2103.
        Harry Perl, 3907 Calif. Way, Livermore, CA 94550; (415) 447–2253.

ORANGE COUNTY SOARING ASSN.   P.O. Box 1746, Huntington Beach, California 92647; —; 2–22 (2), 2–33, 1–26 (2), LP–46; 143; open; $150; $12; SSA chapter.
Meetings: 3rd Mon. ea. mo., 7:30 P.M., Santa Ana City Library, Ross & Civic Ctr. Dr.
Soaring Site: Perris Valley Airport, Perris, CA.
Contacts: Dianne Rodriguez, 807 Modena, Anaheim, CA 92801; (714) 826–1088.
        C. E. Jennings, 4718 Coke Ave., Lakewood, CA 90718; (213) 429–5676.

PACIFIC SOARING COUNCIL, INC.   c/o H. Ray Gimmey, Pres., 14 Space Court, Sacramento, California 95831; (916) 421–8819. A regional organization of about 450 members. Publishes a monthly magazine, WEST WIND, sponsors camps and contest. Annual dues, $5.00.

Meetings: 1st Mon. ea. mo.; call for time & location.
Contact: Dick Loeper, Sec.-Tres., 3785 Via Granada, Moraga, CA 94556; (415) 284–1776.

PANASOAR, INC. c/o Sky Sailing Airport, 44999 Christy St., Fremont, CA 94538; (415) 656–9900; 2–33A; 12; open; $500; $10; SSA chapter.
Meetings: Quarterly, Sky Sailing Airport. Call for date & time.
Soaring Site: Sky Sailing Airport, Durham Rd. & Nimitz Freeway.
Contacts: John Aikens, 1115 Eden Bower Lane, Redwood City, CA 94061; (415) 368–4384.
    Emil Kissel, 21154 Sullivan Way, Saratoga, CA 95070; (415) 867–3927.

PHOENIX CLUB, INC., SOARING GROUP. 1566 Douglas Rd., Anaheim, CA 92806; (714) 639–1592; Blanik, 1–26, Slingsby T–53B; 60; open; $150; $10; SSA chapter.
Meetings: Mon., 8:00 P.M., 1566 Douglas Rd., Anaheim, CA. Call for date.
Soaring Site: Skylark Field, Elsinore, CA.
Contacts: Reinhard Thiel, 1431 Crown View Dr., Corona, CA 91720; (714) 737–0100.
    Hans Klein, 2702 Hillside, Orange, CA 92665; (714) 522–0101.

SACRAMENTO SOARING CLUB, INC. c/o John Flynn, 4308 "T" St., Sacramento, California 95819; (916) 457–1021; Blanik; 9; 9; SSA chapter.
Meetings: 1st Fri. ea. mo., 8:00 P.M. Call for location.
Soaring Site: Lincoln Municipal Airport & Truckee Municipal Airport.
Contacts: Leland Spalding, 7000 Grant Ave., Carmichael, CA 95608; (916) 944–2423.
    James Lockhart, 10520 Spaulding Way, Rancho Cordova, CA 95670.

SAN FERNANDO VALLEY SOARING CLUB. c/o Jack Jordan, 3920 Albury Ave., Long Beach California 90808; (213) 425–1075; LK–10; 5; —; —; —.
Soaring Site: Skylark Field, Elsinore, CA.

SAN GABRIEL VALLEY SOARING GROUP. c/o Merilyn Winsor, 131 E. Scenic Dr., Monrovia, California 91016; (213) 358–3888; hangar; 25; open; —; —. A social group for "hangar flying."

SANTA YNEZ VALLEY SOARING CLUB. Box 567, Santa Ynez, California 93436; (805) 733–1420; 2–33, 1–26; 39; open; $250; $15; SSA chapter.
Soaring Site: Santa Ynez Airport, Santa Ynez, CA.
Contacts: Al Moreno, 2414 Anacapa St., Santa Barbara, CA 93105; (805) 966–9707.
    Morgan Hetrick, Box 323, Santa Ynez, CA 93460; (805) 967–2668.

SHASTA-ENTERPRISE SOARING CLUB, INC. c/o Joseph Redmon, Box 753, Redding, California 96001; (916) 243–4996; Ka. 7; 12; open; $200; $15.
Meetings: Last Wed. ea. mo., 8:00 P.M., Enterprise Sky Park, Tarmac Rd., Redding, CA.
Soaring Site: Enterprise Sky Park, 5 mi. E of Redding on Hwy. 44.
Contacts: Bill Gelonek, 3809 Traverse, Redding, CA 96001; (916) 243–3640.
    Frank Kosko, 3320 Sacramento Dr., Redding, CA 96001; (916) 241–0261.

THE SOARCERERS, INC. c/o Stan Winsor, 131 E. Scenic Dr., Monrovia, California 91016; (213) 358–3888; P–R; 7; 8; $150; $5.

Soaring Site: El Mirage Dry Lake, El Mirage, CA.
Contact: John Linn, 1205 Birchcrest Ave., Brea, CA 92621; (714) 941–8139.

SOUTHERN CALIFORNIA COMPETITION CLUB (S3G).   c/o G. E. Giddens, Sec., 5805 Lone Grove
Way, La Canada, CA 91011; (213) 790–2211. A regional organization of about 60 members
interested in soaring competition, conducts several flying workshops each year. $15 to
join, $5 annually.
Contact: Einar Enevoldson, 38621 Desert View Dr., Palmdale, CA 93550; (805) 947–
0689.

SO. CALIFORNIA SOARING ASSN.   c/o Barbara Sharpe, 3708 1/2 W. 104th St., Inglewood, CA
90303; (213) 671–3217; 2–33, 1–26, Blanik; 195; open; $5; $5 annually; SSA chapter.
Meetings: 2nd Fri, ea. mo., 8:00 P.M., 810 So. Flower St., Los Angeles, CA.
Soaring Site: El Mirage Field, 12 mi. W of Adelanto, CA.
Contacts: Bill Graves, 16539 Gilmore, Van Nuys, CA 91406; (213) 785–8221.
         Hans Holland, 4666 Varwa Ave., Sherman Oaks, CA 91403.

TRI-VALLEY SOARING GROUP.   c/o John Ludowitz, 23067 Ventura Blvd., Woodland Hills,
California 91364; (213) 340–6751; TG–3A; 9; 12; $215; $4; SSA chapter.
Soaring Site: El Mirage Field, El Mirage, CA.
Contact: Ken LeDuc, 1229 Moncado Dr., Glendale, CA 91207; (213) 241–1441.

29 SOARING CLUB.   c/o 29 Palms Airport, Star Rt. Box 688, Twentynine Palms, California
92277; (714) 367–3932; 1–26, 2–22; 37; open; $50; $10.
Soaring Site: 29 Palms Airport, Twentynine Palms, CA.
Contacts: Noel Roberts, 153 Argonne Ave., Long Beach, CA 90803; (213) 438–6515.
         William Brown, 73758 Siesta Dr., Twentynine Palms, CA 92277; (714) 367–
3186.

UNIVERSITY OF CALIFORNIA AT RIVERSIDE SOARING CLUB.   Campus Activities Office, University
of California, Riverside, CA 92502; —; None; 15; open; None; $1.
Meetings: Wed. ea. wk., 7:30 P.M., U.C.R. campus.
Contacts: Bruce Butterfield, 3398 Lemon St., Riverside, CA 92507; (714) 686–9528.
         Len Motz, 1471 Massachusetts #D, Riverside, CA 92507; (714) 686–0966.

UNIVERSITY OF CALIFORNIA AT SAN DIEGO SOARING CLUB.   University of California, P.O. Box
109, La Jolla, CA 92037; (714) 453–2000, Ext. 1007; 2–22E, 1–26; 60; open; $20; $4.
Meetings: Alternate weeks; call for date, time & location.
Soaring Site: Torrey Pines Gliderport, 12 mi. N of San Diego; Skylark Field, Elsinore,
         CA & Clark Dry Lake, 15 mi. SE of Borrego Springs, CA (private).
Contacts: Pat Rorabaugh, 9791 Genesee Ave., San Diego, CA 92122; (714) 453–2142.
         Anthony Stanonik, 3443 Ottawa Ave., San Diego, CA 92117; (714) 273–4121.

COLORADO

AIR FORCE ACADEMY SOARING CLUB.   c/o Soaring Branch/CWIA USAFA, CO 80840;
(303) 472–2495; 2–33 (6), 1–26 (4), 2–25, 2–22, Phoebus C; 124; 200; SSA chapter.

Meetings: 1st Wed. ea. mo., 7:15 P.M., USAFA Cadet Area.
Soaring Site: USAFA Airfield, 20 mi. N of Colorado Springs, CO.
Contacts: Richard Blanchet, P.O. Box 1492, USAFA, CO 80840.
   Larry Rider, Soaring Branch/CWIA, USAFA, CO 80840; (303) 472–2495.

COLORADO SOARING ASSN. 9990 Gliderport Rd., Colorado Springs, CO 80908; (303) 495–
4144; 2–33, 2–32, 1–26 (2); 54; open; $150; $10; SSA chapter.
Meetings: Call for date and location, 9990 Gliderport Rd., Colorado Springs, CO.
Soaring Site: Black Forest Glider Port, 11 mi. NE of Colorado Springs, CO.
Contacts: Shirley Marshall, 10265 Thomas Rd., Colorado Springs, CO 80908; (303) 495–
   4292.
   Donald Derry, 1005 So. Jamaica #312, Aurora, CO 80012; (303) 366–5114.

C.U. SOARING CLUB. P.O. Box 3061, Boulder, Colorado 80302; —; 2–22E; 25; 40; $100; $7.
Meetings: 2nd Mon, ea. mo., 7:30 P.M., University of Colorado Memorial Center.
Soaring Site: Boulder Airport, 1/2 mi. E of Boulder, CO.
Contacts: Bill Daniels, 3615 High Court, Wheatridge, CO 80033; (303) 423–2716.
   Dennis Haley, 1535 Grove, Boulder, CO 80302; (303) 447–1721.

DENVER SOARING COUNCIL. c/o Max Grassfield, 2058 So. University, Denver, CO 80210;
(303) 733–0677; 2–33; 15; —; $200; $10; SSA chapter.
Meetings: 1st Wed. ea. mo., 7:30 P.M., John's Manville, Greenwood Plaza South.
Soaring Site: Flying D Ranch, 20 mi. N on 80-S to Hudson, 1 mi. W, follow signs.
Contacts: John Trice, 9162 E. Tufts Circle, Englewood, CO 80110; (303) 770–0651.
   Richard Cofrin, 2539 S. Dudley Street, Denver, CO 80227; (303) 985–4185.

THE FRONT RANGE SOARING SOCIETY, INC. c/o Neil Mayfield, 1208 Emigh Street, Ft. Collins,
Colorado 80521; (303) 484–8960; —; 31; open; $10 annually; SSA chapter.
Meetings: 3rd Tues. ea. mo., 7:30 P.M. Call for location.
Soaring Site: Waverly West Soaring Ranch, 12 mi. N of Ft. Collins on Colorado Hwy.
   1, past Waverly to Owl Canyon Rd. & 1 mi. W.
Contacts: B. F. Magsamen, 1200 E. Elizabeth St., Ft. Collins, CO 80521; (303) 493–
   0112.
   Alfred Herr, 2900 Tulane Dr., Ft. Collins, CO 80521; (303) 484–5606.

SOAR ASPEN ASSN. c/o Dieter Bibbig, Box 175, Aspen, Colorado 81611; (303) 925–3418; 2–33;
5; open; $150; $10.
Soaring Site: Aspen Airport, 5 mi. W of Aspen on Hwy. 82.

SOARING SOCIETY OF BOULDER. P.O. Box 1031, Boulder, Colorado 80303; (303) 499–4493;
2–33, Blanik; 50; open; $325; $10; SSA chapter.
Meetings: 1st Mon. ea. mo., 8:00 P.M., National Center for Atmospheric Research,
   Boulder, CO.
Soaring Site: Boulder Municipal Airport, 1 mi. NE of Boulder, CO.
Contacts: C. C. Watterson, 235 Mohawk, Boulder, CO 80303; (303) 499–9069.
   Rich Roberts, 4940 Thunderbird #220, Boulder, CO 80303; (303) 297–6739.

CONNECTICUT

CONNECTICUT CU-CLIMBERS SOARING GROUP, INC.   c/o R. Patenaude, 34 Fenwood Grove Rd., Old Saybrook, CT 06475; (203) 388–3295; 2–22E; 13; open; $300; $50 annually; SSA chapter.
Meetings: Chester Airport, Chester, CT. Call for date & time.
Soaring Site: Chester Airport, 5 mi. W of Chester, CT.
Contacts: George Bosnak, Main St., Ivoryton, CT 06442; (203) 767–1918.
  Harold Parisen, Fall River Dr., Ivoryton, CT 06442; (203) 767–8539.

CONNECTICUT YANKEE SOARING CLUB, INC.   c/o M. Allen Reynolds, Taunton Ridge Rd., Newton, CT 06470; (203) 426–5451; 2–22E; 1–26; 20; 24; $250; $75 annually.
Meetings: 2nd Fri. ea. mo., 8:00 P.M., Taunton Ridge Rd., Newtown, CT.
Soaring Site: Johnnycake Airport, Harwinton, CT.
Contacts: Loren Caddell, 34 Catoonah St., Ridgefield, CT 06877; (203) 438–4324.
  Ronald Goodridge, 3 Long View Heights Rd., Newtown, CT 06470; (203) 426–6345.

NUTMEG SOARING ASSN.   c/o J. W. Sargent, 51 Leaf Ave., Waterbury, CT 06705; (203) 756–6754; 2–22C, 1–23, H–15, 1–26 (2); 56; 56; $300; $7.50; SSA chapter.
Meetings: 3rd Fri. ea. mo., 8:00 P.M., Sikorsky Aircraft Plant, Stratford, CT.
Soaring Site: Johnnycake Airport, 15 mi. W of Hartford, on Rt. 4.
Contacts: W. R. Batesole, 8 Canton Rd., West Simsbury, CT 06092; (203) 658–9992.
  Warren Dion, 40 Vantana Dr., Bristol, CT 06010; (203) 582–8530.

TUNXIS SOARING CLUB, INC.   c/o Warren Dion, 40 Vantana Dr., Bristol, Connecticut 06010; (203) 582–8530; 2–33; 6; open; $900; $13.33.
Meetings: Annually; call for date, time & location.
Soaring Site: Johnnycake Airport, 5 mi. SW of Torrington, CT.
Contacts: John Sargent, 51 Leaf Ave., Waterbury, CT 06705; (203) 756–6754.
  Ransom Thompson, Keighley Pond Rd., Middle Haddam, CT 06456; (203) 267–4003.

FLORIDA

CENTRAL FLORIDA SOARING CLUB, INC.   c/o B. N. Willis, 340 Wilma Circle, Riviera Beach, FL 33404; (305) 848–7115; 2–33, 1–26; 43; open; $135; $10; SSA chapter.
Meetings: 2nd Wed. ea. mo., 8:00 P.M., Boca Raton Airport, Boca Raton, FL.
Soaring Site: Boca Raton Airport, 2 mi. W of Boca Raton, FL.
Contacts: Jose Marin, 700 West 39th Pl., Hialeah, FL 33012; (305) 821–9797.
  E. K. Morice, P.O. Box 1598, Delray Beach, FL 33444; (305) 732–6725.

FLORIDA SOARING ASSN.   c/o John Rubino, Box 12944, Gainesville, FL 32601; (904) 372–6739; 2–22E, 1–26C; 60; open; $25; $5.
Soaring Site: Williston Municipal Airport, 2 mi. SW of Williston on Rt. 121.

Contacts: Mike Madden, 1700 SW 16th Ct., Bldg. "H," Gainesville, FL 32601; (904) 373–6914.

Maurice Sherrard, 1019 NW 94th St., Gainesville, FL 32601; (904) 376–0439.

NORTH FLORIDA SOARING SOCIETY, INC.   c/o Robert Ryan, 5331 Keystone Dr. N, Jacksonville, FL 32207; (904) 396–4291; 1–26, 2–33, 1–34; 30; open; $100; $10.
Meetings: 2nd Wed. ea. mo., 7:30 P.M., Elks Club, 207 Laura, Jacksonville.
Soaring Site: Herlong Airport, 6 mi. W of Jacksonville, FL.
Contacts: Clyde Sharman, 5005 Cleveland Rd., Jacksonville, FL 32210; (904) 771–1271.
Joe D'Accardi, 1100 Universal Marion Bldg., Jacksonville, FL 32202; (904) 354–4481.

SAILPLANES, INC.   c/o W. P. Clarke, 1441 University Blvd. N., Jacksonville, Florida 32211; (904) 743–1944; Blanik; 10; 20; $400; $10.
Meetings: 2nd Wed. ea. mo., 7:30 P.M. Call for location.
Soaring Site: Herlong Field, 6 mi. SW of Jacksonville on Normandy Blvd.
Contact: Tom Elmore, 2423 Doctors Lake Dr., Orange Park, FL 32073; (904) 264–9998.

SKY SAILORS ASSN., INC.   c/o Ernest Terrell, 1646 Pasadena Dr., Dunedin, Florida 33528; (813) 733–5132; —; 18; open; $1; $1 annually; SSA chapter.
Soaring Site: Plant City Air Park, Plant City, FL, 10 mi. E of Tampa on Hwy. 92.
Contact: Russell St. Arnold, c/o Clearwater Aircraft Inc., 1000 N. Hercules Ave., Clearwater, FL 33515; (813) 443–3202.

SOARING SEMINOLES, INC.   Rt. 1, Box 475, Oviedo, Florida 32765; (305) 365–3201; 1–26 (2), 2–22, 2–33 (2); 45; open; $50; $10.
Meetings: 2nd Sat. ea. mo., 6:30 P.M., Flying Seminole Ranch Airport, Oviedo, FL.
Soaring Site: Flying Seminole Ranch Airport, 4 mi. E of Oviedo on Hwy. 419.

THERMAL RESEARCH, INC.   Box 618, South Miami, Florida 33143; —; Blanik; 15; —; —; —.
Soaring Site: Miami Gliderport, 7 mi. N of Homestead, FL.
Contacts: H. Senn, 9600 SW 81st Ave., Miami, FL 33156; (305) 271–4268.
J. Randall, 915 Bayamo Ave., Coral Gables, FL 33146; (305) 666–3141.

GEORGIA

ATLANTA COMPETITION CLUB.   c/o David Culpepper, 4560 Lanark Dr., Atlanta, GA 30331; (404) 344–7428; —; 18; open; none; none.
Meetings: Each Sat., March thru Sept., 10:00 A.M., Monroe Airport, E of Atlanta, GA.
Soaring Site: Monroe Airport, 30 mi. E of Atlanta on Hwy. 78.
Contact: Ed Sessions, 3530 Towanda Trail, College Park, GA 30331; (404) 766–3164.

G.L.E.R.C. SOARING ASSN., INC.   86 So. Cobb Dr., Marietta, GA 30060; (404) 424–3992; K 8B, 2–33; 10; open; $50; $7.
Meetings: Spring & as necessary. Call for date, time & location.
Soaring Site: Monroe Airport, on U.S. 78, 2 mi. SE of Monroe, GA.

Contacts: John Lane, 915 Woodland Trail #D–2, Smyrna, GA 30080; (404) 432–7687.
 Al Barrett, 4312 Lake Laurel Dr. SE, Smyrna, GA 30080; (404) 435–9653.

MID-GEORGIA SOARING ASSN., INC.   P.O. Box W., Monroe, GA 30655; —; Ka. 8, Phoebus B; 30; open; $150; $10; SSA chapter.
Meetings: Call for date, time & location.
Soaring Site: Monroe Municipal Airport, 1 mi. SE of Monroe, GA.
Contacts: Ed Graham, Rt. 1, Box 82, Bishop, GA 30621; (404) 769–5446.
 Woody Woodward, Rt. 1, Box 169, Monroe, GA 30655; (404) 267–6060.

SOWEGA SOARING SOCIETY.   c/o Cliff King, 1511–4th Ave., Albany, Georgia 31705; (912) 432–2879; Ka. 7; 6; open; $500; none.
Soaring Site: Albany Municipal Airport, Albany, GA.
Contact: J. W. Oglesby, 2211 Barnesdale Way, Albany, GA 31705; (912) 435–5349.

HAWAII

MOKULEIA SENIOR SQUADRON (GLIDER) CIVIL AIR PATROL, HAWAII WING.   c/o M. R. Nevin, P.O. Box 664; Waialua, HI 96791; (808) 637–5126; 2–33, 2–33A, 2–22 (2), 1–26; 110; 125; $20; none.
Meetings: 2nd Mon. ea. mo., 7:00 P.M., C.A.P. Wing Headquarters, Lagoon Dr., Honolulu International Airport.
Soaring Site: Dillingham Airfield, 5 mi. W of Waialua.
Contact: Dick Maryott, 1362 Uila St., Honolulu, HI 96818; (808) 422–6393.

OAHU SOARING LTD.   c/o D. H. McCoy, 4999 Kahala Ave. #333, Honolulu, Hawaii 96816; (808) 732–2751; 2–33, 1–26 (2); 18; open; $300; $10.
Meetings: Quarterly; call for date, time & location.
Soaring Site: Dillingham Airfield, 5 mi. W of Waialua.
Contacts: Robert Fox, 1542 Uluhaku Pl., Kailua-Oahu, HI 96734; (808) 262–7923.
 Peter Wheelon, 4564 Kahala Ave., Honolulu, HI 96816; (808) 732–3685.

ILLINOIS

CHICAGO GLIDER CLUB.   c/o Gene Hammond, 274 Terrace Dr., Clarendon Hills, Illinois 60514; (312) 323–7458; Blanik, 2–32, 1–34; 65; open; $200; $10; SSA chapter.
Meetings: Call for date & location.
Soaring Site: Clow International Airport, 5 mi. S of Naperville, IL.
Contacts: Jim Kaufman, 156 Bowman's Court, Bolingbrook, IL 60439; (312) 739–3310.
 Vern Haack, 1136 Sandpiper Lane, Naperville, IL 60540; (312) 355–0059.

CHICAGOLAND GLIDER COUNCIL, INC.   c/o Jim Kaufman, Sec.-Treas., 154 Bowman's Court, Bolingbrook, Illinois 60439; (312) 739–3310. A nonprofit organization providing monthly meetings and a newsletter for Chicago-area soaring enthusiasts, from November thru May. Annual dues, $3.

ILLINI GLIDER CLUB. c/o Dept. of Aero Engineering, 101 Transportation Bldg., University of Illinois, Urbana, IL 61801; —; 2–22C, 2–33A, 1–26 (2); 45; open; $55–$65; $40 per semester; SSA chapter.
 Meetings: Alternate Wed. ea. mo., 7:30 P.M., 121 Animal Science Lab., Univ. of IL campus, on Gregory Dr.
 Soaring Site; Univ. of IL Willard Airport, 1/2 mi. S of Willard, W 1 1/4 mi. past I–57, S 1/2 mi.
 Contacts: Tom Page, 2022 Burlison Dr., Urbana, IL 61801; (217) 344–1133.
  Phil Schmalz, 55 Wilson Trailer Park, Champaign, IL 61820; (217) 367–1494.

SKY SOARING, INC. c/o Vernon Sutfin, 213 W. Main St., Dundee, Illinois 60118; (312) 426–2825; 2–22, 1–26; 30; 33; $250; $7; SSA chapter.
 Meetings: Quarterly, call for date, time & location.
 Soaring Site: Clarence Wesley Aavang Airport, 2 mi. E of Huntley, IL on Algonquin-Huntley blacktop.
 Contacts: Richard Utzke, 721 Webster, Algonquin, IL 60102; (312) 658–7593.
  Roger Miller, 327 Sharon Lane, North Aurora, IL 60542; (312) 896–2319.

WABASH VALLEY SOARING ASSN., INC. 287, Lawrenceville, Illinois 62439; (618) 943–2076; AS-K 13, Phoebus A; 30; open; $100; $40 annually; SSA chapter.
 Soaring Site: Lawrenceville-Vincennes Municipal Airport, between Vincennes, Indiana, & Lawrenceville, Illinois, 2 mi. N of Hwy. 50.
 Contacts: Jack Reed, Box 261, Vincennes, IN 47591; (812) 882–2739.
  Larry Jones, 1640 E. St. Clair #2, Vincennes, IN 47591; (812) 886–4171.

INDIANA

CENTRAL INDIANA SOARING SOCIETY. c/o Wm. L. Sprague, 5833 Winthrop Ave., Indianapolis, Indiana 46220; (317) 251–3453; 1–26, 2–22C; 21; open; $100; $11; SSA chapter.
 Meetings: 2nd Tues. ea. mo., 7:30 P.M. Call for location.
 Soaring Site: Terry Airport, 18 mi. NW of Indianapolis on Hwy. 32.
 Contacts: Richard Deitchman, 6320 Brixton Lane, Indianapolis, IN 46220; (317) 253–0310.
  Dorothy Thomson, 6801 Westfield Blvd., Indianapolis, IN 46220; (317) 251–0122.

HOOSIER SOARING CLUB. c/o Russell East, 4072 Grand Ave., Bloomington, Indiana 47401; (812) 332–4120; 2–33, 1–26; 13; 20; $100; $20.
 Meetings: 2nd Wed. ea. mo., 7:30 P.M. Torp Aero, Monroe County Airport, Bloomington.
 Soaring Site: Monroe County Airport, 5 mi. SW of Bloomington, IN, off Hwy. 46.
 Contact: James Allison, 1127 E. 1st St., Bloomington, IN 47401; (812) 336–6671.

LAFAYETTE SOARING SOCIETY, INC. P.O. Box 2263, West Lafayette, Indiana 47906; (317) 474–1183; 2–22C, 1–26; 20; 30; $130; $5.
 Meetings: 2nd Mon. ea. mo., 8:30 P.M., Rm. 104, Armory Bldg., Purdue University.

Soaring Site: Halsmer Airport, 2 mi. E of Lafayette.
Contact: Curt Cole, 1712 Washington St., Lafayette, IN 47905; (317) 474–4725.

THE MANITAU DRAG-N-FLY SOARING CLUB, INC. c/o L. Larson, Fulton Co. Aviation, Box 109, Rochester, Indiana 46975; (219) 223–5384; 2–22; 10; open; $100; $5.
Meetings: 1st Sat. ea. mo., 7:30 P.M., Fulton County Airport Administration Bldg.
Soaring Site: Fulton County Airport, 1 mi. E of Rochester, IN.
Contact: J. Kent Mills, R. #2, Rochester, IN 46975; (219) 223–3308.

MICHIANA SOARING SOCIETY. c/o Edward Meidel, 515 W. Lowell, Mishawaka, Indiana 46544; (219) 259–2169; K 6CR, Ka. 7; 7; open; $150; $4; SSA chapter.
Meetings: Call for date, time & location.
Soaring Site: Mishawaka Pilots Club, 4 mi. SW of Elkhart, IN.
Contacts: Jack Bierman, 16305 Shamrock Dr., Mishawaka, IN 46544; (219) 259–2044.
    Robert Gallatin, RR #4, Box 193, Elkhart, IN 46514.

IOWA

BURLINGTON SOARING ASSN., INC. c/o Dr. Kurt Hahn, 16 Cascade Terrace, Burlington, Iowa 52601; (319) 752–8789; L-Spatz 55; 7; open; $100; $10; SSA chapter.
Meetings: 1st Tues. ea. mo., 8:00 P.M., 16 Cascade Terrace, Burlington, IA.
Soaring Site: Burlington Airport, SE edge of Burlington, IA.
Contacts: George Zimmerman, 302 No. 3rd St., Burlington, IA 52602; (319) 752–7145.
    John Fox, Summer Street Rd., Burlington, IA 52601; (319) 752–8749.

CEDAR RAPIDS SOARING SOCIETY, INC. c/o Bob Kellner, 345 Sussex Dr. NE, Cedar Rapids, Iowa 52402; (319) 377–6155; Ka. 7; 12; open; $450; $10.
Meetings: 3rd Tues. ea. mo., 7:30 P.M., Farmer State Bank, 8th Ave., Marion, IA.
Soaring Site: Evans Field, 2 mi. SE of Marion Airport, Marion, IA.
Contacts: Marv Falk, 323 1/2 South Dodge, Iowa City, IA 52240.
    Don Gurnett, 6 Durham Ct., Iowa City, IA 52240; (319) 338–4738.

CENTRAL IOWA SOARING SOCIETY, INC. c/o Webster Lehmann, 1005 Paramount Bldg., Des Moines, Iowa 50309; (515) 288–1674; 2–33, 1–26; 20; open; $500; $10; SSA chapter.
Meetings: Last Tues. ea. mo., 7:30 P.M. Call for location.
Soaring Site: Greenfield Municipal Airport, 50 mi. SW of Des Moines, IA.
Contact: Robert Nady, 1207 "H" Ave., Nevada, IA 50201; (515) 382–4330.

SILENT KNIGHTS, INC. c/o John Smith, So. Riverside, RR 2, Ames, Iowa, 50010; (515) 232–3013; 2–22, 1–19; 8; open; none; none.
Soaring Site: Ames Municipal Airport, 1 mi. S of Ames, IA.
Contact: Robert Nady, 1207 "H" Ave., Nevada, IA 50201; (515) 382–4330.

KANSAS

HY-PLAINS SOARING CLUB. c/o Harold Kennedy, Rt. #3, Dodge City, Kansas 67801 (316) 227–6040; —; 6; open; —; —.

Soaring Site: Kennedy Gliderport, 4 mi. from Minneola, KS.
Contact: Dean Shelor, Bloom, KS 67865; (316) 885–4446.

KANSAS SOARING ASSN. c/o Robert Carnahan, 2827 S. Osage, Wichita, KS 67217; (316) 522–2701; none; 45; open; $3; none; SSA chapter.
Meetings: 3rd Fri. ea. mo., 7:30 P.M. Call for location.
Soaring Site: Strother Field, 5 mi. N of Arkansas City, KS.
Contacts: Leroy Clay, 958 Lexington, Wichita, KS 67218; (316) 684–4788.
 Glenn Mauch, 612 Winifred, Dodge City, KS 67801; (316) 483–6248.

MID-WESTERN SOARING ASSN., INC. c/o Roy McCann, 2320 N. 83rd, Kansas City, Kansas 66109; (913) 299–4075; 2–22, 1–26, 1–23H, 34; open; $50; $10; SSA chapter.
Meetings: 3rd Tues. ea. mo., 7:30 P.M., East Kansas City Airport, Grain Valley, MO.
Soaring Site: East Kansas City Airport, 20 mi. E of Kansas City, Missouri on I–70.
Contacts: Charles Brock, 8808 E. 62nd St., Raytown, MO 64133; (816) 353–7207.
 A. B. Crank, 1429 W. Scott Pl., Independence, MO 64052; (816) 461–3363.

SILENT SOARERS, INC. c/o S. L. Bredfeldt, 13 Whitmore Rd., Hutchinson, Kansas 67501; (316) 665–8396; Slingsby Swallow; 4; open; —; —.
Soaring Site: Naval Air Station (abandoned), 10 mi. S of Hutchinson on K–17.
Contacts: John McComb, 604 Adair Circle, Hutchinson, KS 67501; (316) 663–9977.
 Bob Main, 13 Paseo St., Hutchinson, KS 67501; (316) 662–2941.

WICHITA SOARING ASSN. c/o Barbara Davis, 1826 S. St. Francis, Wichita, Kansas 67211; (316) 262–2062; TG–3A; 14; open; $50; $2.
Meetings: Annually; call for date, time & location.
Soaring Site: Strother Field, 8 mi. N of Arkansas City on U.S. 77.
Contacts: John Cary, 801 English Court, Derby, KS 67037; (316) 788–0848.
 Robert Leonard, 12002 W. Beaumont, Wichita, KS 78235; (316) 722–2183.

KENTUCKY

BLUEGRASS SOARING CLUB, INC. c/o Virgil Jones, Rt. 3, Box 250–A, Paris, Kentucky 40361; (606) 484–2253; 1–26 (2); 4; open —; —.
Soaring Site: Cynthiana-Harrison County Airport, 2 mi. SW of Cynthiana, KY.

LOUISVILLE SOARING CLUB, INC. c/o Richard Houser, 318 Browns Lane, Louisville, Kentucky 40207; (502) 893–2155; AS-K 13; 8; 15; $200; $10; SSA chapter.
Meetings: 2nd Thurs. ea. mo., 8:00 P.M. Call for location.
Soaring Site: Freeman Field, 3 mi. SW of Seymour, Indiana.
Contacts: Hugh Cohen, 4811 So. 3rd St., Louisville, KY 40214; (502) 368–2463.
 E. J. Schickli, Jr., 75 Valley Rd., Louisville, KY 40204; (502) 451–3748.

LOUISIANA

AERO-NUTZ SOARING CLUB, INC. c/o Jarvis H. Renfrow, Rt. 5, Box 227, Monroe, LA 71201; (318) 373–2442; 2–33A; 25; 40; $150; $7.
Meetings: 1st Fri. ea. mo., 7:00 P.M., Fleeman's Class Room, Selman Field, Monroe, LA.

Soaring Site: Huenefeld's Strip, 3 mi. E of Monroe, LA.
Contacts: Bob Speed, 511 Orleans St., Monroe, LA 71201; (318) 232–7856.
Vernon Rogers, 104 Stevenson Dr., Monroe, LA 71201; (318) 322–1508.

SHREVEPORT SOARING CLUB, INC. c/o Wilbur Anderson, 3733 Catherine St., Shreveport, Louisiana 71109; (318) 635–2746; 2–22E, 1–26B, Tern; 15; open; $300; none.
Meetings: Call for date, time & location.
Soaring Site: Thacker Airport, 3 mi. NE of Oil City, LA, 30 mi. N of Shreveport, LA.
Contacts: Hugh Hunton, 9529 Pitch Pine Rd., Shreveport, LA 71108; (318) 686–7409.
Emory Strong, 1406 Captain Shreve Dr., Shreveport, LA 71105; (318) 868–8424.

MAINE

BERKSHIRE SOARING SOCIETY, INC. c/o Pittsfield Municipal Airport, Pittsfield, MA 01201; —; 2–22E, 1–26 (2); 20; open; $300; $6; SSA chapter.
Meetings: 2nd Tues. ea. mo., 7:30 P.M., Pittsfield Municipal Airport.
Soaring Site: Pittsfield Municipal Airport, 3 mi. S of Rt. 20 on Barker Rd.
Contacts: Len Bugel, 27 1/2 Meadow St., Hadley, MA 01035; (413) 584–5540.
Charles Wales, Box 161–A, Stockbridge, MA 01266; (413) 298–4950.

EASTERN MAINE SOARING CLUB. c/o R. F. Sedgeley, Rt. 2, Bangor, Maine 04401; (207) 942–0911; LK–10A; 9; 12; $150; $25 annually.
Meetings: 2nd Tues. ea. mo., 8:00 P.M., Rt. 2, Bangor, ME.
Soaring Site: Winterport, 9 mi. SW of Bangor, ME.

MARYLAND

MID-ATLANTIC SOARING ASSN., INC. Frederick Municipal Airport, Frederick, Maryland 21701; (301) 663–9753; 2–33, Ka. 8, AS–K 13; 100; open; $200; $30 annually; SSA chapter.
Meetings: 2nd Fri. ea. mo., 8:30 P.M., auditorium of the Perpetual Bldg., Bethesda, MD.
Soaring Site: Frederick Municipal Airport, Frederick, MD.
Contacts: Hope Howard, 5712 S 2nd St., Arlington, Virginia 22204; (703) 671–2027.
Mario Piccagli, 8103 Meadowbrook Lane, Chevy Chase, MD 20015; (301) 589–6420.

PATUXENT NAVY SOARING TEAM. P.O. Box 5, U.S. Naval Air Station, Patuxent River, Maryland 20670; (301) 863–3897; 1–26D, 2–22E; 5; open; $50; $9; SSA chapter.
Meetings: 2nd Wed. ea. mo., 7:30 P.M., Flying Club.
Soaring Site: Naval Air Station, Patuxent River Airport, 1 mi. E of Lexington Park.
Contacts: Mel Pettigrew, 310 Esperanza Dr., Lexington Park, MD 20653; (301) 863–8673.
Bob Miller, 224 Esperanza Dr., Lexington Park, MD 20653; (301) 863–5730.

WALLOPS SOARING ASSN., INC. c/o T. K. Burton, Jr., Dividing Creek Rd., Pocomoke City, Maryland 21851; (301) 957–0805; 2–22E; 4; open; $10; $10.
Soaring Site: Wallops Station, Virginia, 4 mi. E of U.S. Rt. 13 at "T"'s corner.

MASSACHUSETTS

M.I.T. SOARING ASSN. 265 Massachusetts Ave., Cambridge, Massachusetts 02139; (617) 253–1930; Ka. 7, 1–26, 1–34, 2–33 (2); 57; open; $100; $150; SSA chapter.
Meetings: 3rd Tues. ea. mo., 7:30 P.M., M.I.T. Student Center, Cambridge, MA.
Soaring Site: Norfolk Airport, approx. 30 mi. SW of Boston, off Rt. 115.
Contacts: Anne Marie Bleiker, 6 Humphrey Terrace, Swampscott, MA 01907; (617) 599–0817.
   Thomas Keim, 50 Frances St., Boston, MA 02116; (617) 566–5709.

MT. WASHINGTON SOARING ASSN., INC. c/o A. MacNicol, 46 Leewood Rd., Wellesley, Massachusetts 02181; (617) 235–8467; none; 50; open; none; none. (A group for encouraging and sponsoring soaring only.)
Soaring Site: White Mountain Airport, 2 mi. S of North Conway, New Hampshire.
Contacts: Marcia Prest, 376 Cross St., Carlisle, MA 01741; (617) 369–2072.
   Bob Sedgeley, Rt. 2, Bangor, Maine 04401; (207) 942–0911.

NEW ENGLAND SOARING ASSN. Hiller Airport, Barre, Massachusetts 01005; (617) 885–5880; Blanik, 2–22 (2), 1–26; 30; open; $200; $12; SSA chapter.
Meetings: Last Sat. ea. mo., 7:00 P.M., Hiller Airport.
Soaring Site: Hiller Airport, 3 mi. S of Barre, MA.
Contacts: Don Cimon, 169 Marked Tree Rd., Needham, MA 02192; (617) 444–5315.
   Douglas East, 26 Lincoln Circle, Paxton, MA 01612; (617) 757–3348.

MICHIGAN

MICHIGAN STATE UNIVERSITY SOARING CLUB, INC. c/o 101 Student Services Bldg., MSU, E. Lansing MI 48823; (517) 353–7876; 2–22E, 1–26; 25; open; —; —.
Meetings: Wed. ea. wk., 7:30 P.M., Student Union, MSU.
Soaring Site: Ionia County Airport, 1 mi. S of Ionia, MI.
Contact: James Landre, 513 E. Columbia, Mason, MI 48854; (517) 676–1310.

CHARLEVOIX SOARING CLUB, INC. c/o Phil Lawrence, Fairport 307 Belvedere, Charlevoix, Michigan 49720; (616) 547–6553; K 6CR/PE; 5; open; $200; $7.50.
Meetings: 1st Wed. ea. mo., 7:30 P.M., Fairport 307 Belvedere, Charlevoix, MI.
Soaring Site: Charlevoix Airport, 3/4 mi. SW of Charlevoix, MI.
Contact: Ray Wood, 302 Michigan Ave., Charlevoix, MI 49720; (616) 547–9447.

SAGINAW VALLEY SOARING SOCIETY, INC. c/o Metrie Mendel, 314 Linton St., Saginaw, Michigan 48601; (517) 754–7921; 2–22E; 7; open; $150; $5.
Meetings: 2nd Sun. ea. mo., 7:30 P.M. Call for location.
Soaring Site: Saginaw Municipal Airport, 2 1/2 mi. E of Saginaw on Janes Road.
Contacts: Dennis Traynor, 1519 Seminole St., Saginaw, MI 48601; (517) 799–6776.
   Harold Burke, 8380 W. McCarty Rd., Saginaw, MI 49636; (517) 793–4268.

VULTURES, INC. c/o Johann Kuhm, 30418 Whittier, Madison Heights, Michigan 48071; (313) 588–7085; Ka. 7, Ka. 8; 40; open; $250; $60 annually; SSA chapter.

Meetings: 4th Tues. ea. mo., 8:30 P.M., Birmingham Comm. House at Bates & Town-
    send.
Soaring Site: (Private strip) 3 mi. N of Oxford, MI, on Hwy. M–24.
Contact: Jim Sumner, 1878 W. Tahquamenon Ct., Bloomfield Hills, MI 48013; (313)
    851–0185.

MINNESOTA

MINNESOTA ASSN. OF SOARING CLUBS. 5249 Chicago Ave., Minneapolis, Minnesota
55417; (612) 824–0223; —; —; —; —; —.
Meetings; 5249 Chicago Ave., Minneapolis, MN. Call for date & time.
Contact: Harris Holler, 3901 Harriet Ave., Minneapolis, MN 55409; (612) 822–5605.

MINNESOTA SOARING CLUB, INC. c/o Dale Fletcher, 555 Harriet Ave., St. Paul, MN 55112;
(612) 484–8967; AS–K 13; Ka. 7, Ka. 8; 63; open; $350; $5.50; SSA chapter.
Meetings: 7:30 P.M. Call for date & location.
Soaring Site: Carleton Airport, 8 mi. E of Northfield, 35 mi. S of Minneapolis.
Contacts: Eugene Chatelaine, 872 Como Ave., St. Paul, MN 55103; (612) 489–1118.
    Ray Schroeder, 5400–42nd Ave. So., Minneapolis, MN 55417; (612) 727–1827.

NORTHERN SOARING, INC. c/o James Solsten, 118 N. Kendall, Thief River Falls, Minnesota
56701; (218) 681–4253; 2–22; 8; 15; $300; $5.
Meetings: 1st Thurs. ea. mo., 7:00 P.M., Municipal Airport, Thief River Falls, MN.
Soaring Site: Thief River Falls Municipal Airport.
Contacts: Jerry Wedul, 410 St. Paul Ave. So., Thief River Falls, 56701; (218) 681–1076.
    Larry Eck, 1240 Edgewood Dr., Thief River Falls, MN 56701; (218) 681–7601.

RED WING SOARING ASSN. c/o Ed Finegan, 1867 Simpson Ave., St. Paul, Minnesota 55113;
(612) 645–9678; 2–22, 2–32, 1–26, BG–12; 25; open; $150; $75 annually; SSA chapter.
Meetings: Benson's Airport, White Bear Lake, MN. Call for date & time.
Soaring Site: Benson's Airport, 2 mi. N of White Bear Lake on Hwy. 61.
Contacts: Larry Rodgers, 3054 Benjamin St. NE, Minneapolis, MN 55418; (612)
    781–1389.
    George Marks, 3424 NE Silver Lake Rd., Minneapolis, MN 55418; (612)
    788–0137.

MISSISSIPPI

STATE COLLEGE GLIDER CLUB. c/o Mississippi State University, Drawer A.P.; State
College, Mississippi 39762; (601) 325–3624; 1–26; 5; open; $40; $10.
Soaring Site: Bryan Field, 2 mi. SW of Starkville, MS, on Hwy. 12.
Contact: Larry Mertaugh, 2001 Pin Oak Dr., Starkville, MS 39759; (601) 323–7287.

MISSOURI

SAINT LOUIS SOARING ASSN. c/o A. A. Cacciarelli, 332 Huntleigh Forrest Dr., Kirkwood, Missouri 63122; (314) 966–2283; 2–33, 1–26, 1–34, Ka. 13, LP–49; 58; 70; $200; $11; SSA chapter.
Meetings: 2nd Wed. ea. mo., 8:00 P.M., Community Federal Savings & Loan, 8944 St. Charles Rock Rd., St. Louis, MO or Highland-Winet Airport, Highland, IL.
Soaring Site: Highland-Winet Airport, Highland, Illinois.
Contacts: Larry Orbin, 14494 Pettycoat Lane, Florissant, MO 63034; (314) 741–4064.
David Plotky, 4055 Chartley Dr., Bridgeton, MO 63044; (314) 739–7381.

MONTANA

BIG SKY SOARING. c/o Robert Neils, 220 Yerger Dr., Bozeman, Montana 59715; (406) 587–2228; 2–33A; 13; open; $200; none; SSA chapter.
Meetings: 1st Sat. ea. mo., 10:00 A.M., Flite Line, Inc., Bozeman Airport.
Soaring Site: Bozeman Airport, 8 mi. NW of Bozeman on U.S. Hwy. 10.
Contacts: Greg Mecklenburg, Box 824, Bozeman, MT 49715; (406) 587–4755.
John Neils, 2219 W. College #61, Bozeman, MT 59715; (406) 586–5597.

NEBRASKA

FRELIN SOARING ASSN. c/o Ed Weaver, 1600 Center Park Rd., Lincoln, Nebraska 83208; (402) 432–5321; Ka. 7, SF–26; 12; 25; $100; $12.
Soaring Site: Arrow Airport, 5 mi. NE of Lincoln, NE.
Contacts: Glen Hattan, 7541 Old Post Road #3, Lincoln, NE 68520; (402) 488–5324.
Duane Funk, 1630 Jannsen Dr., Lincoln, NE 68520; (402) 489–7334.

MCCOOK SOARING ASSN., INC. c/o Don Morgan, Box 491, McCook, Nebraska 69001; (308) 345–1480; —; 9; open; $15; none.
Meetings: Call for date, time & location.
Soaring Site: McCook Municipal Airport, 1 mi. E of McCook, NE.
Contacts: Ray McKee, P.O. Box 115 Star Route, Lexington, NE 68850.
Milt Johnson, McCook Flying Service, McCook, NE 69001; (308) 345–1999.

NEBRASKA SOARING ASSN. c/o Ed Weaver, RFD #1, Roca, NE 68430; (402) 435–4276; none; 21; open; $15; none; SSA chapter.
Meetings: Annually, McCook Municipal Airport. Call for date & location.
Soaring Site: McCook Municipal Airport, 1 mi. E of McCook, NE.
Contact: Glenn Hattan, 7541 Old Post Rd., Lincoln, NE 68520; (402) 488–5124.

PANHANDLE SOARERS, INC. c/o C. S. Ostenberg, 1708 Ave. "G," Scottsbluff, Nebraska 69361; (308) 635–2355; 2–33, K 6CR; 15; open; $200; $3.
Meetings: Semi-annually; call for date, time & location.
Soaring Site: Scottsbluff Municipal Airport, 3 mi. E of Scottsbluff, NE.
Contact: Jack Benger, Rt 1, Scottsbluff, NE 69361; (308) 635–1504.

NEVADA

NEVADA SOARING ASSN., INC. c/o Charles Glattly, P.O. Box 2952, Reno, NV 89505; (702) 329–8441; Blanik; 20; open; $150; $10; SSA chapter.
Meetings: Call for date, time & location.
Soaring Site: Douglas County Airport, 12 mi. S of Carson City on U.S. 395;
        Stead Airport, 8 mi. N of Reno on U.S. 395.
Contacts: A. Joseph Killian, 13623 Mt. Baldy, Reno, NV 89506; (702) 972–0185.
        Dave Ellis, 385 Greenstone Dr., Reno, NV 89503; (702) 322–3223.

NEW HAMPSHIRE

KEARSARGE SOARING ASSN., INC. c/o Harold Smith, Crocketts Corner, New London, New Hampshire 93257; (603) 526–4219; 2–22, 1–26; 19; open; $250; $7; SSA chapter.
Meetings: 4th Thurs. ea. mo., 7:30 P.M., Gray House Restaurant, New London, NH.
Soaring Site: New London, 33 mi. W of Concord, NH on Rt. 89.
Contacts: Charles Whitcomb, 32 Pillsbury St., Concord, NH 03301; (603) 225–9043.
        Harold Buker, Shaker St., New London, NH 03257; (603) 526–4421.

NEW MEXICO

ALBUQUERQUE SOARING CLUB, INC. P.O. Box 11254, Albuquerque, New Mexico 87112; 1–26, 2–33, Slingsby Swallow; 52; open; $100 Class A/None Class B; $7; SSA chapter.
Meetings: 3rd Mon. ea. mo., 7:30 P.M., Conference Rm., Cutter Flying Service, Albuquerque International Airport.
Soaring Site: Moriarty Municipal Airport, 2 mi. SE of Moriarty, NM.
Contacts: John Wheatley, 3517 Parisian Way NE, Albuquerque, NM 87111; (505) 298–7268.
        Charles Burnett, 1008 Adams SE, Albuquerque, NM 87108; (505) 268–9762.

HOBBS SOARING SOCIETY, INC. c/o Jack Gomez, P.O. Box 831, Hobbs, New Mexico 88240; (505) 393–3252; 2–33A; 12; open; none; $25.
Meetings: Will Rogers Recreation Center, 300 E. Clinton, Hobbs, NM. Call for date and time.
Soaring Site: Crossroads Continental Airport, 5 mi. NW of Hobbs.
Contacts: Don Yarbro, P.O. Box 1136, Lovington, NM 88260; (505) 396–3389.
        Hank Wunsch, P.O. Box 220, Hobbs, NM 88240; (505) 393–2171.

WHITE SANDS SOARING ASSN. P.O. Box 1200, Alamogordo, New Mexico 88310; —; 2–22, 1–26; 10; 15; $100; $13; SSA chapter.
Meetings: 2766 Sandoval LP, Hollman A.F.B., New Mexico. Call for date & time.
Soaring Site: Alamogordo Municipal Airport, 89 mi. N of El Paso, Texas.
Contacts: Charles Dugan, P.O. Box 51, Alamogordo, NM 88310.
        C. J. Stephens, 2766 Sandoval LP, Holloman A.F.B., NM 88330; (505) 473–4115.

NEW JERSEY

AERO CLUB ALBATROSS, INC.   P.O. Box 123, Pluckemin, New Jersey 07978; —; 2–33, T–58B, 1–23H–15, 1–26 (2); 40; 50; $300; $10 annually; SSA chapter.
Meetings: 2nd Wed. ea. mo., 8:00 P.M., Willow Tree Inn, Gladstone, NJ.
Soaring Site: Somerset Airport & Blairstown Airport.
Contacts: A. Scarborough, 361 Walnut Street, Nutley, NJ 07110; (201) 667–9234.
    J. C. Dellicker, 24 Emmans Rd., Ledgewood, NJ 07852; (201) 584–6277.

CENTRAL JERSEY SOARING CLUB, INC.   c/o Frank Fine, 3311 Belmar Blvd., Wall, New Jersey 07719; (201) 681–5286; 1–26, 2–22E; 20; open; $150; $5.
Meetings: 3rd Fri. ea. mo., 8:00 P.M., Colts Neck Airport, Colts Neck, NJ.
Soaring Site: Colts Neck Airport, 1/2 mi. W of Hwy. 34.
Contacts: Bernard Golden, 506–7th Ave., Asbury Park, NJ 07712; (201) 775–7611.
    Alan Wood, 28 Rosalie Ave., Lincroft, NJ 07738; (201) 741–0974.

ICARUS SOARING CLUB, INC.   c/o Adolf Beins, James Dr., Mt. Arlington, New Jersey 07856; (201) 398–4525; 1–23, 2–33E; 8; open; $200; $5; SSA chapter.
Meetings: Caldwell Airport, Fairfield, NJ, N of Caldwell on Passaic Ave. Call for time & date.
Soaring Site: Caldwell Airport, Fairfield, NJ.
Contact: Ronald Schwartz, 169 Morris Ave., Denville, NJ 07834.

SOUTH JERSEY SOARING SOCIETY.   c/o A. Heavener, 1102 Hickory Dr., Vineland, New Jersey 08360; (609) 692–3212; 2–33; 16; open; $100; $5; SSA chapter.
Meetings: Call for date, time and location.
Soaring Site: Millville Municipal Airport, 3 mi. SW of Millville, N.J.
Contacts: Clayton Shoemaker, 26 Lakeview Dr., Alloway, NJ 08001; (609) 697–0950.
    Otto Zauner, 489 Weymouth Rd., Vineland, NJ 08360; (609) 697–0950.

NEW YORK

DANSVILLE SOARING CLUB, INC.   c/o Dansville Airport, Dansville, New York 14437; (716) 987–9970; Ka. 7, Ka. 8; 14; 14; $200; $150 annually.
Soaring Site: Dansville Airport, N of Dansville, NY.
Contacts: James Flaitz, 112 So. Lackawanna, Wayland, NY 14572; (716) 728–2922.
    James Blum, 64 Park Ave., Dansville, NY 14437; (716) 987–5134.

HARRIS HILL SOARING CORP.   Harris Hill, R.D. #1, Elmira, New York 14903; (607) 734–0641; 2–33 (2), 2–22E, 1–26D; 85; open; $100; $2.50; SSA chapter.
Meetings: 3rd Sat., ea. mo., 7:30 P.M., Administration Bldg., Harris Hill, Elmira.
Soaring Site: Harris Hill, 3 mi. NW of Elmira on Rt. #17 or #352, 10 mi. E of Corning.
Contacts: L. Roy McMaster, Rt. #352, R.D. #1, Elmira, NY 14903; (607) 732–6418.
    Dietrich Ennulat, Brown Rd., R.D. #1, Horseheads, NY 14845; (607) 739–8578.

IROQUOIS SOARING ASSN.   1 Nouvelle Park, New Hartford, New York 13413; (315) 736–5466; 1–26, 2–22; 30; open; —; —; SSA chapter.

Meetings: 3rd Thurs. ea mo., 7:30 P.M., Shurkatch Fishing Tackle Co., Richfield Springs, NY.
Soaring Site: Cooperstown-Westville Airport, 7 mi. S of Cooperstown, NY.
Contacts: Leland Jones, RD #1, Box 343, Valley View Rd., New Hartford, NY 13413.
William Amols, RD #1, Cooperstown, NY 13326; (607) 547-9545.

ITHACA SOARING CLUB, INC. c/o Robert Keech, Box 175, Etna, New York 13062; (607) 347-3495; 2-33 (2), 2-22C, 1-26; 72; open; $25; $4.
Meetings: 2nd Wed., 7:30 P.M., Club Hangar, Mecklenburg Rd., Ithaca, NY.
Soaring Site: Grund Field, 1765 Mecklenburg Rd., Ithaca, NY, 4 mi. W.
Contact: Siegfried Werners, RD #5, Box 2290, Ithaca, NY 14850.

LONG ISLAND SOARING ASSN., INC. c/o James Kade, 53 Cedar St., Babylon, NY 11702; (516) 669-0885; 1-26 (2), 2-33 (2), 2-32; 100; $450; $10; SSA chapter.
Meetings: 3rd Wed. ea. mo., 8:00 P.M., Sky Lounge, Deer Park Airport, Deer Park, L.I.
Contacts: Rudy Suehs, Jr., 820 James Pl., Uniondale, NY 11553; (516) 483-3369.
Rowland Cross, 333 W. 57th St., New York, NY 10019 (212) 265-1248.

METROPOLITAN AIRHOPPERS SOARING ASSN. P.O. Box 188, Wurtsboro, NY 12790; A social club, providing BBQ's & a bunkhouse ($35 per season); 59; open; $10; none; SSA chapter.
Soaring Site: Wurtsboro Airport, approx. 12 mi. W of Middletown on Rt. 17, & 2 mi. N on 209.
Contacts: Florence Dietz, 4 Skyline Dr., Morristown, New Jersey 07960; (201) 539-7363.
William Moroney, 136 Senator St., Brooklyn, NY 11220; (212) 748-5655.

MOHAWK SOARING CLUB, INC. c/o F. P. Bundy, Box 55, RD #1, Scotia, New York 12302; (518) 374-8635; 2-33 (2), 1-23, 1-26; 52; 50; $100; $7; SSA chapter.
Meetings: Last Thurs. ea. mo., 8:00 P.M., Schenectady County Airport, Scotia, NY.
Soaring Sites: Saratoga County Airport, 6 mi. S of Saratoga Springs, NY; North Adams Airport, 2 mi. W of North Adams, MA.
Contacts: R. Edwin Joynson, Box 56, RD #1, Scotia, NY 12302; (518) 377-4238.
F. Richard Ellenberger, 2476 Poersch Ct., Schenectady, NY 12309.

ROCHESTER SOARING CLUB. c/o S. F. Lambers, 15 Tuxford Rd., Pittsford, New York 14534; (716) 381-6983; 2-33, 1-26 (2), 1-34; 37; 40; $100; $8; SSA chapter.
Soaring Site: Dansville Airport, Dansville, NY.
Contacts: Lloyd Hunter, 10 Schoolhouse Lane, Rochester, NY 14618; (716) 442-1493.
Neil Atkins, 20 Portsmouth Terrace, Rochester, NY 14607; (716) 442-5325.

SOARING CLUB OF SYRACUSE, INC. c/o Robert Brittain, 512 Oswego St., Liverpool, New York 13088; (315) 457-2561; 2-22, Slingsby T-53; 15; open; $200; $10; SSA chapter.
Meetings: 2nd Wed. ea. mo., 6:30 P.M. Call for location.
Soaring Site: Canastota Municipal Airport, 1/4 mi. W of Canastota, NY, on Hwy. 5.

TRI-CITIES SOARING SOCIETY, INC. c/o Tri-Cities Airport, Endicott, New York 13760; (607) 785-8353; 1-26, 2-33; 15; open; $250; $6.
Meetings: 1st Mon. ea. mo., 7:30 P.M., AmVets Bldg., Tri-Cities Airport, Endicott, NY.
Soaring Site: Tri-Cities Airport, 2 mi. W of Endicott on Rt. 17-C.

Contacts: Karen Augustitus, 805 Imperial Woods Dr., Vestal, NY 13850; (607) 748–7687.
Jim Lippincott, 297 Prospect St., Owego, NY 13827; (607) 687–4327.

WARREN E. EATON SOARING SOCIETY OF NORWICH. c/o Ron Latham, 11 Eaton Ave., Norwich,
New York 13815; (607) 334–9630; TG–2; 3; —; —; —.
Soaring Site: Cooperstown-Westville Airport, 7 mi. S of Cooperstown, NY.
Contacts: Robert Moore, Lyonbrook Rd., Norwich, NY 13815; (607) 334–6337.
Howard Latham, Maple Knoll Apts. #G–39, Johnstown, NY 12095; (518) 762–3356.

NORTH CAROLINA

TARHEEL SOARING CLUB. c/o Herbert Walls, 2278 The Circle, Raleigh, North Carolina
27608; (919) 833–0669; 2–22, Slingsby Skylark 4; 19; open; $300; $10; SSA chapter.
Meetings: Alternate Wed. ea. mo., 7:00 P.M., K & W Restaurant, Holley Hill Mall,
Burlington, NC. Call for date.
Soaring Site: Burlington Municipal Airport, 3 mi. SW of Burlington, NC.
Contacts: Gerald Dodson, Rt. 6, Box 425–20, Burlington, NC 27215; (919) 228–8997.
Arch Schoch, Jr., 1012 Country Club Dr., High Point, NC 27261; (919) 883–9652.

OHIO

ADRIAN SOARING CLUB. c/o H. R. Jost, 2456 Orchard Rd., Toledo, Ohio 43606; (419)
531–6244; AS–K13 (2), 1–23D, 1–26; 81; open; $150; $75 annually; SSA chapter.
Meetings: C.A.P. Bldg., Adrian Airport, Adrian, MI. Call for date & location.
Soaring Site: Adrian Airport, 1 mi. SW of Adrian, MI.
Contacts: John Van Schaik, 216 N. Broad St., Adrian, MI 49221; (313) 263–9498.
Wayne Westra, 17329 Helen, Allen Park, MI 48101; (313) 388–2583.

BRYAN SOARING CLUB. P.O. Box 488, Bryan, Ohio 43506; (419) 636–1340; Ka. 7 (2); 28; open;
$200; $4; SSA chapter.
Meetings: Call for date & location.
Soaring Site: Williams County Airport, 2 1/2 mi. E of Bryan, Rd. "D."
Contacts: Robert Jackson, 10619 Pine Mills Rd., Fort Wayne, Indiana 46800; (219)
637–6742.
Ed Frappier, 118 E. Mulberry, Bryan, OH 43506; (419) 636–3857.

CANTON SOARING EAGLES. c/o H. Buytendyk, 401 Holmes Blvd., Wooster, OH 44691; (216)
262–8301; SFS–31, Pilatus B4, RF–5B; 5; 25; $500; $15.
Meetings: Fri., 8:00 P.M., Wayne County Airport, OH. Call for date.
Soaring Site: Wayne County Airport, 6 mi. N of Wooster, OH.
Contact: Robert Graham, 1432 Sand Run Rd., Akron, OH 44313; (216) 864–9031.

CENTRAL OHIO SOARING ASSN. Box 194, Columbus, OH 43216; —; 2–33 (2), 1–26; 65; open;
$50; $7.50; SSA chapter.

Meetings: 3rd Thurs. ea. mo., 8:00 P.M., Buckeye Federal Savings & Loan.
Soaring Site: Marion Municipal Airport, 3 mi. E of Marion, OH.
Contacts: Pat Skeele, 4802 Colonel Dr., Columbus, OH 43229; (614) 885–1464.
    Warren Kniepkamp, 4206 Glenmawr, Columbus, OH 43224; (614) 267–5191.

CLEVELAND SOARING SOCIETY, INC. c/o Howard Graves, 6633 Somerset Dr., Cleveland, Ohio 44141; (216) 526–1023; 2–33 (2), 1–26; 32; open; $5; none; SSA chapter.
Meetings: 1st Fri. ea. mo., 7:30 P.M., Horizons Research, Inc., 23800 Mercantile Rd., Beachwood, OH.
Soaring Site: Geauga County Airport, Middlefield, OH.
Contacts: Sunny Vegso, 1949 Greed Rd., #205, Cleveland, OH 44121; (216) 531–3055.
    Jack Conroy, 2409 Greenvale Rd., Cleveland, OH 44121; (216) 531–0826.

FREEDOM'S SOARING THUNDERBIRDS, INC. c/o Earl Mitchell, 265 Aqua Blvd., Akron, Ohio 44319; (216) 644–1139; K–8B, Blanik; 15; 25; $200; $11.50; SSA chapter.
Meetings: 3rd Fri. ea. mo., 7:30 P.M., American Bank of Commerce, 1908 State Rd., Cuyahoga Falls, OH.
Soaring Site: Martin Field, 4 mi. E of Canton, OH on Old Rt. 62 (No. Canton, OH).
Contacts: John Mansfield, 4162 Claridge Dr., Youngstown, OH 44511; (216) 793–1453.
    John C. Yeagle, 1247 Argonne Rd., South Euclid, OH 44121; (216) 382–8775.

KITTY HAWK SOARING, INC. c/o Don Morrison, 5071 Mosiman Rd., Middletown, Ohio 45042; (513) 423–3142; 1–26B; 4; 8; —; —.
Meetings: Annual. Call for date, time & location.
Soaring Site: Soaring Society of Dayton Gliderport, 5 mi. E of Waynesville, OH.
Contact: Ken Bassett, 2195 Rockdell Dr., Fairborn, OH 45324; (513) 879–0678.

NORTHERN OHIO SOARING ASSN. c/o Alfred Davis, 418 Williams St., Niles, Ohio 44446; (216) 652–4861; 1–26A; 12; open; $150; none.
Soaring Site: Price Field, 3 mi. S of Youngstown Municipal Airport, off Rt. 193.
Contacts: Loyal D. Rawlings II, 1618 W. Park Ave., Niles, OH 44446; (216) 652–5575.
    Jay A. Carter, "Glenmore" Rt. 267, East Liverpool, OH 43920; (216) 385–8519.

SOARING SOCIETY OF DAYTON, INC. c/o Box 581 Far Hills Branch, Dayton, Ohio 45419; (513) 299–1943; 2–22 (2), Ka. 7; 195; open; $100; $7; SSA chapter.
Meetings: 2nd Tues. ea. mo., 8:00 P.M., State Fidelity Savings & Loan Assn. Bldg.
Soaring Site: Soaring Society of Dayton Gliderport, 5475 Elbon Rd., Waynesville, OH.
Contacts: Julian Allen, 3700 Strathmoor Dr., Dayton, OH 45429; (513) 299–1943.
    Robert Phillips, 400 E. Church St., Oxford, OH 45056; (513) 523–4639.

OKLAHOMA

TULSA SKYHAWKS SOARING CLUB. c/o Ronald Hanna, 6793 East 66th Pl., Tulsa, Oklahoma 74133; (918) 622–6910; Bergfalke III, Ka. 8B; 24; open; $100; $10; SSA chapter.
Meetings: 1st Mon. ea. mo., 7:30 P.M., Admiral Rm., Sooner Federal Savings & Loan, 7878 E. Admiral Pl., Tulsa, OK.
Soaring Site: Harvey Young Airport, 10 mi. E of Tulsa on 11th St.

Contacts: Paul Schaeffer, 2128 East 31st St., Tulsa, OK 74133; (918) 742–0132.
        Robert Warren, 5770 East 26th St., Tulsa, OK 74114; (918) 835–4602.

OREGON

WILLAMETTE VALLEY SOARING CLUB.   c/o Dick Bowen, 852 NW Albermarle Terrace,
Portland, Oregon 97210; (503) 223–0040; Bergfalke; 12; open; $200; $5.
Meetings: Last Fri. ea. mo.; call for time & location.
Contacts: Laird Smith, 782 NE Sunrise Lane, Hillsboro, OR 97123; (503) 648–7449.
        Dennis Jurries, 958 NW Sycamore Ave. #39, Corvallis, OR 97330.

PENNSYLVANIA

BUTLER SOARING CLUB, INC.   P.O. Box 1, Nixon Branch, Butler, PA 16001; —; 2–22E,
1–26B; 27; open; $150; $12; SSA chapter.
Meetings: Semi-annual, Board meets monthly. Call for date & location.
Soaring Site: Butler-Graham Airport, 6 mi. S of Butler, PA.
Contacts: Robert Bollinger, 106 Roberts Dr., Corapolis, PA 15108; (412) 457–7428.
        Mark Moore, 3235 Thayer St., Pittsburgh, PA 15204; (412) 922–3412.

LANCASTER COUNTY SOARING SOCIETY.   c/o Ken Herskey, 112 So. Main St., Manheim, Penn-
sylvania 17545; (717) 665–2401; 2–22E; 13; open.
Meetings: 2nd Tues. ea. mo., 7:30 P.M., 112 So. Main St., Manheim, PA.
Soaring Site: Elizabethtown-Marietta Airport, 1 mi. N of Maytown.
Contact: Leroy Lovelidge, 201 E. Orange St., Lancaster, PA 17602; (717) 393–4121.

MIFFLIN COUNTY SAILPLANE ASSOCIATES.   c/o Wayne Haubert, Box 205, Mexico, Pennsyl-
vania 17056; (717) 436–8266; 2–33; 5; open; —; —.
Soaring Site: Mifflin County Airport, 8 mi. N of Lewistown, PA.
Contact: Robert Rawdon, Box 193, Reedsville, PA 17084; (717) 667–2128.

NITTANY SOARING CLUB.   c/o Clark Motor Co., Box 556, State College, Pennsylvania 16801;
(814) 238–3014; 2–22, 1–26; 15; open; $200; $10; SSA chapter.
Meetings: 2nd Wed. ea. mo., 8:00 P.M. Call for location.
Soaring Site: State College Airport, 1 mi. SW of State College, PA.
Contacts: Suzanne Striedieck, RD #1, Port Matilda, PA 16870; (814) 237–7996.
        Frank Dachille, 1420 Park Hills Ave., State College, PA 16801; (814) 238–9663.

1–26 ASSOCIATION.   c/o Alberta Sterling, Sec., 5911 Fox St., Harrisburg, Pennsylvania
17112. A national, one-design association for those interested in the Schweizer 1–26
sailplane. Publishes a monthly newsletter, promotes regattas, and sanctions an annual
North American 1–26 Championships. Annual dues, $4.00.

PHILADELPHIA GLIDER COUNCIL, INC.   934 Route 152, Perkasie, Pennsylvania 18944; (215)
822–9974; 1–26 (2), 2–33 (2), 1–34; 64; open; $500; $8; SSA chapter.
Meetings: Call for date, time & location.
Soaring Site: Philadelphia Gliderport, 20 mi. N of Philadelphia on Rt. 152.

Contacts: Jack Shafer, Seven Oaks Farm, Chalfont, PA 18914; (215) 822–3948.
Art Millay, 106 Carleton Rd., Wallingford, PA 19086; (215) 566–6753.

PITTSBURGH SOARING CLUB, INC. c/o Douglas Fraser, 269 Foxcroft Rd., Pittsburgh, Pennsylvania 15220; (412) 279–1008; 1–26A, 2–22E; 32; open; $250; $5.
Soaring Site: Bandel Airport, 8 mi. SE of Washington, PA & 3 mi. NE of U.S. 40 & 519.
Contacts: Bruno Cerceo, 258 Edmond St., Pittsburgh, PA 15224; (412) 361–5307.
Frank Hoist, 3512–5th Ave., Pittsburgh, PA 15213; (412) 682–7637.

THE SOARING DUTCHMEN, INC. c/o Kutztown Airport, Kutztown, Pennsylvania 19530; (215) 683–3821; 1–26, 2–33; 30; open; $250; $18; SSA chapter.
Meetings: 3rd Fri. ea. mo., 8:00 P.M., Kutztown Airport, Kutztown, PA.
Soaring Site: Kutztown Airport, 1 mi. W of Kutztown on Rt. 222.
Contacts: Hugh Johnston III, Box 293 Exeter Rd., Haverford, PA 19041; (215) 649–7165.
Lark Bonelli, Box 97, Breiningsville, PA 18031; (215) 682–7583.

RHODE ISLAND

BROWN UNIVERSITY SOARING CLUB. c/o Student Activities Office, Brown University, Providence, Rhode Island 02912; —; Blanik; 15; open to Brown University students & alumni; $5, $10/alumni & staff; None.
Meetings: Irregular. Call for date & location.
Soaring Site: Plymouth Municipal Airport, S of Boston on Rt. 3 to 44.
Contact: Brian Clark, Box 577, Brown University, Providence, RI 02912.

SOUTH DAKOTA

WEST RIVER SOARERS, INC. c/o Jim Campbell, RR 4, Box 815–A, Rapid City, South Dakota 57701; (605) 342–1904; Ka. 7; 14; 20; $250; $5.
Soaring Site: Black Hills Airport, 5 mi. E of Spearfish.
Contact: Lowell Thomas, Box 396, Kadoka, SD 57543; (605) 837–2232.

TENNESSEE

MEMPHIS SOARING SOCIETY. c/o Dolph Clark, Box 4418, Memphis, Tennessee 38104; (901) 278–7900; 1–26, 1–34, 2–32, 2–33 (2); 32; open; $150; $10; SSA chapter.
Meetings: 2nd Sat. ea. mo., 10:30 A.M., Finley Gliderport, Marion, Arkansas.
Soaring Site: Finley Gliderport, 4 mi. W of Marion, AR.
Contacts: James Finley, Jr., 133 Walnut, Marion, Arkansas 72364; (501) 735–2449.
Charles Mann, Box 155, Memphis, TN 38101; (901) 332–3587.

TEXAS

BROWNSVILLE SOARING CLUB, INC. c/o Robert E. Velteh, 1345 Coral Court, Brownsville, Texas 78520; (512) 564–6423; 2–22E, 1–26D; 10; open; $50–$250; $5–$15.

Meetings: Annual & when necessary. Call for date & location.
Soaring Site: San Benito Municipal Airport, SE of San Benito, TX.
Contacts: George Lipe, 1454 Central Blvd., Brownsville, TX 78520 (512) 542–2061.
    Charles Langston, 1003 Pamela Dr., Mission, TX 78520; (512) 585–2772.

DALLAS GLIDING ASSN., INC. c/o N. B. Noland, 1111 Frito Lay Tower, Dallas, TX 75235;
(214) 357–3851; —; 25; open; —; —.
Contacts: M. S. Griffith, Jr., 4031 Fawnhollow, Dallas, TX 75234; (214) 247–7297.
    Othmar Schwarzenberger, 912 Walnut Lane, Arlington, TX 76010.

DENTON SOARING ASSN., INC. c/o Jim Rudis, 3941 High Summit, Dallas, TX 75234; (214)
247–0378; Blanik; 7; open; $200; $25; SSA chapter.
Meetings: Vary. Call for date, time & location.
Soaring Site: Oliver Farms, 6 mi. N of Ft. Worth, W of Saginaw, TX.
Contacts: Jim Sherwood, 510 Norman Dr., Euless, TX 76039; (817) 283–3295.
    John Suttle, 3317 Woodthrush, Denton, TX 76201; (817) 387–4997.

EL PASO SOARING SOCIETY, INC. P.O. Box 9041, El Paso, Texas 79982; —; 2–22, 1–26; 27; open;
$100; $10; SSA chapter.
Meetings: 1st Tues, ea. mo., 7:30 P.M., 18th Floor, El Paso National Bank Bldg., 400 No.
    Mesa, El Paso, TX.
Soaring Site: Skysport, on McCombs Rd., 3 1/2 mi. N of Dyer St., El Paso, TX.
Contacts: James Moore, 7737 Rosedale, El Paso, TX 79915; (915) 778–6195.
    Jorgen Andersen, 225 Lancer Way, El Paso, TX 79912; (915) 584–2096.

FAULT LINE FLYERS. c/o Dennis Scheidt, 4415 Newcome, San Antonio, TX 78229; (512)
696–1559; —; 7; open; $20 annually.
Meetings: Call for date, time & location.
Soaring Site: San Marcos Municipal Airport, 4 mi. E of San Marcos on Hwy. 21.
Contact: Bill Snead, 12702 Tomanet, Austin, TX 78751; (512) 255–2785.

HIGH PLAINS SOARING SOCIETY, INC. c/o Bob Grant, 4202 E. 31st, Amarillo, TX 79103; (806)
374–3404; 2–33, 1–26; 30; open; $50; $10; SSA chapter.
Meetings: Last Sat. ea. mo., 7:30 P.M. Call for location.
Soaring Site: Palo Duro, 2 mi. S of Amarillo, off South Washington.
Contacts: Jerry Hopson, 4409 Charlene, Amarillo, TX 79106; (806) 352–6682.
    Jim Foreman, 4335 Mesa Circle, Amarillo, TX 79109; (806) 352–8546.

MESILLA VALLEY SOARING ASSN. c/o R. L. Carver, 415 Bayou View, Seabrook, TX 77586;
(713) 334–1764; HP-14 (2), Austria SH-1; 6; open; none; none.
Meetings: 1st Wed. ea. mo., 7:00 P.M., 415 Bayou View, Seabrook, TX.
Soaring Site: San Marcos Municipal Airport, 3 mi. NE of San Marcos, TX.
Contacts: Gary Meester, 2007 Savannah Court No., League City, TX 77573; (713) 554–
    4068.
    Harold Shelton, 507 Newport Blvd., League City, TX 77573; (713) 332–2091.

NORTH DALLAS GLIDERS, INC. c/o John Price, 610 Northhill, Richardson, TX 75080; (214)
231–5554; 1–26 (3), 2–33, 2–22; 34; open; $50; $10; SSA chapter.

Soaring Site: Heath Gliderport, 20 mi. E of Dallas, 5 mi. S of Rockwall.
Contacts: Jesse Womack, 3417 Canson St., Dallas, TX 75233; (214) 331–2132.
Bob Gibbons, 14038 Peyton Dr., Dallas, TX 75240; (214) 233–2430.

PERMIAN SOARING ASSN. 201 First Savings Bldg., Midland, Texas 79701; (915) 682–4316; 1–26; 12; open; $50; $5; SSA chapter.
Soaring Site: Ector County Airport, N of Odessa, TX.
Contacts: Henry Tillett, Rt. 2, Box 840, Midland, TX 79701; (915) 694–1717.
Tom Dollahite, 3607 Sinclair, Midland, TX 79701; (915) 694–2075.

REFUGIO SOARING CIRCLE. Box 366 Refugio, Texas 78377; —; AS-W15; 1–34, 2–33; 39; 45; $150; $10; SSA chapter.
Meetings: 2nd Mon. ea. mo., 7:30 P.M., Lambert Plaza, Refugio, TX.
Soaring Site: Rooke Field, 2 mi. SW of Refugio, TX.
Contacts: Paul Elliott, Box 566, Bishop, TX 78343; (512) 584–2764.
Ken Arteburn, Drawer X, Refugio, TX 78377; (512) 526–4445.

ROCKWALL SOARING COUNCIL, INC. Box 245, Rockwall, Texas 75087; (214) 722–8819; (corp. owns hanger and is manager of soaring site used by local clubs & private owners).
Soaring Site: Rockwall Municipal Airport, 20 mi. NE of Dallas on U.S. 67.
Contact: Robert McNeill, 215 Joe White St., Rockwall, TX 75087; (214) 722–4501.

SAN ANTONIO SOARING SOCIETY. c/o C. E. Earnhardt, 138–99th St., Stinson Field, San Antonio, Texas 78214; (512) 924–4519; TG-3; 15; open; $35; $6.
Meetings: Sun., 1:00 P.M., 138–99th St., San Antonio, TX. Call for date.
Soaring Site: Horizon Airport, 10 mi. S of San Antonio, TX.

SIGNAL MOUNTAIN SOARING SOCIETY. c/o O. C. Shapland, 2701 Cactus Dr., Big Spring, Texas 79720; (915) 267–8893; 1–26; 5; open; —; —.
Soaring Site: Moss Creek Gliderport, 10 mi. ESE of Big Spring, TX.
Contact: R. H. Weaver, 105 W. 4th, Big Spring, TX 79720; (915) 267–8203.

TEXAS SOARING ASSN., INC. P.O. Box 1452, Grand Prairie, Texas 75050; (214) 264–9420; 2–32, 2–22C, 2–22E, 1–26; 85; open; $60; $5; SSA chapter.
Meetings: Last Fri. ea. mo., 8:00 P.M., Texas Soaring Assn. Gliderport.
Soaring Site: Texas Soaring Assn. Gliderport, 5 mi. S of Grand Prairie on Beltline Rd.
Contacts: Bill Stewart, 10021 Gateway Lane, Dallas, TX 75218; (214) 324–0373.
George Coder, 1514 Tulip Dr., Arlington, TX 76013; (817) 261–9272.

UTAH

SOARING SOCIETY OF UTAH. c/o G. A. Flandro, 4589 Wallace Lane, Salt Lake City, Utah 84117; (801) 277–9984; 2–22E, Ka. 8B; 20; open;—; —.
Meetings: 2nd Fri. ea. mo., 8:00 P.M., 4589 Wallace Lane, Salt Lake City, Utah.
Soaring Sites: Nephi Municipal Airport, 1 mi. W of Nephi, Utah.
Heber City Airport, 1 mi. SW of Heber City, Utah.
Contacts: Lila Fielden, 3718 S. 9th East, Salt Lake City, UT 84106; (801) 266–7097.
John Apps, 1436 Federal Way, Salt Lake City, UT 84112; (801) 364–4453.

TIMP GLIDER CLUB   c/o Leon Duste, 35 East 300 South, Provo, Utah 85601; (801) 373–1686; HP–16; BG–12; 10; open; —; —.
Soaring Site: Nephi Municipal Airport, 1 mi. W of Nephi, Utah.

UNIVERSITY OF UTAH SOARING CLUB, INC.   Jerrold Foote, 112 E. Marie Dr., Midvale, Utah 84047; (801) 225–8611; 2–22E, Cherokee RM; 30; 35; $125; $8.
Meetings: 2nd Fri. ea. mo., 8:00 P.M., Exec. Terminal, Salt Lake Airport.
Soaring Site: Heber Valley Airport, 1 mi. S of Heber City, Utah.
Contact: Karren Kessler, 1840 Hillcrest Ave., Salt Lake City, UT 84087; (801) 225–8611.

VERMONT

SUGARBUSH SOARING CLUB.   c/o Jim Herman, Sugarbush Inn, Warren, Vermont 05674; (802) 496–3301; 1–26, 2–22; 12; —; $500; —.
Soaring Site: Warren-Sugarbush Airport, 1 mi. NE of Warren, VT.
Contact: John Macone, Waitsfield, VT 05673; (802) 496–2209.

VIRGINIA

BLUE RIDGE SOARING SOCIETY, INC.   Box 1099, Salem, Virginia 24153; (703) 389–2305; 2–33, 1–23; 37; open; $200; $15; SSA chapter.
Meetings: 3rd Thurs. ea. mo., 7:30 P.M., in members' homes.
Soaring Site: New Castle International Airport, 1.5 mi. S of New Castle on Rt. 311.
Contacts: Robert Penn, 709 Orchard, Martinsville, VA 24112.
          Timothy Kelly, 775 Virginia Ave., Salem, VA 24153; (703) 389–9796.

RIDGE & VALLEY SOARING CLUB, INC.   c/o C. M. Rohmann, 1525 University Ave., Charlottesville, Virginia 22903; (703) 296–7561; 2–33, 1–26; 18; open; $200; $15; SSA chapter.
Meetings: L. B. Gliderport, Lexington, VA. Call for date & time.
Soaring Site: L. B. Gliderport, 4 mi. S of Lexington, VA.
Contacts: Farren Smith, Rt. 2 Westover Hills, Waynesboro, VA 22980; (703) 942–2384.
          Ron Roberts, P.O. Box 5302, Charlottesville, VA 22903; (703) 973–3142.

SHORT HILLS SOARING CLUB, INC.   c/o Raymond Cramer, 4820 Village Rd., Fairfax, Virginia 22030; (703) 591–8107; 2–22, 1–26; 30; open; $200; $5.
Soaring Site: Scott Airpark, 3 mi. S of Brunswick, Maryland.

TIDEWATER SOARING SOCIETY, INC.   c/o Wolf Elber, P.O. Box 1005, Portsmouth, Virginia 23705; (703) 595–7963; 2–22, 1–26; 21; 100; $200; $7; SSA chapter.
Soaring Site: South Norfolk Airport, 7 mi. S of Norfolk, VA.
Contact: Jack Mills, 409 W. Plantation Rd., Virginia Beach, VA 23454.

WASHINGTON

AIR EXPLORER POST 299.   c/o Gary Connor, 5450–49th SW, Seattle, WA 98116; (206) 935–6405; TG–2; 15; 30; $15 annually.

Meetings: 2nd & 4th Tues. ea. mo., 7:30 P.M., Camp Long, 35th SW & SW Dawson, Seattle, WA 98126.

Soaring Site: Fancher Field, 5 mi. NE of Wenatchee, WA.

Contacts: Richard Kennedy, 22819–17th Ave. S, Des Moines, WA 98188; (206) 878–4186.

Kim Gould, 3808 E. McGilvra St., Seattle, WA 98102; (206) 323–3808.

BOEING EMPLOYEES' SOARING CLUB, INC.   c/o The Boeing Co., Box 3707, Seattle, WA 98124, MS 4H–96; (206) 655–2441; Blanik (2), K 6E, AS-K13; 76; open to Boeing employees: $150; $8.

Meetings: 3rd Mon. ea. mo., 7:30 P.M., DC Recreation Center, Boeing Co.

Soaring Site: summer, Ephrata; winter, Canaday, 5 mi. NE of Arlington, WA.

Contacts: Nelson Funston, 3930–96th Ave. SE, Mercer Island, WA 98040; (206) 232–0741.

John Hope, 9500 Rainer Ave. S #302, Seattle, WA 98124; (206) 723–3127.

COLUMBIA BASIN SOARING ASSN.   c/o Ronald Chitwood, 2406 Dover, Richland, Washington 99352; (509) 943–3658; —; 15; open; SSA chapter.

Soaring Site: Richland Airport, NW of Richland, WA.

Contacts: Robert L. Moore, Rt. 1, Box 351–C, Richland, WA 99352; (509) 967–3773.

Fred Moore, 504 Falley, Richland, WA 99352; (509) 943–1007.

SEATTLE GLIDER COUNCIL, INC.   c/o Robert Chase, 12422–68th Ave. NE, Kirkland, Washington 98033; (206) 822–6600; —; 200; open; $4.50 annually.

Meetings: 1st Mon. ea. mo., 8:00 P.M., Boeing D. C. Credit Union Bldg., 9725 East Marginal Way, Seattle, WA.

Soaring Site: Fancher Field, 5 mi. NE of Wenatchee, WA.

Contacts: John Sager, 240 SW 183rd, Seattle, WA 98166; (206) 246–5225.

Norm Donatt, 16038 NE 27th, Bellevue, WA 98040; (206) 885–3060.

WENATCHEE VALLEY SOARING SOCIETY, INC.   c/o Frank Campbell, 710 Highland Dr., Wenatchee, Washington 98801; (509) 662–5097.

WEST VIRGINIA

CUMBERLAND SOARING GROUP   c/o J. F. Wagner, Rt. 1, Box 53, Ridgeley, West Virginia 26753; (304) 738–9118; 2–33, 1–26; 35; 40; $100; $6; SSA chapter.

Meetings: Last Sat. ea. mo., 7:30 P.M., Cumberland Municipal Airport.

Soaring Site: Cumberland Municipal Airport, 1/2 mi. S of Cumberland on Rt. 28.

Contacts: Esther McGonagle, 107 Peters Dr, McMurray, PA 15317; (412) 941–9834.

Tom Herndon, 1305 Burleigh Rd., Lutherville, MD 21093; (301) 296–9040.

MOUNTAINEER SOARING ASSN., INC.   c/o S. W. Williamson, 1146 Mulberry Circle, Charleston, West Virginia 25314; (304) 346–2797; 2–33A, 1–26C; 30; 40; $300; $5.

Meetings: Call for date, time & location. Scheduled as necessary.

Soaring Site: Robert Newlon Field, 4 mi. NE of Huntington, WV on Rt. 2.

Contacts: Daniel Packard, 1515 W. Summit Dr., Charleston, WV 25302; (304) 346–7157.

Robert Childers, 90 Belmont Dr., Huntington, WV 25705; (304) 523–2308.

WISCONSIN

AEROSPACE EXPLORER POST 309, B.S.A.   c/o P. B. Hammersmith, 2755 N. Stowell Ave.,
Milwaukee, WI 53211; (414) 962–6727; —; 27; open, age limit/21; $3.50 annually.
Meetings: 1st Mon. ea. mo., 7:30 P.M., St. Mark's Episcopal Church, 2618 N. Hackett
Ave., Milwaukee, Wisconsin.
Soaring Site: West Bend Municipal Airport, 35 mi. N of Milwaukee on Hwy. 45, 33.
Contacts: Dave Block, 8620 N. Pelham Pky., Milwaukee, WI 53217; (414) 352–9482.
Bill Norton, 5535 N. Berkely Blvd., Milwaukee, WI 53217; (414) 964–0691.

MONONA GLIDER CLUB.   c/o C. M. Van Airsdale, 407 Sethne Ct., Madison, Wisconsin 53716;
(608) 222–3142; Cherokee II; 3; 3; none; none.
Soaring Site: Lodi Lakeland Airport, 30 mi. NW of Madison on Hwy. 60.

THERMAL SNIFFERS SOARING CLUB, INC.   c/o Gunter Voltz, 5007 N. Bay Ridge Ave., Mil-
waukee, Wisconsin 53217; (414) 962–1340; —; 20; open; —; —; SSA chapter.
Meetings: Mon. ea. wk., 7:00 P.M., St. Mark's Episcopal Church, 2618 N. Hackett Ave.,
Milwaukee, WI.
Soaring Site: West Bend Municipal Airport, 3 mi. E of West Bend on Hwy. 33.
Contacts: Paul Hammersmith, 2755 N. Stowell Ave., Milwaukee, WI 53211; (414) 962–
6727.
Arthur Shanley, 2703 Madison St., Waukesha, WI 53186; (414) 547–7972.

WHISPERING WINGS SOARING CLUB.   c/o Reabe Flying Service, P.O. Box 24, Waupun, Wis-
consin 53963; (414) 324–3519; Ka. 7; 6; open; none; none; $50 annually.
Soaring Site: Waupun Airport, 1 mi. SW of Waupun, WI, on Fox Lake Rd.
Contacts: Glen Dunham, 26 N. Mill, Waupun, WI 53963; (414) 324–3029.
Eugene Sandburg, 815 S. Lapham St., Oconomowoc, WI 53066; (414) 567–
6551.

WINNEBAGOLAND SOARING ASSN., INC.   c/o Frederick F. Flood, 5810 S. Honey Creek Dr.,
Milwaukee, Wisconsin 53221; (414) 282–7502; TG–2, BG–6; 17; open; $100; $5.
Soaring Site: Aero Park Airport, 6 mi. E of Timmerman Field, Menomonee Falls, WI.
Contacts: Rod Diehl, 618 N. 90th St., Milwaukee, WI 53226; (414) 258–6776.
Karl Schaarschmidt, W204 N5022 Lannon Rd., Menomonee Falls, WI 53051;
(414) 252–9992.

Sailplanes

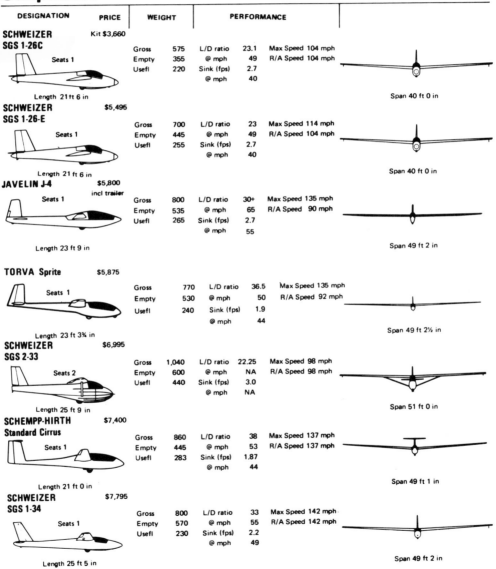

DESIGNATION	PRICE	WEIGHT		PERFORMANCE			
SCHWEIZER SGS 1-26C	Kit $3,660	Gross	575	L/D ratio	23.1	Max Speed 104 mph	
Seats 1		Empty	355	@ mph	49	R/A Speed 104 mph	
		Usefl	220	Sink (fps)	2.7		
				@ mph	40		
Length 21 ft 6 in						Span 40 ft 0 in	
SCHWEIZER SGS 1-26-E	$5,495	Gross	700	L/D ratio	23	Max Speed 114 mph	
Seats 1		Empty	445	@ mph	49	R/A Speed 104 mph	
		Usefl	255	Sink (fps)	2.7		
				@ mph	40		
Length 21 ft 6 in						Span 40 ft 0 in	
JAVELIN J-4	$5,800 incl trailer	Gross	800	L/D ratio	30+	Max Speed 135 mph	
Seats 1		Empty	535	@ mph	65	R/A Speed 90 mph	
		Usefl	265	Sink (fps)	2.7		
				@ mph	55		
Length 23 ft 9 in						Span 49 ft 2 in	
TORVA Sprite	$5,875	Gross	770	L/D ratio	36.5	Max Speed 135 mph	
Seats 1		Empty	530	@ mph	50	R/A Speed 92 mph	
		Usefl	240	Sink (fps)	1.9		
				@ mph	44		
Length 23 ft 3¾ in						Span 49 ft 2½ in	
SCHWEIZER SGS 2-33	$6,995	Gross	1,040	L/D ratio	22.25	Max Speed 98 mph	
Seats 2		Empty	600	@ mph	NA	R/A Speed 98 mph	
		Usefl	440	Sink (fps)	3.0		
				@ mph	NA		
Length 25 ft 9 in						Span 51 ft 0 in	
SCHEMPP-HIRTH Standard Cirrus	$7,400	Gross	860	L/D ratio	38	Max Speed 137 mph	
Seats 1		Empty	445	@ mph	53	R/A Speed 137 mph	
		Usefl	283	Sink (fps)	1.87		
				@ mph	44		
Length 21 ft 0 in						Span 49 ft 1 in	
SCHWEIZER SGS 1-34	$7,795	Gross	800	L/D ratio	33	Max Speed 142 mph	
Seats 1		Empty	570	@ mph	55	R/A Speed 142 mph	
		Usefl	230	Sink (fps)	2.2		
				@ mph	49		
Length 25 ft 5 in						Span 49 ft 2 in	

Sailplanes

DESIGNATION	PRICE	WEIGHT		PERFORMANCE			ENGINE

SCHWEIZER SGS 1-34 RT — $8,390

Seats 1
Length 25 ft 5 in

Gross	840	L/D ratio	34	Max Speed 132 mph
Empty	580	@ mph	55.5	R/A Speed 132 mph
Usefl	260	Sink (fps)	2.1	
		@ mph	49	

Span 49 ft 2 in

BLANIK L-13 — $8,950

Seats 2
Length 25 ft 4 in

Gross	1,102	L/D ratio	28	Max Speed 157 mph
Empty	644	@ mph	58	R/A Speed 87 mph
Usefl	458	Sink (fps)	2.7	
		@ mph	40	

Span 53 ft 0 in

Pilatus B4 — $8,950

Seats 1
Length 21 ft 6½ in

Gross	770	L/D ratio	35	Max speed 149 mph
Empty	506	@ mph	53	R/A speed 149 mph
Usefl	264	Sink (fps)	2.1	
		@ mph	45	

Span 49 ft 2½ in

SCHLEICHER AS-W15B — $9,300

Seats 1
Length 21 ft 6 in

Gross	900	L/D ratio	38	Max Speed 135 mph
Empty	450	@ mph	55	R/A Speed 135 mph
Usefl	450	Sink (fps)	1.8	
		@ mph	42	

Span 49 ft 2 in

GLASFLUGEL Standard Libelle — $9,350

Seats 1
Length 20 ft 4 in

Gross	722	L/D ratio	38	Max Speed 155 mph
Empty	408	@ mph	53	R/A Speed 155 mph
Usefl	286	Sink (fps)	1.8	
		@ mph	47	

Span 49 ft 2.5 in

SLINGSBY Kestrel 19 — $10,665

Seats 1
Length 21 ft 1 in

Gross	1,040*	L/D ratio	44	Max speed 155 mph
Empty	699	@ mph	60	R/A speed 121 mph
Usefl	341	Sink (fps)	1.7	
*with water ballast		@ mph	46	

Span 62 ft 4 in

SCHEMPP-HIRTH Nimbus II — $12,350

Seats 1
Length 22 ft 0 in

Gross	1,036	L/D ratio	47	Max Speed 155 mph
Empty	718	@ mph	56	R/A Speed 155 mph
Usefl	318	Sink (fps)	1.64	
		@ mph	46	

Span 66 ft 7 in

SCHLEICHER AS-W17 — $14,200

Seats 1
Length 24 ft 9 in

Gross	1,035	L/D ratio	49	Max Speed 155 mph
Empty	770	@ mph	65	R/A Speed 155 mph
Usefl	265	Sink (fps)	1.64	
		@ mph	53	

Span 65 ft 7 in
VW. 75 hp/C. 110 hp

Sailplanes

DESIGNATION	PRICE	WEIGHT		PERFORMANCE		ENGINE

SCHLEICHER AS-K16 (powered) — $14,770

Seats 2
Length 24 ft 0 in

Gross	1,540	L/D ratio 25
Empty	1,010	@ mph 55
Usefl	530	Sink (fps) 2.78
		@ mph 45

Max Speed 125 mph
R/A Speed 125 mph

Span 52 ft 6 in

SCHWEIZER SGS 2-32 — $14,995

Seats 2 ½
Length 26 ft 9 in

Gross	1,340	L/D ratio 34
Empty	850	@ mph 59
Usefl	490	Sink (fps) 2.1
		@ mph 52

Max Speed 158 mph
R/A Speed 150 mph

Span 57 ft 0 in

CAPRONI AviAmerica A-15 — $15,995

Seats 1
Length NA

Gross	1,573	L/D ratio 51
Empty	715	@ mph 69
Usefl	858	Sink (fps) 1.5
		@ mph 49

Max Speed 159 mph
R/A Speed 168 mph

Span 75 ft 5 in

CAPRONI-AviAmerica A-21J (jet powered) — $31,995

Seats 2
Length 25 ft 8 in

Gross	1,650	L/D ratio 42
Empty	850	@ mph 67
Usefl	800	Sink (fps) 2
		@ mph 56

Max Speed 208 mph
R/A Speed 155 mph

Sermel Microturbo TRS 18

Span 66 ft 11 in

WORLD AND AMERICAN SOARING RECORDS

RECORD CATEGORY	OPEN SINGLEPLACE WORLD RECORD	OPEN SINGLEPLACE U.S. NATIONAL RECORD	OPEN MULTIPLACE WORLD RECORD	OPEN MULTIPLACE U.S. NATIONAL RECORD
DISTANCE	907.7 mi. (1460.8 km.) Germany West H-W. Grosse AS-W 12 4/25/72	716.952 mi. (1,153.821 km.) Wallace Scott & Benjamin Greene AS-W12&AS-W12 7/26/70	572.874 mi. (921.954 km.) USSR Juri Kouznetsov Blanik 6/3/67	500.64 mi. (805.70 km.) Joseph C. Lincoln 2–32 4/30/67 Prescott, Ariz.
GOAL	652.18 mi. (1,051.2 km.) Germany West Klaus Tesch LS-1C 4/25/72	605.23 mi. (974.04 km.) Wallace Scott AS-W 12 8/22/69 Odessa, Texas	537.399 mi. (864.862 km.) USSR I. Gorokhova Blanik 6/3/67	322.35 mi. (518.78 km.) Edward Minghelli Prue IIA 6/30/67 Cedar City, Utah
OUT AND RETURN	783.20 mi. (1260.44 km.) USA William Holbrook H301 Libelle 5–5–73	Same Lock Haven, Pa.	446.2 mi. (718.2 km.) Poland Edward Makula Caproni A21 8/8/72	425.30 mi. (684.46 km.) Edward Minghelli Prue IIA 7/15/72 Pearblossom, Cal.
GAIN OF HEIGHT	42,303 ft. (12,894 m.) USA Paul F. Bikle 1–23E 2/25/61	Same Lancaster, Cal.	38,320 ft. (11,680 m.) Poland S. Jozefczak Bocian 11/5/66	34,426 ft. (10,493 m.) Laurence Edgar Pratt-Read 3/19/52 Bishop, Cal.
ABSOLUTE ALTITUDE	46,267 ft. (14,102 m.) USA Paul F. Bikle 1–23E 2/25/61	Same Lancaster, Cal.	44,255 ft. (13,489 m.) USA Laurence Edgar Pratt-Read 3/19/52	Same Bishop, Cal.
SPEED OVER 100–KM. TRIANGULAR COURSE	98.94 mph (159.24 kmph) Germany West Klaus Holighaus Nimbus 2 8/14/73	88.621 mph (142.621 kmph) Ross Briegleb Diamant 18 7/25/70 El Mirage, Cal.	81.229 mph (130.726 kmph) Poland Edward Makula Caproni A21 8/6/72	72.932 mph (117.372 kmph) Joseph C. Lincoln 2–32 A 5/24/71 Blanca, Colo.
SPEED OVER 300–KM. TRIANGULAR COURSE	95.34 mph (153.43 kmph) Germany West Walter Neubert Glasflügel 604 3/3/72 (22m)	74.484 mph (119.870 kmph) George Moffat HP–8 8/6/64 Odessa, Texas	70.658 mph (113.717 kmph) Poland Edward Makula Caproni A21 7/31/72	51.169 mph (82.349 kmph) Harland C. Ross R–6 8/13/58 Odessa, Texas
SPEED OVER 500–KM. TRIANGULAR COURSE	84.08 mph (135.32 kmph) South Africa M. Jackson BJ–3 12/28/67	75.488 mph (121.485 kmph) Elemer Katinszky Libelle 8/19/67 29 Palms, Cal.	62.246 mph 101.176 kmph Poland Edward Makula Caproni A21 8/4/72	47.34 mph (76.28 kmph) Paul A. Schweizer 2–32 7/29/66 Odessa, Texas

RECORD CATEGORY	FEMININE SINGLEPLACE		FEMININE MULTIPLACE	
	WORLD RECORD	U.S. NATIONAL RECORD	WORLD RECORD	U.S. NATIONAL RECORD
DISTANCE	465.532 mi. (749.203 km.) USSR O. Klepikova Rot-Front 7 7/6/39	380.06 mi. (611.65 km.) Helen R. Dick HP–14T 7/15/72 Rosamond, Cal.	537.399 mi. (864.862 km.) USSR Tatiana Pavlova Blanik 6/3/67	170.316 mi. (274.100 km.) Betsy Woodward Proudfit Pratt-Read 7/11/52 El Mirage, Cal.
GOAL	454.591 mi. (731.595 km.) USSR Tamara Zaiganova A–15 7/29/66	348.89 mi. (561.48 km.) Helen R. Dick HP-14T 7/24/72 Rosamond, Cal.	537.399 mi. (864.862 km.) USSR I. Gorokhova Blanik 6/3/67	170.316 mi. (274.100 km.) Betsy Woodward Proudfit Pratt-Read 7/11/52 El Mirage, Cal.
OUT AND RETURN	417.68 mi. (672.2 km.) Poland Adela Dankovska Jantar 5/29/73	248.82 mi. (400.42 km.) Helen R. Dick Zugvogel IIIB 7/12/64 Inyokern, Cal.	320.5 mi. (515.8 km.) USSR I. Gorokhova Bocian 6/3/73	None established
GAIN OF HEIGHT	29,918 ft. (9,119 m.) England Anne Burns Skylark 3 1/13/61	27,994 ft. (8,533 m.) Betsy Woodward Proudfit Pratt-Read 4/14/55 Bishop, Cal.	27,657 ft. (8,430 m.) Poland Adela Dankowska Bocian 10/17/67	17,950 ft. (5,471 m.) Janie Oesch 2–32 11/30/67 Colo. Springs, Co.
ABSOLUTE ALTITUDE	39,993 ft. (12,190.2 m.) USA Betsy Woodward Proudfit Pratt-Read 4/14/55	Same Bishop, Cal.	31,230 ft. (9,519 m.) England Anne Burns 2–32 1/5/67	28,150 ft. (8,580 m.) Janie Oesch 2–32 11/30/67 Colo. Springs, Co.
SPEED OVER 100-KM. TRIANGULAR COURSE	74.659 mph (120.53 kmph) Italy Adele Orsi Kestrel 604 8/17/73	68.56 mph (110.338 kmph) Betsy Howell Std. Cirrus 8/14/73 Odessa, Texas	56.51 mph (90.95 kmph) South Africa A. Human Kranich III 12/28/67	None established
SPEED OVER 300-KM. TRIANGULAR COURSE	71.11 mph (114.45 kmph) Australia Susan Martin Kestrel H–401 2/11/72	43.5 mph (70.17 kmph) Henriette Freese Pirat 6/25/73 Leszno, Poland	46.176 mph (74.314 kmph) USSR Olga Manafova KAI-19 6/12/64	None established
SPEED OVER 500-KM. TRIANGULAR COURSE	67.68 mph (108.94 kmph) England Angela Smith Libelle 301 12/18/72	None established	43.246 mph (69.598 kmph) USSR T. Zaiganova Blanik 5/29/68	None established

		MOTORGLIDER		STANDARD CLASS
RECORD CATEGORY	WORLD RECORD	U.S. NATIONAL RECORD		U.S. NATIONAL RECORD
DISTANCE				(None established)
GOAL				
OUT AND RETURN		205.38 mi. (330.54 km.) Bennett M. Rogers AS-K 14 9/12/71 Rosamond, Cal.		
ALTITUDE GAINED				
ABSOLUTE ALTITUDE				
SPEED OVER 100-KM. TRIANGULAR COURSE				
SPEED OVER 300-KM. TRIANGULAR COURSE				
SPEED OVER 500-KM. TRIANGULAR COURSE				

(No other Motorglider records yet established.)

BIBLIOGRAPHY

I. INTRODUCTORY MATERIALS

Soaring in America, by Peter Bowers (Soaring Society of America). Introductory booklet describing the sport; provides basic information for newcomers. 18 pp., 8 photos, 2 drawings, 5 1/2" × 8 1/2".

Complete Book of Sky Sports, by Linn Emrich (Collier, N.Y.). A basic course in five air sports (parachuting, soaring, gyrocopters, ballooning, power planes) includes excellent section on soaring. 8" × 11", 208 pp., 1970.

How to Get Started in Soaring (Schweizer Aircraft Corp., Box 147, Elmira, N.Y. 14902). Booklet tells what Soaring is, how and where it is done. 64 pp., 13 photos, 4 drawings, 5 1/2" × 8 1/2".

Soaring, by Peter L. Dixon (Ballantine, N.Y.). A complete armchair pilot's introduction to the history, joy, and science of soaring flight: Also describes record flights & world competitions. 242 pp., 1970. Paperback.

II. TRAINING MATERIALS

The Joy of Soaring, by Carle Conway (SSA). Flight training manual for all sailplane pilots regardless of experience. Beautifully illustrated, photographs and drawings. New approaches to pilot techniques. 134 pp., 1969.

American Soaring Handbook (SSA). Available as separate chapters, each a comprehensive treatment of the title subject; 5 1/2" × 8 1/2". Paperback; special binder available to hold all ten chapters.

1. "A History of American Soaring," by Ralph S. Barnaby. 1973.
2. "Training," by William R. Fuchs. Syllabus for SSA's ABC Training Program; 107 pp., 1968.
3. "Ground Launch," by William R. Fuchs. 67 pp., 1967.
4. "Airplane Tow," by Tom Page. 45 pp., 1971.
5. "Meteorology," by Harner Selvidge. 44 pp., 1971.
6. "Cross-Country and Wave Soaring," by Richard H. Johnson and William S. Ivans. 52 pp., 1962.
7. "Equipment I, Instruments and Oxygen," by Harner Selvidge. 51 pp., 1963.
8. "Equipment II, Radio, Rope and Wire," by John D. Ryan & Harold Drew. 57 pp., 1966.
9. "Aerodynamics," by Theodore J. Falk and Frederick H. Matteson. 91 pp., 1971.

264

10. "Maintenance and Repair," by Robert Forker. 48 pp., 1965.

The Safety Corner, by Miles Coverdale (SSA). Booklet of reprints of the monthly column on safety in *Soaring* magazine for several years. Good advice for all and especially useful to students and instructors. 44 pp., 1971.

The Art and Technique of Soaring, by Richard Wolters (McGraw-Hill, N.Y.). Step-by-step instructions, drawings, and photographs for the student with no previous experience; also valuable for students preparing for X-C flights. 197 pp., 1971.

Elementary Gliding, by Blanchard (British Gliding Assoc., London). Useful to explain basic gliding and soaring. Excellent information for the beginner. 71 pp., British, paperback.

Federal Aviation Regulations for Pilots (Pan-American Navigation Service, North Hollywood, Ca.). Reprint of key far parts 1, 61, 71, 75, 91, 95, 97, NTSB part 430.

Flight Test Guide—Private and Commercial Pilot—Glider, FAA #AC 61–39.

Glider Flight Instructor Written Test Guide, FAA #AC 61–41.

Glider Pilot Written Test Guide—Private and Commercial, FAA #AC 61–43.

Flying Training in Gliders, by Ann and Lorne Welch (British Gliding Assoc., London). Used by BGA as guide for instruction in gliders. Helps students appreciate training procedures. British, 1956.

Gliding: A handbook on soaring flight, by Derek Piggott (Adam & Charles Black, London). A very popular and widely accepted British textbook; covers all aspects of training and soaring. 263 pp., 1958, revised 1967.

The Gliding Book, edited by Sargent and Watson (Nicholas Kaye, London). From the basics up through achievements; something for all enthusiasts. 109 pp., 1965.

New Soaring Pilot, by Ann and Lorne Welch and F. G. Irving (John Murray, London). Thoroughly revised edition of a comprehensive text covering basic and advanced soaring. 297 pp., 1969.

Oral Test Guide for Glider Pilots, by C. T. McKinnie, Jr. A practice test booklet designed to prepare the student pilot for the private or commercial FAA glider oral exam. 8 1/2" × 11", 8 pp., 1971.

Proceedings of the 1970 Symposium on Competitive Soaring (Soaring Symposia, 408 Washington St., Cumberland, Md., 21502). Tips from top U.S. competition pilots and weather scientists. 155 pp., 1970. Soft cover.

Proceedings of the 1971 Symposium on Competitive Soaring (Soaring symposia, 408 Washington St., Cumberland, Md., 21502). Tips from top U.S. competition pilots and weather scientists. 139 pp., 1971. Soft cover.

Schweizer Soaring School Manual (Schweizer Aircraft Corp., Box 147, Elmira, N.Y. 14902). Standardized training syllabus for private, commercial, and instructor ratings.

Sketchbook of Soaring Flight, by Myrl C. Rupel. An introduction to soaring presented through sketches and accompanying text. 8 1/2" × 11", 104 pp., 1966. Paperback.

Soaring Cross Country, by Ed Byars and Bill Holbrook, 2nd edition (Soaring Symposia, 408 Washington St., Cumberland, Md. 21502). Intermediate text for pilots planning to fly cross country. 177 pp., 1970. Soft cover.

The Theory of Modern Cross-Country Gliding, by Fred Weinholtz (New Zealand Gliding Assoc., Tauranga). Paperback "bible" based on technique of former world champion

Heinz Huth; covers thermaling, optimum distance flying, goal flying, weather forecasting, etc. 61 pp.

Written Test Guide for Glider Pilots, by C. T. McKinnie, Jr. A practice test booklet designed to prepare the student pilot for the private or commercial FAA glider written exam. 8 1/2" × 11", 13 pp., 1971.

III. HISTORIES, BIOGRAPHIES, ANTHOLOGIES, MISCELLANEOUS

British Gliders and Sailplanes, by Norman Ellison (London). 150 drawings, pictures, history of 160 gliders. 1971.

Danny's Glider Ride, by Don Snyder (Follett, Chicago). Beginning reader about a boy who watches a glider land on his father's farm and later gets his first ride. 28 pp., 1968.

Free as a Bird, by Phillip Wills (John Murray, London). Latest anthology by one of the pioneers of British gliding. 1973.

Jonathan Livingston Seagull, A story by Richard Bach with photos by Russell Munson (Macmillan, N.Y.). Delightful fiction and photos about a feathered soaring enthusiast. 93 pp.

On Quiet Wings, A soaring anthology, by Joseph C. Lincoln (Northland Press, Flagstaff, Az.). A beautifully illustrated volume with the best of soaring literature from Greek mythology to today's exciting flights. 397 pp., 1972.

On Silent Wings, Adventure in motorless flight, by Don Dwiggins (Grosset and Dunlap, N.Y.). A new history of the sport including contemporary adventures: includes many black and white photos. 151 pp., 1970.

Once Upon A Thermal, by Richard Wolters (Crown, N.Y.). 1974.

Pilot's Choice, A soaring odyssey, by Gren Seibels (Soaring Symposia, 408 Washington St., Cumberland, Md. 21502). A witty description of U.S. soaring competitions, competitors and competition sites. 208 pp., 1970.

Sailplanes and Soaring, by James E. Mrazek (Stackpole, Harrisburg, Pa.). A new guide to the sport written by a WW II glider infantry battalion commander. 156 pp., 1973.

Soaring, by Dan Halacy (Lippincott, N.Y.). Describes sailplanes and the techniques used in "Sailing the Air." Beautiful color photos: good book for young enthusiasts. 30 pp., 1972.

Soaring for Diamonds, by Joseph C. Lincoln (Northland Press, Flagstaff, Az.). U.S. Pilot's frustrations and triumphs in earning the FAI Gold and Diamond badges; contains many flight stories. 213 pp., 1964. Paperback.

Soaring on the Wind, A photographic essay on silent flight, by Joseph C. Lincoln (Northland Press, Flagstaff, Az.). Beautiful photographs by sailplane artists complemented by statements from various writers in tune with the beauty of the skies. 105 pp., 1972.

Soaring: The Sport of Flying Sailplanes, by William T. Carter (Macmillan Co., N.Y.). A complete sportsman's guide to soaring for beginners. 151 pp., 1973.

Soaring Yearbook—1965, edited by Richard Miller (Soaring International): An absorbing collection of timeless articles on soaring, including distance soaring, sailplane production, etc. 64 pp., 1965. Soft cover.

The Story of Gliding, by Ann and Lorne Welch and Irving (John Murray, London). A comprehensive history of soaring from Da Vinci's theories to today's wave flights. 211 pp., 1965.

Where No Birds Fly, by Philip Wills (Newnes, London). Memorable experiences of former world champion: Many vivid descriptions in words and photos. 141 pp., 1961.

Winning On The Wind, by George B. Moffat, Jr.

IV. TECHNICAL AND METEOROLOGICAL

Aircraft Mechanic's Pocket Manual, by Ashkouti (Pitman, N.Y.). Basic reference handbook in building metal sailplanes from plans or kits or doing maintenance. Gives standards, shop information.

Basic Glider Criteria Handbook (Government Printing Office). Information for designers. Catalog No. FAA 5.8/2:G49/962. 1969 reprint.

Cloud Study, by Ludlam and Scorer (John Murray, London). Explains how clouds are formed. 74 photos of cloud formations, each with a detailed caption. 80 pp., 1957.

Experiment in Flying Wing Sailplanes, by Jim Marske. (130 Crestwood Dr., Michigan City, Ind. 46360.) Report of American postwar tailless sailplane developments. 5-7/8" × 9-3/4", 56 pp., photos, 3-views, 1970.

Fifty Modern Sailplanes. Fifty Powered Sailplanes (Der Flieger, Munich). Pocket editions. Photos and specifications. In German. 3-3/4" × 6".

Glasflugel Repair Manual, by Ursula Hanle. An easty-to-understand primer on maintenance and field repairs of fiberglass sailplanes. Paperback.

Handbook of Airfoil Sections for Light Aircraft, by M. S. Rice (Aviation Publications, Milwaukee). Graphs of L/D, lift and drag vs. angle of attack, and airfoil coordinates for many European and U.S. airfoils of interest in light aircraft design. 134 pp., 1971.

Man-Powered Flight, by Keith Sherwin (Model and Allied Publications, Ltd., England). First textbook primarily aimed at students of man-powered aircraft: Many photos and diagrams. 176 pp., 1971.

Marfa Report, by Wally Scott (1304 Parker Dr., Odessa, Tx. 79760). 16-page booklet and sectional chart showing lift, sink, and no-landing areas in vicinity of Marfa, Texas. 1972.

Meteorology for Glider Pilots, by C. E. Wallington (John Murray, London). A comprehensive treatise on both basics and soaring applications by a soaring met. man. 285 pp., 1961, revised 1966.

Price Lists of items published by Government Printing Office, Public Documents Dist. Ctr. 5801 Tabor Ave., Philadelphia, Pa. 19120. Ask for PL-79 (aviation) and/or PL-48 (meteorology).

Scientific, Meteorological, and Technical Papers on Soaring Presented at Various Ostiv Congresses
  Ostiv Publication VI. Germany, 1960.
  Ostiv Publication VII. Argentina, 1963.
  Ostiv Publication VIII. England, 1965, Part 1.
  Ostiv Publication IX. England, 1965, Part 2.
  Ostiv Publication X. Poland, 1968.

Ostiv Publication: Airworthiness requirements for sailplanes, new edition.

Sailplane Weight Estimation, by Walter Stender (OSTIV, NLM Atoomgebouw, Schiphol

Airport, Netherlands). Covers statistical method of estimating weight for initial computation of load and stress analysis, performance and CG. 46 pp.

Soaring by the Numbers, by Stephen du Pont (Stephen du Pont, Box 234, Fairfield, Ct. 06430). Performance charts, speed rings, final glide tables for five different sailplanes. 30 pp., 1972.

Southland Weather Handbook, by Aldrich and Meadows. So. California weather patterns for outdoorsmen. 51 pp., 1966.

Theory of Flight for Glider Pilots, by R. C. Stafford-Allen (Oliver and Boyd, London). A simple account of the theory of flight. Does not require a mathematical background. New revised edition, 1969.

Theory of Wing Sections, including a summary of airfoil data, by Ira Abbott and Albert Von Doenhoff (Dover, N.Y.). (Contains most of data in NACA Technical Report No. 824, "Summary of Air Foil Data," now out of print.) 693 pp., 1960.

ULTRALIGHT GLIDER BOOKS

Hang Gliding, by Dan Poynter (D. Poynter, 48K Walker St., N. Quincy, Ma. 02171). A comprehensive overview of this phase of ultralight activity, including building, flying, photos & specs. of hang gliders. 205 pp., 1973.

True Flight, by Herman Rice (H. Rice, 1719–S Hillsdale Ave., San Jose, Ca. 95124). Principles and practice of building hang-gliders with emphasis on the Rogallo design. Includes plans for a Rogallo. 47 pp., 1972.

INDEX